A Semiotic Christology

A Semiotic Christology

CYRIL ORJI

☙PICKWICK *Publications* · Eugene, Oregon

A SEMIOTIC CHRISTOLOGY

Copyright © 2021 Cyril Orji. All rights reserved. Except for brief quotations in critical publications or reviews, no part of this book may be reproduced in any manner without prior written permission from the publisher. Write: Permissions, Wipf and Stock Publishers, 199 W. 8th Ave., Suite 3, Eugene, OR 97401.

Pickwick Publications
An Imprint of Wipf and Stock Publishers
199 W. 8th Ave., Suite 3
Eugene, OR 97401

www.wipfandstock.com

PAPERBACK ISBN: 978-1-7252-6917-0
HARDCOVER ISBN: 978-1-7252-6918-7
EBOOK ISBN: 978-1-7252-6919-4

Cataloguing-in-Publication data:

Names: Orji, Cyril, author.
Title: A semiotic christology / by Cyril Orji.
Description: Eugene, OR : Pickwick Publications, 2021 | Includes bibliographical references and index(es).
Identifiers: ISBN 978-1-7252-6917-0 (paperback) | ISBN 978-1-7252-6918-7 (hardcover) | ISBN 978-1-7252-6919-4 (ebook)
Subjects: LCSH: Jesus Christ—Person and offices. | Semiotics.
Classification: LCC BT203 O75 2021 (print) | LCC BT203 (ebook)

03/03/21

Dedicated to
Clement and Olatokunbo Ojo
on the 23rd Anniversary of their Wedding

Contents

Acknowledgments	ix
Introduction	xi
Chapter One: Outlining Some Basic Issues	1
Chapter Two: Setting the Stage for a Theosemiotic Christology	42
Chapter Three: The Christological Titles	73
Chapter Four: Resurrection—The *Sinsign* of Jesus' Identity and Mission	106
Chapter Five: Towards an Evolutionary Christology	134
Chapter Six: The Trinity	166
Chapter Seven: Soteriology	197
Bibliography	225
Index of Names	239
Index of Subjects	243

Acknowledgments

THIS BOOK IS ABOUT an idea. Robert Doran wrote some time ago that an idea is the content of an insight—an act of understanding—and that some acts of understanding are exciting and many others, which are mundane go almost unnoticed.[1] My sincere thanks to all who contributed directly or indirectly to the production of the idea of this book. I will forever be indebted to Steven C. Caton of the Department of Anthropology, Harvard University, for introducing me to the ideas of C.S. Peirce in a way that made lasting impressions on me. There is also Mark Morelli of Loyola Marymount University who always provides platform to test out my ideas at the West Coast Method Institute (WCMI), Los Angeles, CA. Some of the chapters in this book were presented and critiqued over the years at WCMI. I must thank the former Chair of the Department of Religious Studies at the University of Dayton, Daniel Speed Thompson, for his ever- ready willingness to support my research activities with travel fund. There are also many others without whom the idea of this book would not have come to fruition, particularly Robert M. Doran of Marquette University, John D. Dadosky of Regis College of the University of Toronto, and the Lonergan gurus at the Lonergan Center at Boston College— Patrick Byrne, Frederick Lawrence, Kerry Cronin, and Susan Legere. You all demonstrate the functional collaboration to which Bernard Lonergan invites all. In the rat race thing we do in the academy, you will encounter some who embody the worst of the human spirit. But there are also those who embody the best of the human spirit. It is the latter who bring comfort and joy to the academy.

My greatest thanks goes to my Lord and Savior Jesus Christ who gives me strength and in whom I take refuge (See 2 Cor 12: 1–10). Bernard Lonergan could not have expressed divine providence better when he said, "that God knows with equal infallibility, He wills with equal irresistibility,

---

1. Doran, "Two Ways of Knowing," 1.

He effects with equal efficacy, both the necessary and the contingent."[2] In other words, it is not enough to affirm divine omniscience and divine omnipotence without relating it to the human world.

---

[2]. Lonergan, *Grace and Freedom*, 107.

Introduction

IN ONE OF HIS prison letters (April 30, 1944), Dietrich Bonhoeffer wrote that what bothers him "incessantly is the question what Christianity really is, or indeed who Christ really is, for us today."[3] Consistent with his thoughts about Christianity that in his view must jettison ideas about God and the Church that no longer seem adequate in the modern world, Bonhoeffer was bemused that Christians have yet to initiate a turn in the study of Christology. The science of Christology, like all human studies, is always done in the context of a cultural matrix and often influenced by a *großartige Idee* (grand idea). All cultural matrices have their histories, their high point, and a considerable period of atrophy.[4] Nineteenth century Roman Catholic theology, for example, attempted to meet a need, which was to respond to the challenges posed by modernity and the Enlightenment critiques of religion. It did this effectively under the cultural matrix of scholasticism. The ideas of St. Thomas Aquinas, particularly the philosophical system initiated by Joseph Marechal, known as Transcendental Thomism (a blend of Thomism and Kantian metaphysics), became the *großartige Idee* that helped Catholicism overcome these challenges. But what was at one time a solution can at another time become a "problem" (in the Thomas Kuhn sense).

Contemporary Christological discourse has for a while been stymied by the failure to move beyond Transcendental Thomism. In spite of its achievements, Transcendental Thomism is a product of the faculty psychology of the Aristotelian universe. Faculty psychology has obvious counter-positions. Faculty psychology is static and not attuned to new developments in science and semiotics. It does not heed the trend towards an evolutionary universe. Bernard Lonergan framed it best when he observed, using the example of a substance that has been pivotal in the development of civilizations and cultures throughout human history, fire—that fire was conceived

3. Bonhoeffer, *Letters and Papers from Prison*, 279.
4. Lonergan, "Revolutions in Catholic Theology," 233.

by Aristotle as an element, fire was conceived by Antoine Laurent Lavoisier's predecessors as a manifestation of phlogiston, and fire was conceived by later chemists as a type of oxidization. Although all these thinkers who lived across centuries had different conceptions of fire, it would be incorrect to say that Aristotle had an incorrect explanation of what fire is.[5] Though we know today that fire is not an element, but a mixture of hot gasses, among other things, no one can blame another for being a product of their age, for people cannot but be people of their time.[6] That said, we must also admit that conceptions differ, depending on the scientific temper of each age. There is a difference between a descriptive and explanatory conception of a reality.

What I have been alluding to, precisely, is what this book is about —that Christology is like a symphony. This symphony requires both description and explanatory hypotheses. Transcendental Thomism was a description. This book is, therefore, an attempt at an explanatory account of basic issues in Christology, employing a semiotic analysis. A semiotic model is consistent with the evolutionary worldview of contemporary science. This, by no means, disparages theologies constructed out of the old framework. It is rather a recognition that what the times demand is a new direction and that the nineteenth century solution (transcendental Thomism) is in need of a transposition, if we are to ensure that the science of Christology has a future.

The book has seven chapters. The chapters are organized thematically. Chapter 1 explores some basic methodological issues in the study of Christology. The chapter addresses the transcendental Thomism conundrum. It argues that contemporary Christology needs to anchor its study, not on a metaphysics that lends itself to faculty psychology, but on a metaphysics of presence. If theology is to be a science, it needs a method that can accommodate all the revolutions in physics that have occurred from the sixteenth century onwards. These revolutions present us with conceptions of physical nature radically different from that entertained by classical physics. The complexity of the data and genres to be studied in Christology have made it imperative that contemporary Christology be attentive to the Saussurean distinction between diachronic and synchronic exegesis. The chapter contends that Christology should be as synchronic as it is diachronic and that a blend of the two axes is helpful for our understanding of who Jesus really is for us today. The chapter highlights faith as a *sine qua non condition* for understanding who Jesus is. Although non-believers can engage in Christology, their discourse is only a hypothetical discourse that is based on a

---

5. Lonergan, *Insight*, 759.
6. Lonergan, "Revolutions in Catholic Theology," 233.

contrary-to-fact condition. Since faith is what distinguishes theology from other disciplines, like sociology, psychology, and biology, the chapter contends that non-Christians who do not confess Jesus as Lord cannot meaningfully engage in Christology the way Christians do. This is because the intelligibility to be grasped in the science of Christ is not prescriptive, but derives rather from the invariant structure of consciousness of people with a legitimate (physical or spiritual) experience of the risen Christ.

Chapter 2 sets the stage for semiotic Christology. The chapter offers a bird's-eye view of the role of semiotics in Christology. In order not to disrupt the flow of the Christological arguments to be developed in subsequent chapters, the chapter introduces C. S. Peirce and his sign-theory at the outset in order to help readers unfamiliar with semiotics understand some Peircean derived terms we would be applying to Christology. Using Peirce's semiotics as an entry point for understanding "why and how the force of our experiential encounters with reality can be woven indexically into the net of our most sophisticated beliefs," the chapter shows why we need to reconstruct Christian theology in a way that engages contemporary philosophy of science. The traditional way of doing Christology, like some of the ancient Christological debates, is fraught with conceptual logjams due to their overreliance on ancient metaphysical categories. Similarly, the German idealism on which some traditional systems of Christology are built has for long been under the spell of what one writer has described as Teutonic captivity because of its excessive love for transcendental a prioris. Transcendental a prioris not only make theology incapable of engaging in the self-correcting process of knowledge, it also makes Christology incapable of grasping or explicating the practical imports of theological hypotheses. The chapter goes on to show why a metaphysics built on fallibilist theory, as Peirce does, is a corrective to the transcendental theories that assume truth to be a priorily derived. In the end, the chapter uses a semiotic analysis to clarify and shed light on the different kinds of Christology: Ascending v Descending Christology, High v Low Christology, Explicit v Implicit Christology, and Ontological v Functional Christology.

Chapter 3 examines, phenomenologically, some of the Christological titles the early Church applied to Jesus and validates the argument of fusing diachronic and synchronic exegesis in Christology. The chapter uncovers that the early Christians did not merely intuit the descriptors or titles they applied to Jesus, but rather that they derived the titles from their existing usage in both the Jewish and the Hellenistic world. The titles are classified and analyzed under four rubrics, consistent with a semiotic understanding—to show that understanding of these symbolic descriptors is not rigid, but fluid and open to further and deeper meanings. The four rubrics are

(1) the Christological titles that refer to the earthly work of Jesus (2) the Christological titles that refer to the present work of Jesus (3) the Christological titles that refer to the future of Jesus and (4) the Christological titles that refer to the pre-existence of Jesus. These four cluster or schematization helps us work from within the New Testament itself, as opposed to working from extra-biblical or later theological points of view. Our semiotic analysis shows how the titles, taken together, are meant to give a fuller picture of whom Jesus is. A semiotic analysis shows more clearly that there is no one single title that is self-sufficient as to encompass the infinite fullness of Christ. The chapter concludes by showing how each of the titles is related to one or more of the four different functions of Jesus. The chapter ends by pointing out the mutual assimilation of meanings and connotations that may have taken place in the consciousness of the early Christians who first applied the titles to Jesus.

Chapter 4 argues that Jesus' claim to being the messiah and savior cannot in itself alone be the basis of Christology. That claim has to be validated and vindicated by the Father who raised Jesus from the dead. The Resurrection-event is the basis of this validation. Employing a diachronic (historical) approach, the chapter uncovers that the very idea of resurrection in itself is not something new to Christianity, but something already held in the ancient world. In spite of the fact that it was an idea that was already present in the ancient conception of life after death, the disciples still saw Jesus' brutal death on the cross and the bodily resurrection that followed it three days after to be the hermeneutical key for unlocking the identity and mission of Jesus. The chapter proceeds to show that rather than undermine it, the ancient and Jewish notions of resurrection can enhance the Christian understanding of Jesus' identity and mission. In the light of the psychological work W. Dewi Rees, the Welsh general practitioner known as the pioneer of bereavement hallucination and whose experiment and publication in the *British Medical Journal* in 1971 has revived the hallucination hypothesis, the chapter gives considerable attention to the bereavement hypotheses of Gerd Ludeman, Michael Goulder, and Maurice Casey and offers arguments that refute hallucination claims. The chapter applies indexical paradigm to both the ways we speak and understand the Resurrection. If, as C.S. Peirce claims, the highest grade of reality is only reached through signs, then the sublime reality of resurrection can be only be fully grasped with the aid of signs. Although the resurrection is not considered one of the sign-miracles in the Fourth Gospel, the chapter uses Peirce's understanding of signs and symbols to argue that the Resurrection is the proto-sign. Using a term derived from Peirce, the chapter argues that the Resurrection is a *Sinsign* (actual existent that occurs only once). The chapter concludes by showing that in asserting,

"I Am the resurrection and the life" (John 11:25), Jesus embodies what we know about the resurrection of the dead in a unique way—a *Sinsign* in the Peircean true sense of the word.

Chapter 5 argues that evolution matters to theology because evolution affects all facets of human existence: the concepts of creation, the questions of human origins, the question of original sin, the questions of human nature, human behavior and human destiny. The chapter argues that because soteriology and Christology are built on these theological claims, Christology should therefore be examined in the light of the evolutionary view of the world. The chapter gives a bird's-eye view of the theological claims of two groups of Neo-Darwinism: the atheistic group represented by Richard Dawkins and Daniel Dennett and the non-Darwinian group represented by Niles Eldridge and Stephen Jay Gould. The chapter accepts, as paradigmatic, Rahner's thesis that the Chalcedonian definition of the Person and two natures of Christ should be seen, not as an end of Christology, but as the beginning point. Contemporary understanding of person is different from that of the Chalcedonian world that defined the natures of Christ using the available metaphysical framework of the time. This chapter raises questions regarding what will happen to Christology when the metaphysical superstructure of the Chalcedonian world is no longer in place and the ontology of substance that gave it logical consistency is no longer applicable. Using Thomas Kuhn's idea that a paradigm shift is needed when a "crisis" occurs, the chapter argues that Christology needs a paradigm shift that is attentive to the evolutionary view of the world. A paradigm shift is already implicit in Rahner's evolutionary Christology. The chapter examines Rahner Transcendental Christology and ontology of Symbols with a view to connecting contemporary understandings of biological evolution to God. Rahner embraced the evolutionary view of the world, conceiving evolution not as random adaptive process, but as systematic and tailored progress toward God, the final goal of life.

Chapter 6 lends voice to the Trinitarian renaissance that began in the second half of the twentieth century by offering an alternative—a Semiotic Model of the Trinity. The chapter argues that while Christology must begin with the person and mission of Jesus, its basic question has to be about his unity with God. Rahner, to his credit, has long spoken out against inadequate theologies of incarnation and grace that separate Trinitarian theology from Christian spirituality and experience. His goal, as he puts it, is to liberate Trinitarian theology from its Neo-Scholastic bondage, as well as renew interest in the Trinity. It is the renewed interest in Trinitarian theology that the chapter furthers, comparing Rahner's project with that of Andrew Robinson. Robinson built his Trinitarian theology on the metaphysics of

C.S. Peirce. He thought he could connect Peirce's metaphysical categories of Firstness, Secondness, and Thirdness to the Christian understanding of the three divine Persons. Like Rahner who developed his Trinitarian theology with an eye on how to speak of the Trinitarian relations, Robinson shows how the perennial problems associated with the way we approach Trinitarian Persons and Intra-Trinitarian relations can be resolved. He locates the solution in the semiotic model of the Trinity, which he favors. The chapter also shows how the Semiotic Model of the Trinity is both similar and different from Rahner's. Rahner was mindful of the dangers of subordinationism. So was Robinson who thought by correlating the Peircean phenomenological categories to the Trinitarian Persons one would eliminate subordinationism. The chapter ends by showing how Robinson's semiotic model of the Trinity can be both an application and a challenge to Rahner's *grundaxiom*. For the semiotic model of the Trinity, at least, attempts to resolve the problem of the intra-Trinitarian relations and the difficulties of the psychological the social analogies of the Trinity.

Chapter 7 takes as paradigmatic that Christology must have a soteriology. The chapter argues that both the Scriptures and the writings of the Fathers on soteriology anticipate a semiotic understanding, although this has not been made clear in the traditional rendering of soteriology. Arguing that the traditional account of the Christian view of atonement will benefit from a revision that reflects this semiotic understanding, the chapter follows a diachronic and synchronic approach, exposits various New Testament metaphors for soteriology, and argues that the metaphors employed by Paul and the New Testament writers are not to be understood as dialectical, but as semiotic in that they make room for a both-and approach. The chapter also attempts to correct, through a semiotic analysis, a long held mistaken assumption that there are two patterns of soteriology in patristic thought: one that conceives salvation as juridical or legal and the other that conceives salvation as deification. It is not only the language of the New Testament and the Fathers that should be read symbolically, orthodox Protestantism, following the refinements of Fredrick Schleiermacher and Albert Ritschl, and even Luther, has also come to the conclusion that there is room for a both-and approach in these metaphors. The chapter concludes by seeking an ecumenical consensus on what it means to affirm *Christus Victor*—that God in Jesus was reconciling the world to God.

Chapter One

Outlining Some Basic Issues

IT IS HARD TO do Christology today and not be attentive to the major shifts—developments in philosophy and the social and natural sciences—that have affected both the questions that Christology raises and the way of going about answering these questions. It is too simplistic to reduce the shift that occurred in theology to the efforts of one person, but the mathematician and philosophyer Rene Descartes (1596–1690) and the empiricist John Lock (1632–1704) were influential figures in the new anthropological turn that places emphasis in a conscious human subject who thinks, feels, and acts in response to his or her self-consciousness as a subject. Descartes's discoveries on how the human mind comes to know an object became the foundational ground of subsequent developments in philosophy and science. Isaac Newton (1642–1727) built on it and regarded the world as a machine or closed continuum of causes and effects and the French mathematician and physicist Pierre-Simon Maquis de Laplace (1749–1827) summed it all up by suggesting that the universe was mechanistically determined.[1] "Their remarkable progress in physics and the natural sciences in general encouraged many scholars in other disciplines to endorse the search for absolute objectivity. The ideal frequently became a dispassionate, neutral, and value-free version of reality (often conceived in merely physical terms), which reduced or even eliminated personal participation and could establish conclusions in a mathematical way."[2] Their quest for scientific objectivity affected the way both theology and Christology will

---

1. O'Collins, *Christology*, 219.
2. O'Collins, *Christology*, 219.

be done moving forward.³ In its extreme form, their fixation for objectivity became one-sided, such that where in earler generation the maxim was *crede ut intelligas* (I believe in order to understand), the new maxim became " If you believe, you will not understand."⁴

The anthropological turn influenced by Descartes and Locke in the seventeenth century was mediated to the twentieth century through the transcendental analysis of Immanuel Kant (1724–1804) and those that came after him. "Kant challenged classical metaphysics in the sense that whoever makes claims about such matters as God, the immortality of the soul, and its liberty must first inquire whether such an enterprise is at all possible."⁵ In its extreme form, the Kantian transcendetnal method, which attends only to the knowing subject, reduces external reality, i.e., anything not perceptible to the senses, to the product of the human mind.⁶ The twentieth century attempted to correct the nineteenth century science's fixation with objectivity and "began to modify the dream of absolute 'objectivity,' and accept the fact that pure objectivity does not exist, not even in physics."⁷ The German-born theoretical physicist, Albert Einstein (1879–1955) developed in 1905 a Theory of Relativity that rehablitated the observer's viewpoint and dealt a deadly blow to the idea that there are absolute markers for time or space. The German theoretical physicist, Max Planck (1858–1947) discovered what came to be known as the Planck's Law—that energy is emitted from a black body in discrete amount or quanta that is proportionate to the frequency of the radiation that is absorbed by the black body. It was his work that led to Einstein's discovery that lights exist in discrete quanta of energy or photons. The German theoretical physicist, Werner Heisenberg (1901–1976), also developed an Uncertainty Principle (introduced in 1927) to further throw doubt on the notion of absolute objectivity, at least in physics. His Uncertainty Principle states that we cannot know accurately, at the same time, both the position and the velocity of any of the particles which make up an atom because we cannot know with accuracy the position and velocity of atomic particles. The Uncertainty Principle also states that the subatomic processes cannot be explained by causes and effect, but by statistical laws.⁸ Taken together, Planck's Law, Einstein's General Theory of Relativity, and Heisenberg's Uncertainty Principle all brought an end to

3. O'Collins, *Christology*, 219.
4. O'Collins, *Christology*, 219.
5. O'Collins, *Christology*, 218.
6. O'Collins, *Christology*, 218.
7. O'Collins, *Christology*, 219.
8. O'Collins, *Christology*, 220.

the classical Newtonian physics that was built on the idea that there is an objective measurability of causes and effects.[9] They fostered the idea that all knowledge, when all said and done, is properly subjective. "The results of observations and experiments inevitably depend upon the observer's point of view; we get answers only to the questions we put. As forms of our knowledge, scientific laws put together the many observations we have made. There is no such thing as a view 'from nowhere.'"[10] It was left to Vatican I (1869–1870), the first twentieth century Council of Catholicism, to wrestle with the implications of the subjective-objective poles of knowledge for theology and our understanding of the mystery of the incarnate Word, Christ, in the Scriptures.

In its extreme form, the scientific principle that there is no such thing as a view "from nowhere," which was intended to tame the rising tide of excessive objectivity, led to a new form of rationalism, liberalism, and materialism. The net effect was that it challenged the teachings of the Church in a way not seen since the Protestant Reformation three centuries earlier. Vatican I's response was to refute these ideas by defining papal infallibility and the Church's doctrines. Some of the dissentions that followed the Church's definition of its teachings and papal infallibility further fractured the Christian unity, making Vatican II a necessity.

Contemporary discourse in Christology must acknowledge the role of the Second Vatican Council (1962–1965) which taught that it is only in the mystery of the incarnate Word, Christ, "the final Adam" and "the image of the invisible God" (Col 1:15) that the mystery of the human person take on new light.[11] Reading "the signs of the times," the Council addressed the relations of the Church with the modern world and shed new light on some age-old Church doctrines that massively impact contemporary thinking on the science of Christ. When in January 1959 Pope John XXIII announced that there would be an assembly of Roman Catholic bishops and religious leaders, although the idea of a Council was welcomed by many because the Catholic world was in crisis at the time, the very idea of a Council came as a surprise because there had not been an ecumenical council for nearly a century. In the end, Vatican II turned out to be a turning point in both the Catholic Church's self-understanding of its relations to Christ and its relations with the modern world.

Many of the challenges that the Church faced before the Second Vatican Council came from outside of the Church. It was by and large a cultural

---

9. O'Collins, *Christology*, 220.
10. O'Collins, *Christology*, 220.
11. See Vatican Council II, *Gaudium et Spes* 22.

crisis that was three-pronged: epistemic or intellectual, moral, and spiritual. It affected not only Catholicism, but the whole of the western world as well.[12] The origin of the intellectual challenge is a long one. It was set in motion by the revolutions in modern science that began a few centuries earlier. It is hard to dispute its ties to the publication of Nicolaus Copernicus's *De Revolutionibus Orbium Coelestium* (1543) and some seventeenth and eighteenth century developments in mathematics, physics, and astronomy, etc., in particular Isaac Newton's *Philosophiae Naturalis Principia Mathematica* (1687). There is also the matter of Planck's Law, Heisenberg's Uncertainty Principle, and Einstein's theory of relativity that revolutionized in the twentieth century knowledge of the physical universe and our place in it. All together these events revolutionized both modernity's view of the universe and its relationship with the world. The intellectual challenge came with a moral dilemma. The dilemma was triggered by the democratic ideals (equality, liberty, and fraternity) that were inspired by the emerging new democracies in places like France and the United States. The ideals were rising at an unprecedented pace, but there was no unifying moral philosophy on which to validate or at least clarify the moral advocacy that was on the upswing. This further exacerbated the instability in modern culture.[13] A combination of the intellectual and moral challenges led to the third—the spiritual challenge—that came about as a result of rejection of traditional religious allegiances championed by some humanists and naturalists who desired only a society in which discourse about God was removed from the public sphere.

In effect, this three-dimensional cultural crisis dramatically altered both our perception and manner of doing theology. On the positive side, it effected what Karl Rahner and Bernard Lonergan referred to as a shift from a cosmological to anthropological viewpoint. "Where before man contemplated an objective universe and understood himself in terms of the same objective categories, now what is first to be understood is not the universe but man, even though it is man as the principle whence one can come to know the universe."[14] The shift to anthropological viewpoint also demanded that adjustments be made, not to the content of theology, but its forms and structures.[15] Rahner thinks that one of the positive effects of the crisis of modernity is that it made the Church to realize that we no longer live in a

---

12. McCarthy, *Authenticity as Self-Transcendence*, ix.
13. McCarthy, *Authenticity as Self-Transcendence*, ix.
14. Lonergan, "Future of Christianity," 138.
15. Lonergan, "Belief," 84.

world of monoculture, but in "gnoseological pluralism."[16] In the new pluralism, theology, he insists, cannot stand alone, let alone act as if it were the arbiter of all truth. Theology must engage the sciences or risk what he calls "gnoseological concupiscence." Gnoseological concupiscence is Rahner's term for the erotomania that comes about when a discipline accords itself an absolute value, presupposing "that the key which it carries within itself will fit every door."[17] In a nutshell, the positive side of the crisis of modernity is that it made the Church realize that not only must theology engage the sciences, it must also be involved in a relationship of mutual interdependence with all ally disciplines in the social sciences. Not to do so, according to Rahner, is to risk methodological monism (isolation).[18]

Thus, theology's new engagement with ally disciplines must be anchored in philosophy. But not all philosophies can arbitrate the truth of theology. A number of European derived philosophies, since the dawn of modernity at least, has been tinged with the bug of nominalism. These philosophies have abdicated their role as arbiter of truth. For example, a philosophy that makes a priori truth claims, like some Kantian derived philosophies or a philosophy that relies on the power of intuition, is incapable of playing this mediating function. Only a philosophy that adequately accounts for how the highest grade of reality can be grasped metaphysically can play a mediating role between theology and the ally disciplines. Since the goal of Christology is to make credible Christian truth claims of the Christ event, where might we locate a philosophy that adequately accounts for how to grasp metaphysically the highest grade of reality?

SEARCH FOR A METAPHYSICS OF EXPERIENCE

We have made the case that theology must engage the sciences. This is not an argument that undercuts the primal role of philosophy in theological discourse. In fact, theology needs not only philosophy, but also a metaphysics to ground its truth-claims. Josiah Royce (1855–1916) long ago characterized Christianity as a religion in search of a metaphysics.[19] Theology constantly searches for a metaphysics (a philosophical theory of the nature of reality) because it needs a philosophical frame of reference on which to anchor

---

16. Rahner, "On the Current Relationship between Philosophy and Theology," 69.
17. Rahner, "Theology as Engaged in an Interdisciplinary Dialogue with the Sciences," 90.
18. Rahner, "Theology as Engaged in an Interdisciplinary Dialogue with the Sciences," 93.
19. Gelpi, *Gracing of Human Experience*, ix.

Christian teaching. There is precedent for this in both Scripture and tradition. The Fourth Gospel is highly philosophical and employs concepts from Greek and Hellenistic world to explain the pre-existence of Christ. Although the apostle Paul was suspicious of airy philosophical speculations of the Greeks and exhorted his disciples to be alert so that no one takes them "captive through philosophy and empty deception, which are based on human tradition and the spiritual forces of the world rather than on Christ" (Col 2:8), early Greek and Latin Fathers, following Paul's lead, were constantly searching for the best philosophical tradition that can help convey the Christ message to their culture. The Christian apologist Justin Martyr (AD 100—165) equates the *Logos* of the Johannine Gospel with the *Nous* (mind or intelligence) of Middle Platonism. Origen Adamantius, sometimes referred to as Origen of Alexandria (AD 184—253) also equates the Second Person of the Trinity with the *Nous* of Middle Platonism. Throughout the history of Christian theology, the Christian understanding of human condition has been influenced by philosophical systems, such as Platonism, Aristotelianism, and Stoicism.[20] St. Augustine (AD 354—430) built his system on Plato's philosophy and used Plato's theory of participation to develop human participation in divine creative act (nature and grace). Thomas Aquinas (1224/5–1274) and the scholastics re-thought some of the Augustinian teaching using Aristotelian categories. By drawing from Platonism, Aristotelianism, and Stoicism, medieval and scholastic thinkers show that Christian theology needs a rational way of thinking about God, i.e., one that can consistently express what Christian teaching about God means for the human person who exists as a being among other beings in the universe.

The demise of Thomism came after Immanuel Kant (1724–1804) claimed to have cracked the code and destroyed metaphysics. Kant's claim and the demise of Thomism left twentieth century Catholic theology in the dark, for a while at least. In truth, the demise of Thomism was a net effect of the cultural crisis of modernity for which Catholicism was forced to find a response. In what seemed like an irony, Catholic theology attempted a revival of both Thomism and metaphysical way of thinking as its way of responding to the crisis of modernity. It invented Transcendental Thomism. The appeal to Transcendental Thomism, whether or not it proved successful in the long run, underscores the fact that Christian theology needs an inferential way of thinking. In the twentieth century, when the study of anthropology revolutionized contemporary understanding of language and culture, the linguistic and cultural turns it effected paved way for interdisciplinary

---

20. Gelpi, *Gracing of Human Experience*, 25.

cooperation. Some forward-thinking Catholic thinkers also embraced the idea of interdisciplinary cooperation of the disciplines. When Thomism was fading and was no longer tenable, though not without official magisterial backing, some Catholic systematic theologians began to embrace and adapt anthropological "turns" into systematic theological thinking. They embraced the turn to experience. The turn to experience appeared with regularity in the work of those theologians proposing methodological and doctrinal developments, particularly the Jesuits Karl Rahner (1904–1984) and Henri de Lubac (1896–1991) and the Dominican Edward Schillebeeckx (1914–2009).

In general, these writers used the term "experience" broadly to capture a range of cognitional and emotional operations common to all human beings that were hitherto neglected or unaccounted for by mainstream theology. Although they may have used the term "experience" differently, they all agreed that all theology "should be 'experiential' in a manner analogous to the way in which it ought all to be 'scriptural,' 'philosophical,' and 'logical,' and in way in which it cannot all be Roman Catholic, or Anglican, or perspectival in a great variety of ways."[21] Thus, as varied as each of the "turns" were, each in its own way reflected a discovery of a new philosophical approach that undergirds systematic theological thinking.[22] There are, at least, five variants of theologies of the turn to experience:

1. The theologies of experience that appeal to the transcendental. This is found in the various forms of transcendental Thomism, like Rahner and Henri de Lubac.
2. The theologies of experience that appeal to the hermeneutical. This is found among perspectival theologians, like Barth's discourse on the place of experience in theology in the *Church Dogmatics*.
3. The theologies of experience that appeal to the constructive. This is found in some contemporary narrative theology, like Barth's work on Anselm.
4. The theologies of experience that appeal to the confessional. This is found in the various forms of homiletic and devotional literature, as well as popular literature by certain forms of evangelism.
5. The theologies of experience that appeal to the mystical. This is found in the writings of Schleiermacher, as well as in some New Age writings.[23]

---

21. Schner, "Appeal to Experience," 40.
22. Gelpi, *Turn to Experience in Contemporary Theology*, 1.
23. See Schner, "Appeal to Experience," 51–57.

The most common of these variants of theologies of experience is the appeal to the transcendental— a hall mark of transcendental Thomism. Transcendental Thomism is built on ideas derived from the Aristotelian worldview and its faculty psychology. It is complemented by a Kantian epistemology. Aristotle thought that human beings had only five faculties: common sense, imagination, memory, active mind, and passive mind. Faculty psychology was built on this classical Greek powers of the mind and metaphysical categories of spirit-matter dualism. Its superstructure is the Platonic-Aristotelian notions of first principles and a priori ideas, a superstructure that runs contrary to the discursive nature of knowledge. The Jesuit Donald Gelpi (1934–2011), like many others who identify counter-positions in faculty psychology, has vehemently offered reasons why contemporary theology has to abandon transcendental Thomism. He also insists that in spite of their best attempts to move beyond faculty psychology, many transcendental Thomists have not succeeded in extricating themselves from the failures and inadequacies of Kantian epistemology on which it is built.

A word about Gelpi the theologian may help us determine why we should take his admonition seriously. Like many Jesuits of the post-conciliar period, Gelpi was trained in Neo-Scholastic theology. An offshoot of this Jesuit training was the transcendental Thomism that was already gaining current even before the Second Vatican Council. Needless to say, Gelpi began his theological vocation as a devotee of Rahner and his Transcendental Thomism, but had to abandon Transcendental Thomism when he saw through it. When he abandoned Rahner's Transcendental Thomism, Gelpi integrated, with some degree of success, the classical American philosophy of the likes of William James, Josiah Royce, George Santayana, and Alfred North Whitehead into Catholic theological thought.

There are also other theologians in the mold of Gelpi who think the introduction of transcendental Thomism into theology has skewed Catholic theology. They contend that this is what is responsible for the confusion in contemporary Catholic understanding of the relationship between nature and grace, among other things. The Kantian transcendental logic, which is rooted in classical metaphysics, they argue, was what forced Rahner to employ an inadequate, prescriptive approach to human experience. If Gelpi and Rahner's critics are right, then we must contend with the fact that the failure to take into account contemporary philosophy's critique of the inadequacies of the Kantian logic do have Christological implications. Gelpi pointed out that what inadequate critique of Kantian logic fails to realize is that human nature and supernatural grace are correlative terms, such that as our conception of the human person shifts, so must our conception of how the human person is related to divine grace. It is precisely the failure to realize that contemporary understanding of the human person is constantly evolving and that changes in our conception of the human nature must force a revision in our theological understanding of the correlative reality of divine grace that calls into question the continued reliance of Transcendental Thomism.[24] Is there an alternative to Transcendental Thomism?

For the purpose of Christology, let me argue tentatively that contemporary theology will be better served by a philosophy with an in-built metaphysics for reaching the highest grade of reality. One of such philosophy is the semiotic philosophy built on the triadic logic of the American pragmatist and scientist, Charles Sanders Peirce (1839–1914). Peirce's metaphysics makes no claim to grasp realities intuitively and immediately as the many variants of Platonic-Aristotelian derived philosophical thoughts do. Before I advance this argument further, it is imperative that I lay bare the conundrum of Transcendental Thomism, particularly as advanced by the Belgian Jesuit Joseph Marechal (1878–1944) and supported by his German Jesuit confrere, Karl Rahner. If there was one who employed Transcendental Thomism but who also know fully well the limitations of that procedure, it was none other than the Jesuit Bernard Lonergan (1904–1984). Lonergan stands unique among the so-called Transcendental Thomists (and I hesitate to call him one) because of his awareness of the limitations of faculty psychology, which he painstakingly avoided by making a transition to intentionality analysis. Although trained in scholastic theology, Lonergan charted a new approach to Christology, abandoning scholastic Christology, which was dominated by the role of truth, for a phenomenological Christology, which is dominated by the role of affections. Lonergan was on course to developing this new Christology when suddenly the plan was disrupted because he had to fight a battle with cancer. Frederick Crowe tells us that this bout with cancer confined Lonergan mostly to lecturing in course on Christology, instead of producing treatises. Most of Lonergan's thoughts in Christology would be confined to articles and lecture notes he gave from 1935 to 1982. Even as voluminous and scattered as these articles appear to be, they show a conceptual unity in his thought on Christology. If I do not cite much of Lonergan's Christology in this work, it is precisely for the reason that he never had time to develop it fully the way he would have wanted. To return to the Kantian transcendental analysis, one thing about Lonergan is, he engages with a broad spectrum of thinkers, makes them his interlocutors, and takes a further step of making his interlocutors better than they really are. So with respect to Kant's transcendental analysis, Lonergan interprets "Kant's transcendental imagination as inquiry transforming mere

---

24. Gelpi, *Gracing of Human Experience*, 133.

experiencing into the scrutiny of observation, trying to promote something imagined into something intelligible."[25] Those who have been trying to establish a relationship between Lonergan and Kant ought to know that the relationship is more complex than they make it out to be. Lonergan transforms Kant's transcendental imagination without however fusing Kant's horizon into his own transcendental method.

Like we see in Lonergan's phenomenology, Peirce's foundational metaphysics of grasping reality, is grounded in fallibilistic logic. Although it aspires to a universal verifiability, both Peirce and Lonergan eschew any claim to a priori necessity. Peirce's fallibilistic logic is a pragmatic admission "that the human mind has a much better chance of reaching the truth if it admits its capacity for error than if it denies that capacity."[26] Lonergan's methodic thinking also shows how through human deliberation (acts of understanding and judging) we can possibly reach the question of God and arrive at intellectually satisfying answers.[27] How they showed this will be discussed next only after we resolve the transcendental Thomism conundrum.

The Transcendental Thomism Conundrum

Ever before there was such a thing as Transcendental Thomism, there existed in the United States a philosophical system that was engendered by the Enlightenment critique of religion. It began in the eighteenth century and flourished in the nineteenth century under the banner of Transcendentalism. It lasted well into the twentieth century. The different thinkers that came under this umbrella movement shared a common philosophical and theological concerns and each elaborated a kind of religious doctrine of intuition, though they all understood intuition in a variety of ways.[28] Far from being monolithic, Transcendentalism developed in a series of intellectual waves, different thinkers riding each wave, claiming to deconstruct or go beyond both the Enlightenment and Modernist projects. Among the many thinkers who took part in this deconstruction were Ralph Waldo Emerson (1803–1882), Theodore Parker (1810–1860), and Orestes Augustus Brownson (1803–1876).[29] Emerson "elaborated a Platonic doctrine of intuition which claimed for the human mind the power to ascend to the realm of eternal truth and to discover there a purely subjective grasp of the unchanging

---

25. See Doran, "Two Ways of Being Conscious," 4; see n5.
26. Gelpi, *Gracing of Human Experience*, vii.
27. See ch. 4 of Lonergan, *Method in Theology*.
28. Gelpi, *Grace as Transmuted Experience and Social Process*, 2.
29. See Gelpi, *Varieties of Transcendental Experience*, vi–vii.

laws of the universe. Parker believed that the human mind possesses the power of grasping within subjectivity the objective truth of . . .religion: the existence of God, the immortality of the soul, and the universal principles of morality."[30] Brownson developed a robust incarnational doctrine of intuitive religious enlightenment.[31]

The shared concern of the Transcendentalists was how to move beyond (transcend if you will) the limitations of Enlightenment critique of religion. To this end, they all adopted different strategies to rescue religious experience from the skepticism and nominalistic tendencies perpetuated by Enlightenment thinkers, like John Locke, David Hume, and Immanuel Kant.[32] Their Transcendental critiques called into question the Enlightenment's nominalism, individualism, naïve claims to objectivity, what is verifiable, and foundational ontology. It was the philosophy of Charles Sanders Peirce that "brought to its culmination the critique of the American Enlightenment begun in the 1830s by the American Transcendentalists."[33] Peirce, to be clear, did not go along with the doctrine of religious intuition of the Transcendentalists. What Peirce did rather was launch a vigorous and well calibrated assault on transcendental intuitionism by developing a metaphysical realism that addresses their shared concerns. Peirce was concerned that some modern and enlightenment induced philosophies have been harvesting, to use Gelpi's phrase, "a cornucopia of dualistic conceptions of reality" and that they have been steeped in dualistic systems of thought that conceive realities in ways that make their interrelationships to one another lose all intelligibility.[34] Thus, Peirce not only rejected the theories of intuitionism popularized by the American transcendentalists, he also "censured them for their failure to take into adequate account the historical and symbolically mediated character of human cognition."[35]

It is wrong to speak of the Enlightenment and modernist projects in monolithic terms, as if they took only one form. Just as modernism had different forms and variations, depending on time, place, and circumstance, Enlightenment in British Isles, for example, had distinct flavors that made it different from the Enlightenment in, say Germany or France. Although Enlightenment took more than one form, the various varieties of Transcendentalism that Peirce vigorously tried to combat attempted different ways of

---

30. Gelpi, *Gracing of Human Experience*, 139.
31. Gelpi, *Grace as Transmuted Experience and Social Process*, 2.
32. Gelpi, *Varieties of Transcendental Experience*, vii.
33. Gelpi, *Gracing of Human Experience*, 264.
34. Gelpi, *Grace as Transmuted Experience and Social Process*, 3.
35. Gelpi, *Grace as Transmuted Experience and Social Process*, 35.

deconstructing the Enlightenment and modernist projects. At the back of the mind of Transcendentalists was how to overcome the bug of nominalism that had infected continental philosophy.

Although quite different from Transcendentalism, but nonetheless a deconstructionist project, Transcendental Thomism took its cue from Transcendentalism. The Belgian Jesuit, Joseph Marechal (1878–1944), who taught for many years at the Jesuit faculty of Philosophy at Louvain, is generally considered the father of Transcendental Thomism. His work, *Le Point de Depart de la Metaphysique*, is especially significant in this endeavor. The influence of this work on Marechal's fellow Jesuits in continental Europe in the years between the First and the Second World Wars cannot be overstated. Quite often deconstructionist projects take their inspiration from different sources and from different philosophies. Marechal took his inspiration, not from the New England Transcendentalists, but from St. Thomas Aquinas. He laid the philosophical foundation for Transcendental Thomism by blending Kantian logic and epistemology with Thomistic metaphysics.[36] In a philosophical revolution likeable to the Copernican revolution in physics, Kant moved the gravitational epicenter of the cognitional universe away from the object and centered it on the subject, ushering in a turn to the subject. Marechal's "principal thesis was that if Kant's transcendental reflection on human knowledge is applied consistently, it leads to metaphysical realism and not to critical idealism, as Kant had mistakenly supposed."[37]

Marechal's re-grounding of Thomistic metaphysics in Kantian epistemology and logic, in Gelpi's view, should be seen for what it is— an apologetic work. There is evidence on Gelpi's side on this matter. Like Rahner and other speculative theologians of the pre-Vatican II era, Marechal worked in the shadows of Leo XIII's encyclical, *Aeterni Patris* (1879), which called for new ways of thinking about Thomism and which had established Thomism as the official Catholic philosophy and theology. These speculative theologians did not dare to risk the wrath of the Holy Office.[38] Although at the time of Marechal's writing, the Modernist crisis was beginning to subside and the hunting of heretics was no longer carried out openly by the hierarchy, "cautious integralists kept their weather-eyes cocked for signs of modernist deviance among Catholic intellectuals."[39] Marechal may be considered one of the conservative integralists who attempted apologetic work on behalf of the Church.

---

36. Gelpi, *Turn to Experience in Contemporary Theology*, 91.
37. See McCool, *Rahner Reader*, xiii.
38. Gelpi, *Turn to Experience in Contemporary Theology*, 92.
39. Gelpi, *Turn to Experience in Contemporary Theology*, 92.

In the century before, Kant claimed to have destroyed metaphysics and that he had confined the idea of God to the waste basket of unverifiable concept. For Kant, God, immortality of the soul, and human freedom are postulates of practical reason of which speculative reason can have no objective knowledge. Showing disinterest in metaphysics, Kant sought to reground metaphysical thinking in the "turn" to the subject, thereby replacing "metaphysical thinking with a transcendental deduction a priori of the conditions for the possibility of knowing, of making moral judgments, and of having aesthetic experiences."[40] Kant's legacy was to leave a gulf between the noumena and phenomena, sense and intellect, and speculative and practical reason. His assault on metaphysics had far-reaching implications. If we do not have objective knowledge and the human mind cannot know reality, as Kant purportedly claimed, then we cannot know religious truths and we are left in the dark regarding the realities of the Trinitarian God who revealed self as Father, Son, and the Holy Spirit.

Marechal taught he could reconcile Kant's speculative and practical intellect through the dynamism of the human spirit. He, therefore, contended that the metaphysics of knowledge is an integral part of a general metaphysics of finite and infinite reality.[41] Marechal argued that a Thomist theory of knowledge already anticipates the kind of problems raised by Kant and also that a Thomistic theory of knowledge invalidates Kant's notion that the idea of God is an unverifiable proposition. Pointing our key limitations of the Kantian proposition, Marechal argued that Kant's error was that he reduced human cognition only to an analysis of concrete sense images and abstract universal concepts. Kant, in Marechal's view, had therefore overlooked "a more fundamental a priori structure of consciousness, a structure which Thomistic theory of knowledge supplies."[42]

Marechal concluded that "a consistent application of the transcendental method to human knowledge should lead to a remarkably similar dynamic structure of human knowledge in both Kant and in St. Thomas and to the metaphysical affirmation of the Pure Act of Being."[43] Thus, Marechal taught that the transcendental method could be extended beyond epistemology and can be used to ground a general metaphysics whose form and structure could resemble Aquinas's own metaphysics. He also taught that he could show that Kant and Aquinas both agreed that the human person is a

---

40. Gelpi, *Gracing of Human Experience*, 269.
41. McCool, *Rahner Reader*, xiv.
42. Gelpi, *Grace as Transmuted Experience and Social Process*, 68.
43. McCool, *Rahner Reader*, xv–xvi.

receptive knower whose knowledge begins with sense sensation.[44] "Consequently the unity of sense and intellect in the single act of the receptive knower's existential affirmation demands as the condition of its possibility that both the receptive knower and the sensible objects of his knowledge be composed of matter, form, and existence."[45] Thus, the possibility of such a transcendental metaphysics, which Marechal indicated, became the origin of what would be known as Transcendental Thomism.

In general, metaphysical hypotheses formulate theories about the nature of human and celestial realities. Classical Greek philosophy thought all of reality was a great chain of being, which are hierarchically structured, fixed and unchangeable. Classical Greek metaphysics also thought of its hypotheses as universal and necessary truth, claiming to grasp a priori universality and necessity with respect to the nature of Being.[46] Plato and Aristotle reified essences. Plato reified them as transcendent, subsistent ideas and Aristotle reified them as unchanging principles of being that are immanent in all things. Since classical Greek metaphysics thought of its hypotheses as universal and necessary truth, Marechal's error, as Gelpi points out, was that he thought he could use Kantian transcendental logic to reground metaphysics.[47] There is also the added fact that justifying faculty psychology, as Marechal did, forces one to justify equally the world of classical Greek metaphysics that it presupposes. Unfortunately, that world builds on the essence fallacy and a person who reifies essences, Gelpi insists, commits essence fallacy.[48] "Philosophical acquiescence in the essence fallacy inclines the rational mind to think in equally fallacious dualistic categories. The essence fallacy reifies ideas by treating them as objects of thought rather than as modes of perceiving the realities and actualities which the human mind knows."[49]

Be that as it may, at the heart of Thomistic faculty psychology is an operational dualism that stemmed from Aquinas who recalibrated the Aristotelian notion of the five sensory faculties in terms of the powers of the will and the intellect or spiritual powers. "The sense powers include the five external senses, sensible memory and imagination, as well as the concupiscible and irascible appetites. The active and passive intellects as well as the

---

44. McCool, *Rahner Reader*, xvi.
45. McCool, *Rahner Reader*, xvi.
46. Gelpi, *Gracing of Human Experience*, 266.
47. Gelpi, *Turn to Experience in Contemporary Theology*, 95.
48. Gelpi, *Turn to Experience in Contemporary Theology*, 100.
49. Gelpi, *Gracing of Human Experience*, 3.

will qualify as spiritual and therefore lack any organic basis."[50] The spiritual powers of the soul are ontologically superior to the sensible powers. Gelpi correctly points out that if one accepts faculty psychology's account of the human psyche, then one would be unable to explain how intellectual knowledge arises from the senses. Gelpi also takes time to point out the problems of essentialism and dualism—two interrelated problems he conceives as fallacies, which have bedeviled Christian anthropology and long confused theological thinking about the graced transformation of the human person:

> When the human mind not only reifies essences but chooses to define one essence as the logical contradiction of another, it teaches itself to misconceive reality by understanding two interrelated realities in such a way as to render their real relationship subsequently unintelligible. I call all such things dualistic. For example, by defining "spiritual" as "immaterial" and by reifying these two essences, Platonic philosophy made it subsequently impossible to find anything in common between material and spiritual realities and vice versa. By definition, the spiritual must negate the material, the physical, in reality. A convinced Platonist had no choice, then, but to understand physical reality as the negation of spiritual reality and spiritual reality as the negation of the physical. This understanding of the relationship between spirit and matter exemplifies dualistic thinking because it defines two interrelated realities, e.g., the body and the soul, in such a way that their real relationship to one another becomes subsequently unthinkable.[51]

Gelpi argues coherently that what Marechal did in responding to Kant should be seen as an apologetic attempt to rehabilitate Aquinas in a world that was fast losing interest in Thomism. To some extent, this explains why some contemporary theologies that are built on faculty psychology continue to gain acceptance and popularity in Catholic circles, in spite of the obvious flaws of faculty psychology. "The political situation of the church," Gelpi argues, "conspired with the confusion of Kantian logic to betray Marechal and his followers into confusing the enunciation of an epistemological hypothesis with its validation."[52] Gelpi attributes this to a problem of ego-inertia he thinks is apparent in Catholic theology. "A theological community habituated for over a century to thinking almost exclusively in Thomistic patterns

---

50. Gelpi, *Turn to Experience in Contemporary Theology*, 102.
51. Gelpi, *Gracing of Human Experience*, 4.
52. Gelpi, *Turn to Experience in Contemporary Theology*, 96.

of thought seems to find it virtually impossible to shift to more inculturated patterns of philosophical reflection."[53]

Gelpi credits the developmental psychologist Jean Piaget (1896–1980) as one who understands more than his peers why modern European philosophy after Descartes continue to foist one contradiction after another on the nature of the human mind. Gelpi also castigates mainstream philosophy for the failure to understand how human thinking works. The reason why they fail to understand how human thinking works is because the philosophers proposing the hypotheses fail to ask anyone whether their minds do in fact operate in the manner philosophers say they do.[54] He argues that Piaget had sought to correct this "bubble of philosophical illusion" by suggesting a "multi-disciplinary validation of philosophical theories of knowledge through the empirical techniques like those he employed in his developmental psychology."[55] It is apt to add that quite independently of each other, both Peirce and Lonergan have reached the same conclusion regarding interdisciplinary cooperation that Piaget suggested. As a corrective to Kant's fatal error and the methodological illusions that have dogged philosophy, Peirce suggested a critical realism that brings to bear induction, deduction, and abduction. Lonergan also suggested an inferential reasoning similar to that of Peirce, espousing eight interrelated set of operations he calls the functional specialties as a means of arriving at a satisfying metaphysical theory of knowledge.

To return to Gelpi's criticism of Marechal, Gelpi thinks the illusions that Marechal popularized in laying the foundations of the intellectual movement that came to be known as Transcendental Thomism negatively impacts the development of Transcendental Thomism as such. Kantian logic teaches the mind to confuse the mere enunciation of a hypothesis with its validation. Since most Transcendental Thomists ground their assumptions on faculty psychology, Gelpi reasons that those assumptions are fundamentally flawed because "the polymorphic character of human consciousness makes it impossible to deal adequately with human evaluative responses by using Kantian transcendental method alone."[56]

It is hard not to agree with Gelpi that there is no place in contemporary theology for a metaphysics that is built on faculty psychology. Lonergan reinforced the notion that scholastic faculty psychology was a metaphysical

---

53. Gelpi, *Turn to Experience in Contemporary Theology*, 103.

54. Gelpi, *Gracing of Human Experience*, 269. Here Gelpi is referencing Piaget's *Insights and Illusions of Philosophy*.

55. Gelpi, *Turn to Experience in Contemporary Theology*, 96.

56. Gelpi, *Turn to Experience in Contemporary Theology*, 112.

psychology built on "a doctrine of the essence of the soul, of its potentialities, of their informing habits and acts, and of the objects of the acts. So little did consciousness enter into this psychology."[57] It is this psychology that has underpinned Christian theological accounts of the person of Christ, his human perfection, and the grace that God gives superabundantly to Christ. If contemporary challenge to traditional Christology is to be met, Lonergan argues, "then one must go beyond a metaphysical view of the person, a metaphysical account of human perfection, a metaphysical account of the life of grace."[58] To do this, we must first acknowledge that a person is a psychological subject of interpersonal relations and "that human development is entry into a symbolic world, a world mediated by meaning."[59] What would serve contemporary theology better, therefore, is a theology built on a metaphysics on fallibilistic logic, like that of Peirce. It is quite easy to forget, in theology at least, that the revolutions in physics that occurred from the sixteenth century to the present day present us with conceptions of physical nature "so radically different from that entertained by classical physics that the philosophical outlook conditioned by the latter is no longer viable either as a metaphysical theory or as tacit presupposition of other sciences."[60] So it is no longer justified or profitable to attempt to find out the nature of things as they are in themselves, as many who employ the transcendental analysis tend to do, by beginning with metaphysical assumptions about the nature of the world and our knowledge with respect to it, and then attempt to interpret it scientifically. To continue in that fashion is to remain steeped in intellectual incongruency.[61] Apart from the fact that he avoids this pitfall, what sets Peirce apart is that his phenomenology and inferential thinking accounts for both the spatio-temporal realities and realities that transcend space and time without appealing to and avoiding the confusion arising from the classical Greek categories of spirit and matter. As Gelpi argued convincingly, evolutionary understanding of the universe calls into serious question the classical Greek understanding of essence that derives from both Plato and Aristotle. "In an evolving universe essences exist but neither as subsistent realities nor as metaphysical principles of being. Rather, the term 'essence' designates a human evaluative response—a sensation, image, or conceptual perception—abstracted from the reality it perceives

---

57. Lonergan, "Christology Today," 75.
58. Lonergan, "Christology Today," 76.
59. Lonergan, "Christology Today," 76.
60. Harris, *Foundations of Metaphysics in Science*, 37.
61. Harris, *Foundations of Metaphysics in Science*, 20.

and from the one who does the perceiving."[62] Unlike the static, hierarchical conception of reality that prevailed in Greco-Roman world, an evolutionary understanding of the universe understands that the dynamism present in all reality results from the revolving histories, not from some fixed, unchanging essence within them. "What a thing is results, not from some fixed essence lurking underneath its activity, but from its history. Each emerging self embodies a developing, more or less integrated complex of tendencies."[63] Thus, an evolutionary understanding speaks rather of development and growth.

Gelpi's criticism of Transcendental Thomism is quite helpful. Where he misses the mark, however, is with respect to his unqualified remarks about Lonergan on the issue of Transcendental Thomism. Gelpi mistakenly lumps Lonergan together with other Transcendental Thomists who regarded Marechal's thought as philosophically *avant garde* and acquiesced in its oversights and fallacies.[64] Granted Rahner may have accepted Thomistic metaphysics and its faculty psychology, but it was not without nuance. It would be a stretch to include Rahner, as Gelpi does, in the list of those transcendental Thomists with "fatally flawed transcendental method."[65] The objection rings even louder with respect to Lonergan who very early on understood and escaped the fallacies of Kantianism or Transcendental Thomism by effecting a shift from faculty psychology to intentionality analysis. Lonergan even objected to Otto Muck's characterization of his work as a Transcendental Thomist,[66] though he did not completely avoid subsequent use of the term "transcendental" to describe his method.[67] He employed the transcendental method in ways different from Rahner and the so-called Transcendental Thomists. There are certainly differences between Rahner and Lonergan's use of the transcendental method. In fact, Lonergan distinguished between three meanings or uses of the term "transcendental:" the Scholastic, the Kantian, and his own (Lonergan's), which he says he derived from Husserl's intentionality analysis. In the Lonergan-Husserl version of transcendental, *noesis* and *noema* are correlative.[68] Rahner, whose version of transcendental analysis is Kantian, perhaps writes more generally of how we can go beyond ourselves through knowledge and freedom, while Lonergan writes more specifically on how we do it through understanding

---

62. Gelpi, *Turn to Experience in Contemporary Theology*, 100–101.
63. Gelpi, *Turn to Experience in Contemporary Theology*, 101.
64. Gelpi, *Turn to Experience in Contemporary Theology*, 96.
65. Gelpi, *Gracing of Human Experience*, viii.
66. See Muck, *Transcendental Method*.
67. Morelli, *At the Threshold of the Halfway House*, 231.
68. See Crowe, *Appropriating the Lonergan Idea*, 149.

and conversion.[69] When Lonergan employed the transcendental method, he used the term "transcendental" in two senses: in the first as an attempt to bring to light the *a priori* conditions of the possibility of knowing an object, and in the second as the dynamic unfolding of the structure of human consciousness and the common core and foundation of all special methods.[70] Thus, while he did not disavow of those who think his procedures may share commonalities with the works of theologians who employ transcendental method, Lonergan was clear that he understood the limitations of the procedure: "I do not consider it very pertinent to an understanding of my own intentions."[71] In various works, Lonergan demonstrates how his method is different from that of Transcendental Thomists like Rahner, arguing that contemporary context has necessitated a shift in theology—that the shifts needed in theology's new engagement mean that scholastic categories and the old-style dogmatic theology are no longer adequate in the new context.[72] In the new context, he insists, theology must replace scholastic metaphysical dogmatics with more appropriate categories from related fields of study, like phenomenology, existentialism, personalism, and linguistics, and even the science of evolution. One of the arguments to be fleshed out later is how Lonergan understood far more than his peers that evolution is not irrelevant for theology and that Christology needs to be aware of its possible implications and the extent and limits of these implications.[73] It is precisely the possible implications of revolution in the science of evolution that makes imperative application of semiotics to Christology.[74] Lonergan, therefore, offers a critical realism that is in accord with the Peircean semiotic triadic structure, which is more viable for the kind of Christology Christian theology needs. Christianity, after all, is religion of a community of persons, not a religion of isolated individuals. Redemption or salvation always occurs in the context of a community.[75] What Lonergan and Peirce did, albeit independent of each other, is replace the Transcendental Thomists' "turn to subject" with the critical realists' "turn to community" of collaborators.

69. See Mueller, *What Are They Saying About Theological Method?*
70. Morelli, *At the Threshold of the Halfway House*, 233.
71. See Lonergan, *Method in Theology*, 17; particularly n11.
72. See Lonergan, "Revolutions in Catholic Theology," 20.
73. Peterson, "Whose Evolution? Which Theology?" 221–32.
74. Revolution in the science of evolution was inaugurated in 1972 with the publication of Punctuated Equilibrium (PE) by Niles Eldridge and Stephen Jay Gould. See Eldridge and Gould, "Punctuated Equilibria."
75. Gelpi, *Gracing of Human Experience*, 194.

FUSION OF DIACHRONIC AND SYNCHRONIC EXEGESIS

So far we have demonstrated why contemporary theology does not need a theology constructed on faculty psychology, but one that can be anchored in a metaphysics that can grasp the highest grade of reality semiotically. Peirce was one who demonstrated the conceptual adequacy of such a metaphysics. A distinguishing feature of the Peircean metaphysics is not just that it is experience-based, but also that it has the ability to take into account the insights and concerns of other philosophical constructs of experience, while still correcting their limitations and oversights. Furthermore, a triadic construct of experience in the Peircean mold avoids the spirit-matter dualism that bedevils Transcendental Thomism and replaces it with an experiential language of relationship and community. Unlike faculty psychology, a triadic construct of experience does not define certain human faculties as essentially spiritual and others as merely organic. Rather, what a triadic construct of experience does is discover "a continuum of evaluative response stretching from basic sensory experience to abstract modes of thinking; and it portrays the growth of consciousness as the acquisition of increasingly complex patterns of perception and of interpretation."[76]

Since theology needs to adjust to a triadic construct of experience, any adjustments in theology (doctrine of God) willy-nilly affects Christology (doctrine of Christ), for theology and Christology are bound together. The goal of theology and Christology is to make this connection.[77] Theology is the science whose object is God. Christology is a sub-division of theology. It is also the science whose object is Christ, his person, and his work.[78] As Wolfhart Pannenberg has made clear, one speaks about Jesus only from the point of view of his significance for the idea of God in the context of the history of that idea as has been philosophically elaborated. "What one might otherwise say about Jesus would have to be presupposed as already known. The procedure of Christology, on the contrary, begins with Jesus himself in order to find God in him. In this case, in turn, the idea of God must be presupposed historically and in substance."[79]

The distinction between synchronic and diachronic exegesis is now very common in modern biblical scholarship. But it was the Swiss scholar and semiologist and the widely acclaimed founder of modern linguistics, Ferdinand de Saussure (1857–1913), who first introduced the distinction

---

76. Gelpi, *Turn to Experience in Contemporary Theology*, 137.
77. Pannenberg, *Jesus—God and Man*, 20.
78. Cullmann, *Christology of the New Testament*, 1.
79. Pannenberg, *Jesus—God and Man*, 20.

in his semiology.[80] The goal of the Swiss master was to provide "a theoretic foundation to the newer trend in linguistics study."[81] The linguistic structuralism, which he founded, was a response to the Neo-grammarian approach to language that dominated the field for a long time. Saussure studied under the Neo-grammarians before he started refuting their atomistic approach to linguistics and began framing a coherent science of linguistics.[82] Today, Saussure's views on theoretical problems are widely consulted by scholars from a wide variety of disciplines. Our interest in Saussure here will be limited only to the descriptive-explanatory relevance of linguistic structuralism to theology and Christology, i.e., the Saussurean distinction between synchronic and diachronic exegesis.

In his posthumous *Cours de Linguistique Generale* (1916) [published in English in 1959], Saussure made an important distinction between diachronic and synchronic approaches to linguistics. A diachronic approach is the study of linguistics over a period of time. Diachronic approach is very historical in nature. It investigates the history of language, paying particular attention to the etymological derivations of words. The synchronic approach is the study of language at a given point in time. Synchronic approach is systematic and contemporary in nature. It investigates how language changes over time, paying particular attention to regional variations of language (dialects) and contemporary usage of words. Saussure saw the two approaches as different; "they are not of equal importance."[83] He, however, considered the diachronic and synchronic axes to be legitimate and necessary. Although he considered the two approaches as legitimate and necessary, "it was on the synchronic axis that the emphasis of his thinking lay."[84] Saussure not only privileged the synchronic over the diachronic, he also thought that the two were "not of equal importance"[85] and that the "synchronic viewpoint predominates."[86] For Saussure, only synchronic linguistics can be considered a rigorous science in the strict sense of the term. He thought that diachronic linguistics, although systematic, represents only a collection of facts that does not reveal authentic nature of language.[87]

---

80. Joyce, "Synchronic and Diachronic Perspectives in Ezekiel," 115.
81. See Saussure, *Course in General Linguistics*, xi.
82. See Saussure, *Course in General Linguistics*, xi.
83. See Saussure, *Course in General Linguistics*, 90.
84. Barr, "Synchronic, the Diachronic and the Historical," 1.
85. Saussure, *Course in General Linguistics*, 90.
86. Saussure, *Course in General Linguistics*, 90.
87. See Graffi, "Again on Saussure and Dilthey," 151–58.

Although Saussure created the impression that synchronic linguistics is to be "regarded as methodologically prior,"[88] his aim was to highlight the distinction between the two axes. The contrast Saussure drew between the diachronic and synchronic approaches has led linguists to question whether synchronic and diachronic explanations of language are contrastive or complementary. In other words, is the study of language a diachronic and synchronic entity that complement each other or are they dichotomies? This is also a relevant question for Christology. Christian theology is a body of knowledge that covers about two millennia years of activities. The complexity of the data and genres to be studied in our quest to understand who Jesus truly is suggests that something similar to the Saussurean approaches to linguistics be adopted.[89] Biblical and historical exegesis fall within the diachronic axis. A systematic approach to the dogmas of faith falls within the synchronic axis. Perhaps in part due to the Saussurean privileging of synchronic approach, "diachronic interests have come to be down-valued, and these tendencies have come to be associated with a more general anti-historical trend in modern culture—something that may have been quite absent from Saussure's own intention."[90]

There are some who think Christology should be more synchronic than diachronic. Our contention here is that Christology should be as synchronic as it is diachronic, for a blend of the two axes is helpful for our understanding of who Jesus really is. The tendency to down-value the diachronic is an anti-historical trend and should have no place in Christology. Synchrony, in the Saussurean sense, must not be antithetical to the historical; rather it must support historical approach. In one sense, the synchronic meanings of some biblical texts are often the historical meanings of the texts.[91] The Prologue of John is a good case in point: "In the beginning was the Word, and the Word was with God, and the Word was God. The same was in the beginning with God. All things were made by him; and without him was not anything made that was made" (John 1:1–3). How did the Johannine community understand the text in their time and how do we understand the text today? The diachronic meaning of "in the beginning" must be the same as the synchronic meaning of the phrase denoting the eternity of the Second Person of the Trinity.

---

88. Barr, "Synchronic, the Diachronic and the Historical," 1; quoting Mühlhäusler, "Linguistics: Diachronic," 355.

89. Edward Oakes may have been one of the early pioneers of this position. See *Infinity Dwindled to Infancy*, 26–27.

90. Barr, "Synchronic, the Diachronic and the Historical," 2.

91. Barr, "Synchronic, the Diachronic and the Historical," 2.

There is no denying that there are some weaknesses in the Saussurean conception of linguistics. There is also no denying that the terms diachronic and synchronic, which Saussure introduced to linguistics, have sometimes been used and applied differently in modern literary studies. The various usages can at times be ambiguous and confusing. However, a recovery of the two Saussurean axes of synchrony and diachrony bodes well for Christology because it fuses the two axes of history and systematics. This recovery can also be a corrective to the current of anti-historical thinking that is ideologically powerful in western culture.[92] Any ahistorical or binary opposition between the diachrony and synchrony has no place in Christology. Irrespective of the fact that Saussure coined the terms synchronic and diachronic in the twentieth century, the realities they denote can be traced back to the nineteenth century and beyond.[93] Admittedly, "the Christ-event, of which Jesus is the center, must not be submerged in the vast misty ocean of two millennia of church history,"[94] the data of the Christ-event to be studied is as complex as the history of the Church itself. The complexity of the data and genres to be studied makes imperative that we adopt diachronic and synchronic investigations without necessarily privileging one over the other. It is by so doing that we can come to a fuller understanding of the person and mission of Jesus and how divine grace is mediated both to those within and outside the visible confines of the Church.

THE QUESTION OF THE IDENTITY AND MISSION OF JESUS

The question of the identity and mission of Jesus is at the heart and center of Christology. Christology (the study of Jesus Christ) is a science in the same way physics and geology or anthropology and linguistics are considered a science. Some themes in Christology (e.g., the incarnation, resurrection, atonement, eschatology, etc.) can either be subjected to some scientific analysis or be understood in the light of new understandings in the science of evolution. However, although Christology is a science in the same way physics or linguistics is considered a science, it is a different kind of science. In the natural sciences (physics and biology for example) and the social sciences (sociology and psychology for example), the fields of investigation are open and accessible to everyone. But not so with Christology. The science of Christ, strictly speaking, is accessible only to people of faith, i.e., those who

---

92. Barr, "Synchronic, the Diachronic and the Historical," 8.
93. Rogerson, "Synchrony and Diachrony in the Work of De Wette," 145.
94. Anderson, "Christology," 83.

confess that Jesus is Lord.⁹⁵ This is because theology is not only an exercise of faith, "it is conducted in the service of faith—that of the individual and of the Church as the community of faith."⁹⁶ Since faith is what distinguishes theology from other disciplines, like sociology, psychology, and biology, there is a sense in which it is fair to say that non-Christians who do not confess Jesus as Lord cannot meaningfully engage in Christology. This is because the intelligibility to be grasped in the science of Christ is not prescriptive but derives rather from the invariant structure of consciousness of those who claim to have a legitimate (physical or spiritual) experience of the risen Christ. For this reason, this intelligibility is not necessarily open to non-believers and not easily accessible to them, since faith is a *sine qua non condition* for understanding who Jesus is. By saying that faith is *sine qua non condition* for Christology, it does not mean that nonbelievers could not discuss what they might hold if they had believed there was God. "But this would only be a kind of hypothetical discourse, based on a contrary-to-fact condition."⁹⁷

Furthermore, non-Christians cannot meaningfully engage in Christology because the data for the science of Christology comes almost entirely from what Christians call the Old Testament (Christian reading of the Hebrew Bible) and the New Testament. Historically, non-Christians, like Pliny the Younger (c. AD 61–160), have made references to Jesus and have contributed to our stock of knowledge on who Jesus is. There was also the Roman historian Publius Tacitus (AD 56–120) who referenced the execution of Jesus by Pontius Pilate in his *Annals* (c. AD 116). In the case of Tacitus, like Pliny the Younger, their knowledge of Jesus's existence "stems entirely from their prior knowledge of Christianity, that is, from Christian witness to Jesus; so their testimony must be regarded as entirely derivative."⁹⁸ We can say the same thing of the Jewish historian Flavius Josephus (AD 37–100) who mentions Jesus a couple of times in his apologetic work of Jewish religion, *The Antiquities* (c. AD 78). His references to Jesus as a whole tell us "little that one would not already have gleaned from the Gospels."⁹⁹ There is, therefore, no denying that the data for Christology is found almost exclusively in the New Testament. The fact that this data derives almost exclusively from the believing Christian community already suggests that

---

95. Oakes, *Infinity Dwindled to Infancy*, 1–2.
96. Dulles, *Faith of a Theologian*, 12.
97. Dulles, *Faith of a Theologian*, 11.
98. Oakes, *Infinity Dwindled to Infancy*, 24.
99. Oakes, *Infinity Dwindled to Infancy*, 25.

the scientific status of Christology is problematic.[100] It is problematic for non-Christians and Christians alike. Thus, if Christology is to be considered a science, it must be called a sapiential science. This sapiential science is made possible only by the gift of the Holy Spirit.[101] In addition, this sapiential science is confessional (belief in Jesus) and ecclesial; it both springs from and returns to Christian life and worship.[102]

Diachronic and Synchronic Study of Jesus

We have hinted that there are two important terms that cannot easily be dismissed in any genuine Christian Christological investigation. These are "faith" and "intelligibility" (reason). The question of who Jesus is in Himself and who He is in relation to us is an intelligibility to be grasped. We have argued that this intelligibility is more accessible to a person of faith than a non-believer. If there is a place where historical investigation and faith must meet in the same person,[103] there is no place more suitable than in the study of Christology. However, that is not to say that a non-believer cannot grasp aspects of it. The intelligibility to be grasped is still wide open, regardless of whether one professes belief in Jesus as the Second Person of the Blessed Trinity. In other words, both believers and non-believers who pose the question regarding the person and mission of the man from Nazareth who lived roughly from 4 BC to 33 BC may seek intelligibility. But how they grasp it is a different question entirely.

To grasp meaningfully this intelligibility, we need to embark on a diachronic and synchronic study of the life of Jesus Christ. In the world of Palestine where Jesus was born and reared, Jesus fully lived out his life in a world mediated by Palestinian cultural meanings and values. He lived out the historicity of his life in a human world controlled at the time by the Roman Empire and under the very conditions that the ruling Roman authorities determined make a world a human world. We need to be reminded that Christ did not begin his life here on earth as an adult, but as an infant and that he made himself an adult by his own acts of experiencing, understanding, judging, and deciding. As an adult, he formed his own dispositions and his own character by his own choices. "He formed himself, not by natural acts alone (as though he existed in a state of pure nature), and not by the light of faith (as though he were not the head but a member of his body), but

---

100. Oakes, *Infinity Dwindled to Infancy*, 2.
101. Oakes, *Infinity Dwindled to Infancy*, 8–9.
102. Oakes, *Infinity Dwindled to Infancy*, 20–21.
103. See Crowe, *Appropriating the Lonergan Idea*, 194.

out of his immediate knowing of God, so that he might incarnately display the divine mystery in such a way that he could say to everyone, 'Follow me' (Luke 2:52)."[104] Also, Christ not only accepted his humanity as an infant, he accepted his lineage from the dynasty of David. He accepted the historicity of his time as one born in the time of Caesar Augustus and embraced the peculiarity of his culture, speaking Aramaic and going through rabbinical education. "We say not only that he was born in that determinate human world, but also that he made that world, that language, that culture, his own. Just as 'making it his own' involves acceptance and assimilation, so too it means a personal adaptation and refashioning."[105]

For these reasons, Christology needs a synthesis of diachronic (historical) and synchronic (systematic) investigations. The mere fact that we (believers and non-believers alike) possess intellect makes us desirous of knowledge. Our natural desire to know is manifested in questions that Lonergan, following Thomas Aquinas and Aristotle, reduces to the pair *an sit* and *quid sit*. The question *quid sit* expresses a natural desire to understand and to know the cause of a thing.[106] *Quid Sit* (what is it), i.e., the examination of data and formulation of hypothesis, with respect to Jesus, must be followed-up with *An Sit* (is it so?), i.e., weighing the evidence and making judgment that will hopefully lead to a responsible action on the part of the Christian. In other words, how could an unchanging eternal God possibly become man when in the true sense of the word "becoming" means to change or even corrode?[107] Those who have pointed out this paradox are quick to point out that what Christians claim God "becomes" in Jesus is conceptually opposite to the unchanging and infinite connotations of what it means to be God.[108] How can the infinite become finite without losing its infinity?[109] How can the eternal become temporal? How can a little baby boy born in a manger at a particular point in time be worshipped as the creator of the world?[110] Can one even conceptualize these questions without involving oneself in contradictions? The complexity of these questions makes imperative a fusion of diachronic and synchronic investigations in the quest to uncover the identity and mission of Jesus. The interpenetration

---

104. Lonergan, *Incarnate Word*, 591.
105. Lonergan, *Incarnate Word*, 593.
106. See Lonergan, "Natural Desire to See God," 81–82.
107. Oakes, *Infinity Dwindled to Infancy*, 2.
108. Oakes, *Infinity Dwindled to Infancy*, 2.
109. Oakes, *Infinity Dwindled to Infancy*, 2.
110. Oakes, *Infinity Dwindled to Infancy*, 8.

of diachrony and synchrony will involve a careful attention to a whole range of issues, including the following:

(a) Study of Historical Data

In studying the life of Jesus, we must ask all relevant questions and ask them in a very satisfying way. The *historische Jesus-Frage* or what is now traditionally known as the first Quest for the Historical Jesus was a failure because it was undertaken by rationalists and agnostics who were not interested in asking all the relevant questions but were simply out to discredit historical Christianity. The Quest was sparked by the writings of the German enlightenment thinker and deist, Herman Samuel Reimarus (1694–1768), who attacked the historical reliability of the Gospels and claimed that the death of Jesus was a conspiracy and a forgery on the part of the disciples who wanted to keep the movement going for their own selfish interest. On this came the basic assumption of the first Quest by subsequent writers like David Strauss 1801–1874) who engaged in historical reconstruction, bypassing the Gospels, to get to "the facts behind the texts." In *The Life of Jesus Critically Examined*, Strauss denied any notion that Jesus was divine and held that Christianity was based on forgery. Following Reimarus's claim, Albert Schweitzer's (1876–1965) attempted to reconstruct the life of Jesus and ended up with the same thesis that early Christian claims about the resurrection were fraudulent.[111] Martin Kahler (1835–1921) who went a step further and distinguished between "Jesus of history" and the "Christ of faith" suggested in the end that there is little that can be known about the Jesus of history because the gospel records are not historical accounts of Jesus, but expressions of faith of the Gospel writers.[112] The error of the first Quest was that in the attempt to get to "the facts behind the texts," it willfully refused to give credence to the Gospel narrative, ignoring "both the overall theological intention of the evangelists and the literary intention of their texts. The theological and literary whole is greater than the sum of its (historical) parts."[113] Scripture must be read and interpreted in the sacred spirit in which the evangelists recorded their narratives. Therefore, to disregard the content and unity of the whole of Scripture, as the first Quest did, is to compromise the meaning of the sacred text itself.[114]

The renewed Quests, i.e., the second and third Quests for the historical Jesus, realized the limitations of the first Quest—that you cannot divorce

111. See Schweitzer, *Quest of the Historical Jesus*.
112. See Kahler, *So-Called Historical Jesus and the Historic*.
113. O'Collins, *Christology*, 53–54.
114. See *Dei Verbum*, Dogmatic Constitution on Divine Revelation, No. 12.

the Christ of history from the Christ of faith— and sought to correct them. In *Jesus of Nazareth*, Maurice Casey memorably remarked that all the attempts, by scholars like Albert Schweitzer, John Meier, and Martin Hengel, to situate Jesus within the background of first century Judaism have not succeeded. The reason why it has not succeeded, according to Casey, is largely due to "insufficient study of Jesus' language" and "the cultural background of scholars themselves."[115] Maurice argued that it is precisely because a vast number of the scholarship in Jesus has "not been Jewish enough" that we need a fresh study of the life of Jesus.[116] Casey may be wrong in many things concerning Jesus's Resurrection, but was right on this point because if we need to understand who Jesus is, it is essential to locate him against the cultural background of the first century Palestine, in addition to stressing the Jewishness of Jesus. Any attempt to understand who Jesus is must involve a study of historical data of the events of his life, death, and resurrection, including how he was perceived and understood by his contemporaries and even generations after him. We have to do this by paying attention to the responses he evoked from the time he lived in the first century to the present day. This means studying the Christian communities— their liturgies, hymns, Scriptures, and traditions that emerged following their understandings of the Jesus-event. Early Christians celebrated their basic belief of who Jesus is in their liturgies and formulated their confessional statements in their creeds and various professions of faith.[117] The responses he evoked are by no means limited to the Christian circles. He has also evoked responses in Jewish, Muslim, Hindu, and other non-Christian circles, in so far as these people have in one way or another attempted an answer to the question posed by Jesus himself: "Who do you say that I am?" (Mark 8:29).[118] In addition to paying attention to responses he evoked, both short term and long term by the Jesus-event, our investigation of the identity and mission of Jesus must also pay attention to antecedents of the Jesus-event in the history of Israel and the Ancient Near East of which Israel was a part.[119] Such antecedents may include the Ancient Near Eastern understanding of prophets and the phenomenon of prophecies, as well as Jewish Messianism. Thus, the Jewish Scriptures and/or what is traditionally referred to in Christian circles as the Old Testament (no supersessionism implied) "is essential for grasping

---

115. Casey, *Jesus of Nazareth*, 3.
116. Casey, *Jesus of Nazareth*, 3.
117. O'Collins, *Christology*, 4.
118. O'Collins, *Christology*, 4.
119. O'Collins, *Christology*, 2.

both the matrix of Jesus' life and what the New Testament witnesses have to say about him."[120]

The first generation of Jesus's disciples relied on ideas, beliefs, and expectations of Judaism that were in both the Old Testament and the Aprocrypha writings to articulate their convictions about the identity and divine mission of Jesus.[121] The Old Testament particularly provided them the theological language and concepts they used in speaking of the identity of Jesus, granted that these images, concepts, and language would later be illuminated by other sources from the world around them, principal among which are the writings from Qumran, Greco-Roman thoughts and writings, and non-Canonical literature from Hellenistic Judaism.[122]

Ancient philosophers like Plato (c. 428 BC—348 BC) and Aristotle (384 BC—322 BC) left a host of writings behind that generations after them scour to discern who they were and what they thought. Plato wrote a lot on various subjects and so did Aristotle. Socrates was an exception because he left no writings. To discern what Socrates believed and taught scholars rely on the writings of his most famous disciple, Plato, and perhaps the writings of the Greek historian Herodotus (484 BC–425 BC). In spite of the amount of data that have been gathered from Plato and Herodotus, scholars still do not claim to have gotten a fuller picture of life of Socrates. In spite of what we know of Socrates from these sources, there is still a lot that we do not know. To attempt to know a person, including self, is to grapple with a mystery, which always remains obscure and elusive.[123] Very much like Socrates, Jesus left no writings, which makes any attempt to understand his personal life somewhat difficult. The only biblical evidence we have that Jesus wrote is found in the episode of the woman caught in adultery when Jesus stooped down and wrote with his finger on the ground while waiting for the first without sin among the multitude to cast the first stone on the woman caught in adultery (John 8:6–11). While we do not know why and what Jesus wrote, some exegetes think Jesus stooping and writing in the dirt is an allusion to a passage in Jeremiah: "Lord, hope of Israel, those who leave you will be ashamed. People who quit following the Lord will be like a name written in the dust because they have left the Lord, the spring of the living water" (Jeremiah 17:13).

Although non-Christian writers, like the Roman Tacitus, Suetonius, and Pliny the Younger and Jewish Historians like Flavius Josephus give their

---

120. O'Collins, *Christology*, 21.
121. O'Collins, *Christology*, 22.
122. O'Collins, *Christology*, 22.
123. O'Collins, *Christology*, 45.

own accounts of Jesus, our best reliable source for the life of Jesus remains the canonical Gospels and the books of the New Testament. These sources make references to the suffering and death of Jesus. They do not, however, exhaust the mystery of the Man. For this reason, we must take seriously the admonition of those who insist that it is to our peril if we approach our study of Jesus as a problem to be solved by scholarship rather than as a mystery with which to engage ourselves for a lifetime.[124] Our limited and fragmentary data of the life of Jesus is not sufficient to reconstruct his whole life, particularly the years before his public ministry, not to talk of the problematic of getting access to his interior life. We must, therefore, guard against "the illusion that research could yield some nuggets of original, uninterpreted facts about Jesus."[125] Our knowledge of Jesus, even in the most reliable of the gospels, is always a mediated and interpreted account of the author or authors behind the texts. This is precisely why we asserted earlier that Christology cannot ignore how the early generation of Jesus's disciples understood the Old Testament and how they used the images and language of the Old Testament to sharpen their understanding of the identity and mission of Jesus. Having said that, we must, however, note that though Jesus did not leave behind any writing or document, the task of interpreting his identity and mission through Old Testament themes, such as relating his messianic mission to the line of David (Mark 2:23–28; 10:46–52) began with Jesus himself,[126] a point we would make clear later when identifying the Old Testament images of Jesus.

(b) The Role of Philosophy

Christology needs not only critical history, but also a philosophical basis to underpin this historical truth. Augustine and a good number of the Church Fathers were Platonists. Aquinas and the scholastics were Aristotelians. A good number of medieval and modern thinkers found a middle ground in a blend of Platonism and Aristotelian philosophy. While the Platonic-Aristotelian derived philosophies do have a place in theological discourse, we cannot deny the inadequacies of these philosophies for the modern context, particularly in the light of the new heights the semiotic realism of C. S. Peirce can take us. Implicit in Platonism is a dualism, and as in many European philosophy, there is over reliance on the power of intuition and denial of the power of introspection. Peirce called into question philosophies that rely on intuition for the very fact that they deny the

---

124. O'Collins, *Christology*, 46.
125. O'Collins, *Christology*, 52.
126. O'Collins, *Christology*, 23.

power of introspection. Intuition, for Peirce, is "a cognition not determined by a previous cognition, and therefore so determined by something out of consciousness."[127] Intuition violates the discursive nature of human knowledge. Peirce not only denounces intuition, he states categorically that we have no power of thinking without signs. This Peircean assertion is a also a rejection of the Kantian nominalism that the mind cannot grasp reality as it exists (Ding an sich).[128] Although not a Peircen, but nonetheless very much in the tradition of critical realism that Peirce inaugurated, Lonergan's generalized empirical method (GEM) foregrounds the kind of philosophy theology needs.

A proper human knowing constitutes of the three acts (experience, understand, judge) in Lonergan's intentionality analysis. For the acts of experiencing, understanding, and judging are three human acts that make up one intentional whole. "For the proportionate object [of human knowing] is a quiddity existing in corporeal matter, where corporeal matter is known through experiencing, quiddity is known through understanding, and existence is known through judging."[129] To arrive at true judgment of who Jesus is in Himself and in relation to us, the data and truth of history must be supplemented by philosophical reason.[130] The Christian confessional statement that Jesus is fully human and fully divine is a claim. In making this claim Christians appeal to concepts that can portray as clearly as possible the claim they are making. While it is not the role of philosophy to attest whether a person can be simultaneously human and divine, philosophy can help us with concepts that can help us not only to examine and clarify whether our claims are coherent, but also to judge whether these claims are "incoherent to the point of impossibility."[131] Some of the terms we use to speak of the salvific role of Christ, like liberation, expiation, sacrifice, transformation, omni-presence, love, etc., belong to the realm of philosophy.[132] Nevertheless, according to the teachings of the First Vatican Council, reason, illumined by faith can by God's grace, attain a highly fruitful understanding of the mysteries of God both from the analogy of what it naturally knows and from the interconnections of the mysteries with one another and with our last end [DS 3016].

---

127. See Peirce, "Questions Concerning Certain Faculties Claimed for Man," 103–114.
128. Gelpi, *Gracing of Human Experience*, 140.
129. Lonergan, *Incarnate Word*, 377.
130. O'Collins, *Christology*, 10.
131. O'Collins, *Christology*, 11.
132. O'Collins, *Christology*, 11.

(c) Problem vs. Mystery Polarity

The classic distinction between a problem and a mystery comes to bear as we try to understand who Jesus is.[133] Kant claimed to have destroyed metaphysics and by so doing thought he had rendered impossible our ability to know things belonging to the celestial realm. If Kant did achieve anything, he helped to further the collapse of a priori metaphysical thinking. However, we know "that the collapse of a priori metaphysical thinking does not preclude the legitimacy of formulating fallible metaphysical hypotheses whose claims to universal applicability one tests systematically both against the experience and against the results of close scientific and scholarly investigations of different realms of human experience."[134] What Kant did was create a metaphysical problem, making it difficult to make objective claims about things of God. But Peirce recalibrates metapysics, making it possible to make objective claims about things of God. Also, in reconstituting metaphysics as a form of inquiry, Peirce's inferential reasoning refutes Kantian and Cartesian dualism, making it possible for us to make claims to understanding mysteries.

The Christian existentialist philosopher, Gabriel Marcel (1889–1973), was one who made an important distinction between problem and mystery in his attempt to refute Cartesianism (skepticism). He also established in the process how the mind comes to know reality. Marcel writes, "A problem is something which I meet, which I find completely before me, but which I can therefore lay siege to and reduce. But a mystery is something in which I am myself involved, and it can therefore only be thought of as a sphere where the distinction between what is in me and what is before me loses its meaning and initial validity."[135] For Marcel, a problem is something outside of our intimate experience. Our attitude towards a problem is always impersonal because it lies outside of us. In other words, the subject asking the question is clearly different from the object of inquiry. The identity of the questioner does not matter because it makes no difference who is asking the question. For this reason, a problem is an object of inquiry for which there exists an objective solution. Thus, a problem can be overcome because it is something definite and fixed and in need of a solution. If subjected to scientific experimentation, the solution can be tested and verified. If something is to be considered a solution to a problem, certain empirically verifiable conditions must be met. In so far as the conditions can be satisfactorily fulfilled, the solution can be verified. If

---

133. O'Collins, *Christology*, 46.
134. Gelpi, *Gracing of Human Experience*, 270.
135. Marcel, *Being and Having*, 117.

given the same problem and conditions for solution, any de-personalized subject will reach the exact same conclusion because of the objectivity of knowledge. "When I am dealing with a problem," writes Marcel, "I am trying to discover a solution that can become common property, that consequently can, at least in theory, be rediscovered by anybody at all. But...this idea of a validity for "anybody at all" or of a thinking in general has less and less application the more deeply one penetrates into the inner courts of philosophy."[136]

On the other hand, a mystery, according to Marcel's distinction, is a problem in which the identity of the questioner becomes an issue. In mystery we are no longer dealing with a de-personalized objective question, rather we are dealing with a question that we are deeply personally involved in. Marcel calls mystery "meta-problematic" and speaks of it as a "problem that encroaches on its own data."[137] Mystery, according to Marcel, can be found in the question of Being. The question regarding what is being is intrinsically connected to the question who am I? Just as the question of being is related to the question of who I am, the question of who I am is also a question concerning the totality of being. Because these subjective and objective questions intersect in this case, Marcel suggests that when dealing with Being we are dealing not with a problem, but a mystery. In a nutshell, the mystery of being reveals the matter of subject-object relationship. What this means then is that a mystery transcends a problem. Because a mystery encroaches into the data of investigation it makes it difficult to be resolved through a rational process. Thus, when we inquire about the identity and mission of Jesus we are dealing not with a problem that can be resolved through scholarship, but with a mystery that engages us for the whole of our life.[138]

Earlier we alluded to the fact that non-Christians cannot meaningfully engage in Christology because the intelligibility to be grasped in this sapiential science is not easily accessible to them. In the light of Marcel's distinction between a problem and a mystery, we might also add that part of the reason why non-Christians cannot meaningfully engage in this sapiential science is because non-Christians who engage in this sapiential science approach it as a problem (in the Marcel sense), not a mystery. Take for example, one of the passages Muslims use to dismiss the divinity of Jesus and the Christian doctrine of the Trinity is the 112th chapter of the Quran, *Surah al-Ikhlas*, one of the shortest (if not the shortest) in the Quran which reads:

136. Marcel, *Mystery of Being*, 213.
137. See Cain, *Gabriel Marcel's Theory of Religious Experience*, 19.
138. O'Collins, *Christology*, 46.

1. Say: He is Allah, the One and Only;
2. Allah, the Eternal, Absolute;
3. He begetteth not, nor is He begotten;
4. And there is none like unto Him.

Muslim scholars are very quick to admit that the divinity, which Christians ascribe to Jesus, and we should add, which Jesus ascribes to Himself, poses a problem for the their understanding of monotheism. Christians, on the other hand, do not see this as a problem. Rather, for Christians, it is a mystery. The mystery of the Trinity again proves our point that Christians are better attuned to understanding this sapiential science because they are better placed to understanding the mystery than a non-believer would.

(d) Paradox

It was Edward Oakes who suggested that in the light of the Christian claim we make that in Jesus God became man, the fundamental problem of Christology centers around the juxtaposition of the infinite with the finite.[139] The title of Oakes's book *Infinity Dwindled to Infancy* is meant to capture the paradox to which Oakes draws our attention: "an infinite God who is a finite man, a virgin who is a mother, a God who dies, a dead man Jesus who lives, a baby born into the very world it made, a prince who is a pauper, in short, Infinity dwindled to infancy."[140] To Oakes's credit, he reminds us that poets employ paradox because they are "best endowed to see the value of paradox as a valued avenue to truth."[141] There is no denying that poetic use of paradox does not necessarily justify theological paradox, but if we can recognize worldly truth lurking in poetic paradox then we can at least be open to the possibility that there are truths embedded in theological paradoxes.[142] For paradox is a foundation stone of Christianity and Christology. According to Cyril of Alexandria, in Christ we find "'the strange and rare paradox' of a master who serves and abased in divine glory.'"[143] Ignatius of Antioch also spoke of Christ as the "only one physician, who is both flesh and spirit, born and unborn, God in man, true life in death, both from Mary and from God, first subject to suffering and then beyond it."[144]

---

139. Oakes, *Infinity Dwindled to Infancy*, 2.
140. Oakes, *Infinity Dwindled to Infancy*, 6.
141. Oakes, *Infinity Dwindled to Infancy*, 9.
142. Oakes, *Infinity Dwindled to Infancy*, 9.
143. Oakes, *Infinity Dwindled to Infancy*, 16.
144. Oakes, *Infinity Dwindled to Infancy*, 17.

(e) Methodological Issue

What Christians today confess about Jesus (i.e., as God-Man) is the same kerygma that the first generation of Jesus's disciples proclaimed. Hence it is apt to speak, as Lonergan does, of "the permanence of dogma"—the mysteries that God alone knows that have been revealed to the Church, defined by the Church, and understood by the faithful.[145] However, while the kerygma is ever the same, it has been proclaimed at different times and at different periods only according to the modes of expression of the time and period. Since each age brings with it new modes of expressions and new modes of understanding, the different ways of expressing faith in the Jesus-event suggests that Christological reflection requires a methodological consideration.[146] The role method plays in Christology is essentially twofold. The first is to examine what in earlier Christological understandings were inadequate. The second is to indicate a better procedure that might best serve Christology in the new context.[147] Take for example, the dogmatic decrees of the early Councils (Nicaea 325 and Chalcedon 451)—that Jesus is the Second Person of the Blessed Trinity. Medieval understanding of "person" was based on metaphysical assumptions of what they understood at the time constituted a person. Medieval metaphysical understanding of a person did not take into account the fact that a person is a psychological subject who is involved in interpersonal relations with others. It also did not underscore what we know today as a fact, thanks to developments in modern psychology and linguistics, "that human development is entry into a symbolic world, a world mediated by meaning."[148] This brings us back to our critique of faculty psychology vis-a vis Transcendental Thomism. Transcendental Thomists think that transcendental method gives a priviledged access to the dynamic structure of the human psyche. They assume that just because they interpret that structure in categories derived from Thomistic faculty psychology, they can locate opennes to mystery in the power of the spirit, and especially in the intellectual apprehension of Being as such. But a more psychologically plausible account of the experience of mystery does not locate it in the intellect, finite as it actually is, but in the imaginative and appreciative forms of knowing.[149] Thus, a contemporary Christology, which pays attention to the question of method, will attempt to go beyond (not reject) the medieval metaphysical view of person and incorporate

---

145. Lonergan, *Method in Theology*, 325.
146. See Lonergan, "Christology Today," 74–99.
147. Lonergan, "Christology Today," 74.
148. Lonergan, "Christology Today," 76.
149. Gelpi, *Grace as Transmuted Experience and Social Process*, 77.

contemporary understanding that a person is first and foremost a subject, a human being involved in psycho-social relations with others.

Another crucial aspect of methodological consideration may in fact be in the way historical facts are reconstructed and understood. Our understanding of history and the way historical investigations are carried out have changed since the linguistic and cultural turns in anthropology. In a dualist nominalist construct of experience, abstract ideas can only be verified in concrete historical facts and verification terminates all cognitive action.[150] But in a Peircean-Lonergan construct, the process of interpretation never ends. Every new event provides an opportunity for interpretation and every interpretation of event invites still further interpretations until a truly satisfactory answer is reached.[151] To put the contrast sharply, where in earlier times history was understood merely as a matter of believing testimonies and was to a large extent pre-critical, the new method we are advocating takes history to be a matter of critical understanding of evidence. For example, where Scripture speaks of Jesus as one who is "like us in every way except sin," the new method takes an approach that understands Jesus as "a historical being, as growing in wisdom, age, and grace in a determinate social and cultural milieu, as developing from below as other human beings and from above on the analogy of religious development."[152]

(f) Religious Language

Ludwig Wittgenstein (1889–1951), the Austrian-British philosopher who revolutionized the philosophy of language, wrote in the *Tractatus Logico-Philosophicus* that we need to "pass over in silence those things of which we cannot speak."[153] There are some who think that the realm of God belongs to a realm of things we need to pass over in silence, lest one falls prey to the idolatry of anthropomorphism through excessive labelling of God with human qualities and terms.[154] Some of the theologies that were developed by Eastern Christianity, i.e., Apophatic or Negative theology, recognized the inadequacies of our language about God. They remind us that we since we are dealing with divine mystery with respect to God, "any affirmation about God has to be qualified with a corresponding negation and with the recognition that God infinitely surpasses our human categories."[155]

---

150. Gelpi, *Gracing of Human Experience*, 192.
151. Gelpi, *Gracing of Human Experience*, 192.
152. Lonergan, "Christology Today," 82.
153. See Wittgenstein, *Tractatus Logico-Philosophicus*, 188.
154. Oakes, *Pattern of Redemption*, 15.
155. O'Collins, *Christology*, 13.

This raises the question: do religious language state facts and/or do they make factual claims?[156] There is no denying that religious language can and do state facts. The creedal statements "Jesus is Lord" and "For our sake he was crucified under Pontius Pilate; he suffered, died, and was buried" are factual claims. But how do our factual claims address the concerns of the empiricists who insist on limiting reality only to what is visible? In claiming that all reality is limited to the visibly perceptible or to the empirically verifiable, empiricists are essentially saying that religious language can never state facts involving the invisible and that what Christians mean when they speak of an empirically verifiable realm of God must be something other than what Christians purportedly claim.[157] Now we are back to the problem of human language. The early Christian understanding of Jesus has evolved over time and language has played a key role in both our understandings and expressions of who Jesus really and truly is. Developments in our thinking about Jesus has been characterized by two features that stem from "linguistic ambiguities and early intimations."[158] Gerald O'Collins has helpfully stated that linguistic ambiguities stem from "ways of describing the incarnation as (1) an appearing; (2) a being clothed (with flesh); (3) a dwelling within the (humanity of Jesus); and (4) a mixing or blending of divinity and humanity."[159] It is no wonder that the Christological councils of the early church appealed to Greek terms like *ousia* (substance), *hypostasis* (subsistent reality), and *physis* to help clarify these. The extent to which the terms employed succeed or fail in this clarification effort speaks to the extents and limits of language. In the main, we must be attentive to the fact that there are different ways of conceiving language, as can be gleaned even from the little we have said so far about the Structuralist School of Saussure that pays attention to structures of language and the Neogrammarian School from which he departed that followed atomistic approach to linguistics. For our purpose here, therefore, we iterate three primal ways of understanding biblical language concerning Jesus:

1. **Christological language as analogical**

    The matter of the right way to speak about God is one of the most basic questions in theology.[160] In ordinary language, we use words in many senses. We ascribe quality to things in different ways. When we ascribe quality to things the senses in which we use words may be divergent.

---

156. O'Collins, *Christology*, 84.
157. O'Collins, *Christology*, 84.
158. O'Collins, *Christology*, 169.
159. O'Collins, *Christology*, 169.
160. See Pannenberg, *Basic Questions in Theology*, 1:211.

But even when words are used divergently, they can still be related in meaning. Philosophically, this raises the distinction between univocal, equivocal, and analogical use of words.

- Univocation: When the same word is used as a referent to two different things but still retaining the same meaning the word is said to have been used univocally (univocation). Univocal language tries to reduce language into a simple empiricism. It ignores differences in its attempt to reduce everything to a sameness.[161]
- Equivocation: When the same word is used to mean two different things, we have equivocation. This occurs when the same word is used as a referent for two different things that have nothing in common. For example, the word "throw" can be used in a sentence to mean Jack threw the ball to Jane. But it can also be used to mean Jack threw the game, i.e., Jack deliberately lost the game. In the two senses of the word "throw" we have an equivocation.
- Multivocation: When the same word is used to mean different things, we have multivocation. Equivocation and multivocation both belong to the "accident of language."[162]
- Analogy: Language does, however, have some flexibility. "There are occasions when the same word can refer to different things that are neither utterly divergent nor identical, but are related somehow to each other, a relatedness which can be graded according to a certain proportionality of reference, that is, according to the fullness of the object to which the term refers."[163] This flexibility, which language has to apply to related things in different ways, is what Biblical writers and religious people capitalize on in speaking about God. The technical term for this is analogy: "Just as health applies primarily to the body and only secondarily to what indicates or promotes it, so too terms like 'good' and 'just' refer primarily to God and only secondarily to us and to the universe, who serve to 'indicate' true goodness: the goodness that is God's."[164] Unlike univocal language that ignores differences and reduces language to sameness, analogical language, by contrast, tries to hold differences and similarities in dynamic tension.[165]

---

161. Little, "Anthropology and Art in the Theology of Karl Rahner," 945.

162. Oakes, *Pattern of Redemption*, 16.

163. Oakes, *Pattern of Redemption*, 16.

164. Oakes, *Pattern of Redemption*, 16.

165. Little, "Anthropology and Art in the Theology of Karl Rahner," 945. See also Lynch, *Christ and Apollo,* 156–68.

As [human] beings, we can know objects that lie within being. "An object that is adequate but not proportionate can be known by us in this life inasmuch as we proceed analogically."[166] Plato developed the analogy of form. Aristotle developed the analogy of substance. Thomas Aquinas developed the analogy of being. The Platonic forms, which are eternal, immutable, subsistent, immaterial, and intelligible, are posited to account for the validity of universal and eternal knowledge.[167] Aristotle developed substances as either material (composed of mater and form) or immaterial (separate from matter) and reasoned that in the cosmos separated substances are the unmoved movers of the heavens. Aquinas developed the idea that the object of the intellect is being (everything that can be understood). For Aquinas, the "intellect is in act or in potency depending on its relation to universal being. It follows that no intellect except God's is purely and simply in act, since no created intellect is infinite being, the principle of the whole being."[168] Employing the doctrine of analogy as developed by Plato, Aristotle, and Aquinas, Lonergan developed the argument that the Chalcedonian distinction of the two natures of Christ after the Incarnation that are unconfused and unchanged is a distinction drawn by analogy.[169] He reads Aquinas as suggesting that when we employ analogy in theological discourse, at some point analogy is transcended and we are confronted with mystery to which we must bow our heads in adoration.[170]

While analogy might prove useful in theological enterprise, it still needs to be pointed out that since God remains an incomprehensible mystery there is still the problem of determining the standard by which one might judge the appropriateness of applying various terms to God.[171] It is for this reason that some theologians, Wolfhart Pannenberg especially, find analogy to be problematic. They consider its use to be a fundamental question in theology "because when used in speech about God it calls into play a whole understanding of the relationship between God and the world."[172]

---

166. Lonergan, *Incarnate Word*, 377.
167. Lonergan, *Incarnate Word*, 395.
168. Lonergan, *Incarnate Word*, 399. See Aquinas, *Summa Theologiae*, 1, q.79, a.2.
169. Lonergan, *Incarnate Word*, 253.
170. See Lonergan, *Verbum*, 208.
171. Oakes, *Pattern of Redemption*, 16–17.
172. See Johnson, "'Right Way to Speak about God,'" 673.

2. Christological language as metaphorical

We pointed out earlier that it is hard to deny that religious language makes factual claims. The creedal statements "Jesus was born in Bethlehem of Judea. He was crucified under Pontius Pilate and rose after three days" are factual claims. Beyond making factual claims, religious language also has metaphorical meanings. Words used metaphorically can at times seem like an equivocation. The difference, however, is that in this case the equivocation is intended and amplified. This is true of many of the words we use when we speak of God anthropomorphically. For example, we speak of God as listening or answering prayers (1 Kgs 18:24). But God does not "listen" or "answer" in the same way we apply the word "listening" or "answering" to human beings who perform these activities. Take another example, Christian believers speak of themselves as "slaves of Christ" (Eph 6:6; Col 3:24; 1 Pet 2:16). When we speak of ourselves as slaves of Christ, although the word slave may evoke memories of oppression, inferior status, vassalship, and even tendency to run away,[173] "slave" here is not used in the same sense as chattel slavery that we know from the Trans-Atlantic Slave Trade. Because the word is used metaphorically in reference to our relationship with Christ, slavery becomes something desirable.

3. Christological language as symbolic

Within the Christian tradition there is the understanding that Christological language is symbolic. The Church Fathers raised the question whether Christ, as man, was ignorant of anything. The consensus among them was that Christ, as man, was not ignorant of anything. Medieval theologians accepted the opinion of the Fathers, and going beyond the Fathers made a distinction between Christ's divine knowledge and human knowledge. They divided his human knowledge into three parts: beatific knowledge (immediate knowing of God), infused knowledge (immediate knowing of all things), and acquired knowledge (knowledge naturally acquired).[174] These are all symbolic representations of the knowledge Christ had in this world.

Following Aquinas who spoke of God in symbolic language—Being itself— some twentieth century theologians, like Paul Tillich and John Macquarie, support the claim that discourse about God is by its very nature symbolic.[175] Human language is symbolic. The Christian

---

173. See Bridge, "Metaphoric Use of Slave Terms in the Hebrew Bible," 13–28.
174. Lonergan, *Incarnate Word*, 603–5.
175. Alston, "Being-Itself and Talk about God," 9–25.

church is also by nature symbolic.[176] The sacraments of the Church of which Christ is the proto sacrament is also symbolic.[177] Since language is symbolic, and we live in a world of symbols, much of Christological language is symbolic. What does it mean, for example, to say Jesus is the Good Shepherd, the Suffering Servant, Rock of Ages, the Light of the World, the Proto-Ancestor, and the Bread of Life, etc., if these were not symbolic representations of our understanding of the person and mission of Jesus? This is why Lonergan argued, using symbolic representation that since Christ Himself is life eternal (1 John 1:2), "he had not the hope of eternal life, although he had another hope."[178]

176. See Tavard, "Papacy and Christian Symbolism," 345–58.
177. See Paschal, "Sacramental Symbolism and the Physical Imagery in the Gospel of John," 151–76.
178. Lonergan, *Incarnate Word*, 553.

Chapter Two

Setting the Stage for a Theosemiotic Christology

IN THE DECONSTRUCTIONIST PROJECT he initiated, the French philosopher and deconstructionist theorist, Jacques Derrida (1930–2004), demonstrated how the structures of language and their meanings are far from clear because they are unstable and are subject to mutation. Language, when translated, is often engulfed in slippage of meanings.[1] Derrida castigates the entire Western philosophical tradition, from its Platonic-Aristotelian origins to the phenomenology of Edmund Husserl (1859–1938). He questions the founding assumptions and aspirations of this philosophical tradition and claims that its "metaphysics of presence" was fatally flawed.[2] Derrida argues further that the Western philosophical tradition does violence to reality by the way it arbitrarily imposes dichotomous and hierarchically structured bipolar categories, such as sacred/profane, mind/body, and sign/signifier. These dichotomous categories, he argues, repress and exclude a whole range of meanings.[3] Derrida locates a solution to this Western philosophical problem in what he calls deconstruction. He coins the term *differance* (from the French, to differ and to defer) to argue his point "that meanings of signifiers were unstable in the sense that they could always mean something else in another linguistic juxtaposition or historical context."[4] Though there are differ-

---

1. See Derrida, *Positions* and Derrida, *Edmund Husserl's Origin of Geometry*.
2. Townshend, "Derrida's Deconstruction of Marxism," 128.
3. Coelho, "Non-Violence of Insight," 29–30.
4. Townshend, "Derrida's Deconstruction of Marxism," 128.

ent interpretations to the Derridean deconstruction of the metaphysics of presence, in general, the Derridean deconstruction can be taken to be a critique of western philosophical construction of how things are present to us.

Very much like Derrida, Bertrand Russell (1872–1970) was so miffed by the idealists' adherence to the classical tradition in philosophy that in 1914 he reproached them for their failure to adapt their thoughts to the scientific temper of the age.[5] Russell no doubt believed he himself was developing a philosophy that is in harmony with the scientific temper of the age. Ironically, some of Russell's own writings, like those of many who follow his methods and develop his ideas, frequently run contrary to some of the most significant trends in modern science. Their ideas have frequently been in conflict with their own professed empirical ideals.[6] Rarely do the philosophers who claim to be scientific in their philosophical methods consider carefully what being scientific means and what being scientific requires. Even a few of those philosophers who have taken the leap forward to consider what scientific criteria must be used to discover when and whether a philosophy meets the requirements of science often fall short in their philosophical methods as their so-called critical methods are ill-founded and therefore unacceptable.[7] The German philosopher of science and a leading proponent of logical empiricism, Hans Reichenbach (1891–1953), was moving in the right direction when he offered two criteria a philosophical method must meet to be considered scientific: logical analysis and adherence to verifiability theory of meaning.[8] However, we know today that each of Reichenbach's criteria either suffers from ambiguity and vagueness of meaning or have been discredited, largely because the criteria mean different things to different philosophers who, professing to practice them, do different things in their name.[9]

In this chapter, we introduce Charles Sanders Peirce (1839–1914), a philosopher, logician, semiotician, and scientist who presented an inferential way of reasoning that can withstand the pitfalls of Reichenbach's criteria for philosophical method. Pierce developed a system of inquiry that is built on what he calls fallibilism. Fallibilism is a non-foundationalist epistemology. It has as its starting point the idea that a theory of inquiry should be understood as an attempt to settle an opinion in the face of doubt. The sole object of inquiry, according to Peirce, is the settlement of opinion. It is an

---

5. See Harris, *Foundations of Metaphysics in Science*, 17.
6. Harris, *Foundations of Metaphysics in Science*, 17.
7. Harris, *Foundations of Metaphysics in Science*, 17.
8. Harris, *Foundations of Metaphysics in Science*, 17.
9. Harris, *Foundations of Metaphysics in Science*, 17.

acknowledgment that human knowledge does not rest on "ultimate and indubitable propositions."[10] Peirce writes that the "opinion which is fated to be ultimately agreed to by all who investigate is what we mean by the truth, and the object represented in this opinion is the real."[11] The Protestant theologian, Paul Tillich (1886–1965), tried to express this, albeit without reference to Peirce, in his remark that faith is an act of the human personality, as its centered and total act. "An act of faith is an act of a finite being who is grasped by and turned to the infinite. It is a finite act with all the limitations of a finite act, and it is an act in which the infinite participates beyond the limitations of a finite act. Faith is certain in so far as it experiences the holy. But faith is uncertain in so far as the infinite to which it is related is received by a finite being."[12] Faith, according to Tillich, has a dynamic character. Its structure includes an element of doubt, for faith is an "act of knowledge that has a low degree of evidence."[13] Tillich also points out that one sometimes believes something that has low probability of evidence, though low probability of evidence does not necessarily render it improbable. Tillich's notion of faith is fallibilist in the Peirce's sense of the term. Peirce's fallibilist method not only overcomes the pitfalls of transcendental analysis, it also stands to enrich our study of Christology.

Peirce has a robust and nuanced analysis of how things are present to us. His work, however, has often been subject to misunderstanding, and sometimes for good reason. Even in his lifetime, Peirce was highly misunderstood by his peers. His writings are technical and difficult to grasp and some find this off putting. But the truth is that Peirce's groundbreaking work in science, logic, and semiotics has revolutionized the field. Still there are those who think, his groundbreaking work notwithstanding, Peirce has no place in the academic study of religion. Such people will be hard pressed to see any connection between Peirce and Christology. Unbeknownst to many, the science of God plays a central role in the architectonic system of Peirce who saw harmony between science and religion. Modern Peirce scholars, particularly Michael Raposa,[14] Kelly Parker,[15] and Bernando Cantens[16] have

---

10. EP 1.115—Citation here follows the standard convention of citing *The Essential Peirce* whereby reference is to volume and page number. Citation of the *Collected Papers* (e.g. CP 1.4) are by volume and paragraph.

11. CP 5.407.

12. Tillich, *Dynamics of Faith*, 16.

13. Tillich, *Dynamics of Faith*, 31.

14. See Raposa, "Peirce and Modern Religious Thought" and Raposa, *Peirce's Philosophy of Religion*.

15. See Parker, "C. S. Peirce and the Philosophy of Religion."

16. See Cantens, "Prolegomena to Peirce's Philosophy of Religion."

addressed misapprehensions about the value of Peirce to the study of religion or theology. Andrew Robinson[17] and Andrew Southgate have also begun a process of uncovering the rich resource of Peirce studies to Christology. They show how Peirce's semiotics lends itself to a theological method that places emphasis on the recipients of God's revelation. Thus, our attempt to appropriate Peirce's semiotics for the science of Christology is part of this grand effort to show that the human recipient of revelation is constituted in such a way that he or she is capable of interpreting Jesus as a sign, icon, or the "image of the invisible God" (Colosians.1:15).[18] For, if God is the human person's ultimate concern, at least as far as Christians are concerned, this ultimate concern must be expressed symbolically, since symbolic language alone is able to express the ultimate.[19]

A brief background of the man, his ideas, and his influences is important to understanding Peirce's brand of semiotics. Also, in order not to disrupt the flow of the Christological arguments we would be presenting in subsequent chapters, an introductory chapter of Peirce's semiotics is needed. That way when we interject some Peirce's derived terms into our Christological argument the reader unfamiliar with Peirce would, at least, have a context for understanding the argument. Peirce's ideas, like that of many great thinkers, developed over a long period. His semiotics, which has been considered one of this mature thoughts, was not even published during his lifetime. Rather, they have been put together from a variety of Peirce's own unpublished lectures and notes.[20] How Peirce's understanding of signs developed and matured over time requires a genetic study, which is beyond the scope of this work. Also, this introductory chapter does not pretend to offer a full biographical account of the life and works of the American pragmatist. This has already been done by both Joseph Brent,[21] who shows why Peirce should be regarded as the greatest American philosopher of all time, and Kenneth Ketner,[22] whose revision of Peirce's 1898 lectures, *Reasoning and the Logic of Things* remains classic. What this chapter offers, rather, is brief introduction to Peirce's ideas in the overall context of his theory of signs for the purpose of advancing his metaphysics of presence and triadic logic for Christology.

---

17. See Robinson, *God and the World of Signs* and Robinson, "Continuity, Naturalism and Contingency."

18. See Robinson, *God and the World of Signs*, 292.

19. Tillich, *Dynamics of Faith*, 41.

20. Robinson, *God and the World of Signs*, 32.

21. See Brent, *Charles Sanders Peirce*.

22. See Peirce, *Reasoning and the Logic of Things*.

METAPHYSICS OF EXPERIENCE: EARLY INFLUENCES

There is no denying that some of Peirce's predecessors, Immanuel Kant (1724–1804) and Georg F. Hegel (1770–1831) especially, exerted a lot of influence on him. But the extent of these influences has yet to be determined. Moreover, whether or not Peirce's intellectual connection to them is deep or superficial also remains a matter of conjecture. This much, however is clear, Peirce had great respect for German idealism. His respect for German idealism stemmed from what he saw as their strong metaphysical worldview, as opposed to the materialistic tendencies of British nominalism, which he loathed. In spite of his great admiration for German idealism, Peirce thought it rested on poor logic. Peirce tells us that he came unto "the threshing-floor of philosophy through the doorway of Kant,[23] although he differed from Kant with respect to how we acquire knowledge and rejected the Kantian idea "that there are certain impassable bounds to human knowledge."[24] In the *Critique of Pure Reason*, Kant held that although objects can never be given in intuition that would correspond to ideas of reason, such ideas still function as regulative principles that direct our understanding with regard to what it should inquire into next. Peirce takes exception to this, suggesting in an 1868 essay, "Questions Concerning Certain Faculties Claimed for Man," that all knowledge is inferential and susceptible to error and that there is no cognition that is not determined by a previous cognition.[25] Peirce would go on to develop a new list of categories —Firstness, Secondness, and Thirdness — as a corrective to the "lacunae in Kant's reasoning."[26]

23. EP 2.400.
24. EP 2.421.
25. W2:193.
26. CP 1.300.

The Peircean Categories

Firstness	Secondness	Thirdness	
That whose being is simply in itself; not lying behind anything	That which is what it is by force of something to which it is second.	That which is what it is owing to things between which it mediates and which it brings into relation to each other.	The three categories are irreducible.
Very abstractable by nature.	A phenomenon that involves otherness or difference.	It bridges the chasm between the absolute first and the absolute last and brings them into relationship.	The presence of one of the categories gives rise to the other two.
Can never be adequately grasped.	Cannot be without first.	The source of meaning and intelligibility in the universe.	First is phenomenologically (and logically) prior to Secondness and Thirdness, but not necessarily causally prior.
Characterized by an airy nothingness.	Characterized by brute actuality of things and facts.	Characterized by ability to establish connections between different objects.	The logical priority of Firstness does not mean that all phenomena originate causally from Firstness.
Feeling is a manifestation of phenomenon of Firstness.	Brute reaction is the manifestation of the phenomenon of Secondness.	Intelligibility is the manifestation of the phenomenon of Thirdness.	
		Thirdness is the basis of continuity (synechism).	

Having distanced himself from Kant, Peirce conceives experience broadly—that it is "that which is compelling, surprising, unchosen, brute, involuntary, or forceful."[27] He links his theory of experience to his categories, suggesting that there is no experience that is not tied to cognition. The categories of Firstness, Secondness, and Thirdness are present in everything that is present to the mind, i.e., present to everything that is experienced.[28]

> Firstness is the mode of being of that which is such as it is, positively and without reference to anything else. Secondness is the mode of being of that which is such as it is, with respect to a second but regardless to any third. Thirdness is the mode of being of that which is such as it is, in bringing a second and third into relation to each other. I call these ideas the cenopythagorean categories.[29]

Whereas Kant claimed to have destroyed metaphysics, Peirce reconstitutes metaphysics, throwing all ideas into the three classes of Firstness, of Secondness, and of Thirdness.[30] He thought what passed for metaphysics in his time was "puny, rickety, and scrofulous science" and should not be made to remain so.[31] In reconceiving metaphysics, Peirce puts forward three metaphysical principles that are scientifically respectable: tychism (the view that there is an element of chance in the universe), synechism (the view that all reality is continuous), and agapism (the view that the evolutionary process is based on love). Tychism is Peirce's own way of refuting mechanistic determinism, like the one espoused today by Neo-Darwinists like Richard Dawkins who would make us believe that what believers call God is actually the blind watchmaker of natural selection.[32] For Peirce rather, the universe is not a static world of laws, but dynamic and ever evolving. Synechism reinforces the evolutionary nature of the universe—that nature is continuous. It is akin to what Pierre Teilhard de Chardin saw as God's design that is woven in a progressive pattern in the evolutionary process, which made him to locate in the universe a Christogenesis.[33] Agapism refutes the notion that the evolutionary process is based on strife, greed, and competition (survival of the fittest), but rather that at its fundamental level the evolutionary process is based on love. Peirce not only suggests that mathematics and logic

---

27. Misak, *Cambridge Pragmatism*, 31.
28. Misak, *Cambridge Pragmatism*, 31.
29. Peirce, "Two Letters to Lady Welby," 96.
30. Peirce, "Two Letters to Lady Welby," 96.
31. CP 6.6.
32. See Dawkins, *Blind Watchmaker* and *Unweaving the Rainbow*.
33. See Teilhard de Chardin, *Christianity and Evolution* (Harvest, 2002).

are connected to experience, he also thinks that just as some metaphysical inquiry is connected to experience, everything present to the mind is interpretable, for all thoughts are in symbols. We shall return later to this idea of interpretable signs in the section on semiotics.

Three Terms at the Heart of Peirce's Evolutionary View of the World

Tychism (Chance)	Synechism (Continuity)	Agapism (Evolutionary Love)
There is no determinism in the universe. The universe is not a static world of laws, but dynamic and ever evolving.	There is continuity in nature.	Evolutionary process is not based on strife, greed, or competition. At its fundamental level it is based on love, such that an entity is predisposed to sacrifice itself to enhance the well-being of others and perfect them.
Tychism could be considered an early anticipation of Werner Heisenberg's Uncertainty Principle.	Synechism could be considered an anticipation of Rahner's evolutionary view of the world.	Agapism could be considered the basis of Rahner's Transcendental Christology.

Kant was not the only German idealist from whom Peirce distanced himself. There was also Hegel whom he thought had things right, except that he did not grasp the category of secondness:

> The truth is that pragmaticism is closely allied to the Hegelian absolute idealism, from which, however, it is sundered by its vigorous denial that the third category. . . suffices to make the world, or is even so much as self-sufficient. Had Hegel, instead of regarding the first two stages with his smile of contempt, held on to them as independent or distinct elements of the trine Reality, pragmatists might have looked up to him as the great vindicator of their truth.[34]

What Peirce calls the cenopythagorean categories are in fact Peirce's own "attempt to characterize what Hegel sought to characterize as the three stages of thought. They also correspond to the three categories of each of the four triads of Kant's table."[35] Distancing himself from both Hegel and Kant's theory of knowledge, Peirce argues that inquiry begins with "the irritation

---

34. CP 5.436.
35. Peirce, "Two Letters to Lady Welby," 96.

of doubt" and ceases when the doubt ends.[36] "The sole object of inquiry is the settlement of opinion."[37] By opinion here, Peirce means true opinion. He writes that the goal of inquiry is settlement of belief and that "real inquiry cannot begin until a state of real doubt arises and ends as soon as Belief is attained, that 'a settlement of Belief,' or, in other words, a state of satisfaction, is all the Truth, or the aim of inquiry consists in."[38] Peirce argues that "if Truth consists in satisfaction, it cannot be any actual satisfaction, but must be the satisfaction which would ultimately be found if the inquiry were pushed to its ultimate and indefeasible issue."[39] He therefore rejects as absurd the notion that there can be one truth in science and another in religion or theology that completely contradicts it.

> It is a damnable absurdity indeed to say that one thing is true in theology and another in science. But it is perfectly true that the belief which I shall do well to embrace in my practical affairs, such as my religion, may not accord with the proposition which a sound scientific method requires me provisionally to adopt at this stage of my investigation. Later, both the one proposition and the other may very likely be modified.[40]

One good example he cites to support this assertion is the origin of the universe. Regarding scientific proposition, he writes, "If we are to proceed in a logical and scientific manner, we must, in order to account for the whole universe, suppose an initial condition in which the whole universe was non-existent, and therefore a state of absolute nothing."[41] He suggests, however, that such "a scientific proposition is merely something you take up provisionally as being the proper hypothesis to try first and endeavor to refute."[42] The only "evidence" for this scientific proposition is none other than the fact "that it is adopted in accordance with a method which must lead to the truth in the long run."[43]

---

36. CP 5.375.
37. CP 5.375.
38. CP 6.485.
39. CP 6.485.
40. CP 6.216.
41. CP 6.215.
42. CP 6.216.
43. CP 6.216.

WHETHER PEIRCEAN CATEGORIES HAVE A PLACE IN THEOLOGY

Peirce was a fallbilist and his idea "that the human mind has a much better chance of reaching the truth if it admits it's capacity for error than if it denies that capacity,"[44] is a corrective to transcendental theories that think of truth as a priorily derived. Peirce's critique of German idealism is significant for theology, particularly when one considers that contemporary Christian theology has long been under the so-called Teutonic captivity. In the view of critics, contemporary theology is still very much dominated by German patterns of thought. This pattern of thought is often characterized by transcendental a prioris and excessive love for transcendental a prioris not only makes theology incapable of engaging in the self-correcting process of knowledge, it also at times makes theology incapable of grasping or explicating the practical imports of theological hypotheses.[45] Peirce, to be clear, is not averse to abstract ideas. But Peirce is convinced that the more abstract an idea, the greater its practicality, for abstract ideas have the greatest number of operational consequences.[46]

Earlier I drew attention to Andrew Robinson and Andrew Southgate as forerunners who have started the process of uncovering the rich resource of Peirce's scholarship to Christology. What they try to do is replace some of our Greek and Teutonic-inspired theological language with a semiotic language. For example, Robinson thinks that the semiotic model can help clarify some contentious issues in our Trinitarian theology. How? In the first place, Robinson sees some neo-Platonic resonances in Peirce's categories of Firstness, Secondness, and Thirdness. In the third century, the Alexandrian School, led by Clement of Alexandria (AD 150—215) and Origen of Alexandria (AD 185—254) incorporated into their Christological thinking concepts drawn from Middle Platonism. Plotinus (AD 204—270), the founder of Neoplatonism held that everything stems from the One and everything will return to the One. He identified the One with the Platonic idea of the Good. From the One emanates Mind (intellect) and Soul. The One (a formless being, indivisible, and without attributes) is the highest element in the hierarchy or chain of Being. Plurality derives from unity and it is from the productive unity of these three Beings (the One, Mind, and Soul) that all existence emanates. There is an ontological hierarchy in Plotinus hierarchy of the three Beings. Emanation is also both causal and

---

44. Gelpi, *Gracing of Human Experience*, vii.
45. Gelpi, *Grace as Transmuted Experience and Social Process*, 42.
46. Gelpi, *Gracing of Human Experience*, 173.

contemplative. Origen found helpful this Middle Platonist idea and used it to argue that the Father is the ingenerate (*agennetos*) transcendent source of all being and that nothing is ungenerate, i.e., nothing is without underived existence, except only God the Father. Origen then went on assert that the Logos was related to the Father by an eternal generation in such a way that the three *hypostases*, Father, Son, and Holy Spirit, are to be "regarded as eternally distinct, not just manifested in the economy of creation and salvation."[47] Not only did Origen introduce innovative ideas drawn from Middle Platonism, he also introduced an argument that would become important in the fourth century Trinitarian debates—that the Father and the Son are correlative terms; the term "Father" implies the existence of a child, and that the Father could not be truly called Father unless this was eternally so.[48]

The concept of "ingenerateness" of the Father and some other concepts that were taken from Platonic philosophical tradition and introduced into Christian theological thinking will become contentious during the Arian controversy in the fourth century. Arius (the father of the Arian heresy) was confused by it: If the Father is ingenerate and the Son is begotten, he reasoned, then "before he was begotten or created or defined or established, he was not. For he was not unbegotten." Without supporting the Arian position, Robinson thinks Arius's argument is a logical outcome of a philosophical commitment to a Neo-Platonic idea that plurality derives from unity—it will lead in a subordinationst direction.[49] Nicaea (AD 325) condemned Arius and affirmed that the Son is "begotten, not made" and of "one substance (*homoousion*) with the Father. The ambiguity of the term *homoousion* created a further problem. Constantinople (AD 381) clarified that the Son is *homousios* (of the same substance) with the Father, not *homoiousios* (of like substance).The Arians, not content with the Nicene-Constantinople clarification, would continue to claim that if the Son was *genetos* (begotten), then it follows necessarily that he was created, not divine. But the Nicene orthodoxy thought the Arians confuse being begotten (*gennetos*) with being created (*genetos*). Athanasius of Alexandria (AD 296—373) tries to mediate by applying the word *agenetos* (uncreated) to both the Father and the Son. Robinson thinks that the Fourth century distinction between *agenetos* and *agennetos* has parallel in Peirce's categories of Firstness and Secondness: Firstness is equivalent to saying the phenomenon is *agennetos* (unbegotteness); the quality of

---

47. Robinson, *God and the World of Signs*, 73.
48. Robinson, *God and the World of Signs*, 74.
49. Robinson, *God and the World of Signs*, 75.

being abstractable from relation to anything else. Firstness is logically prior to other categories. There is ontological mutual dependence between Firstness, Secondness, and Thirdness. The Father is only Father by virtue of having (eternally) a Son who in turn is generated from the Father.

In the fourth century, there emerged a sect holding on to an extreme form of Arianism, the Anomoeans, also known as the Heterousians or Aetians (named after Aetius, a key representative of the sect). Sometimes they are called the Eunomians (named after Eunomius, another key representative of the sect). The common thread among these groups is that they held that Jesus Christ was neither of the same nature as God the Father nor of like nature as the Father (as maintained by the semi-Arians). The Anomeans (literally means "unlike") were so called because they thought that Jesus was "unlike" the Father in nature and identified the essence of God as "unbegottenness" or ingenerateness (agennetos). It was in the attempt to counter the Heterousians that the Cappadocian, Basil of Caesarea (AD 339—379), argued that it is true that ingenerateness is an essential characteristic of the Father, but that is not to say it is an essential characteristic of deity in general. Another Cappadocian, Basil's brother, Gregory of Nyssa, also joined forces against the Heterousians by making clear that "ingenerateness" does not describe the essence of God. "Ingenerateness" is only a characteristic of one hypostasis (the person of the Father). The fatherhood of the person of the Father does not signify divine essence; it only describes the Father's relation to the Son.[50] Together both Basil and Gregory held that the Heterousians are mistaken in identifying the title "Father" as the essence of God when it is only meant to indicate the Father's relation to the Son. They held that "human discussion of God is not about God's un-named and unknowable essence but about his named and knowable energies (*energeia*i)."[51]

Robinson sees both the positive and negative aspects of the Cappadocian argument against the Heterousians. On the positive side, what the Cappadocians accomplished was their ability to show that the essence of God is not in God's ingenerateness. On the negative side, Robinson thinks that the Cappadocian distinction between the unknowable divine *ousia* and the knowable energies of God is symptomatic of the "perennial tendency in Christian theology to disconnect Trinitarian thought from reflection on the economy of salvation."[52] Thus, Robinson argues that the semiotic model of the Trinity can help clarify the Cappadocian objection to the Heterousians

50. Robinson, *God and the World of Signs*, 82.
51. Robinson, *God and the World of Signs*, 82.
52. Robinson, *God and the World of Signs*, 83.

while still avoiding the potential pitfalls of the Cappadocian theology. "The semiotic model illustrates and clarifies the distinction between generate vs. ingenerate (or begotten vs unbegotten) in such a way as to support the idea that this distinction is not the same as the distinction between created vs. uncreated. The semiotic model thus affirms the fourth century insight (championed by the Cappadocians) that ingenerateness is characteristic of the Father specifically, not God in general."[53]

There is, according to Robinson, a notorious theological neglect of a metaphysics of the Holy Spirit. The Christian tradition, Robinson reasons, has given a great deal of attention to the metaphysics of the relation between the Father and the Son. But it has been much less clear about what it wishes to say metaphysically about the Holy Spirit. It is here that the Peirce's category of Thirdness can make a constructive contribution to the tradition.[54] In Peirce's schema, Thirdness is a category of purposiveness and interpretation. If the Holy Spirit is the source of life (Ps 104:29–30; Ezek 37:1–10), as the Christian tradition claims, then there are resonances in the life-giving role of the Spirit (Gen 2:7; Job 33:4) with Peirce's category of Thirdness.[55] The Christian tradition also understands the Spirit in terms of love (Rom 15:30; Col 1:8). St. Augustine (AD 354—430), for example, identified the Spirit as the bond of love between the Father and the Son and Thomas Aquinas (AD 1225—1274) "held that the names *verbum* (word) and *imago* (image) were proper to the Son, and the names *amor* (love) and *donum* (gift) were proper to the Spirit."[56] In Peirce's schema, Thirdness is connected to *agapism* (love). Robinson sees parallels in the roles the Holy Spirit in Christian tradition and Peirce's Thirdness play in relation to history. "The Spirit may be understood theologically as the source of openness to the future (e.g., 2 Cor 3:17; Gal 4:6–7), which coheres with Peirce's notion that Thirdness is the category on which genuine freedom depends."[57] The Christian tradition regards the Spirit as the source of knowledge; it inspires Prophets (Isa 61:1; 2 Sam 23:2). The Spirit is also the source of reason; it is the source insight and understanding (Isa 11:2). The Peircean category of Thirdness is also associated with wisdom and insight.[58] Thus, Robinson argues that given Peirce' notion that Thirdness is the source of intelligibility vis-à-vis the communal nature of knowledge, "the semiotic model makes sense of the

---

53. Robinson, *God and the World of Signs*, 83.
54. Robinson, *God and the World of Signs*, 85.
55. Robinson, *God and the World of Signs*, 85.
56. Robinson, *God and the World of Signs*, 86.
57. Robinson, *God and the World of Signs*, 86.
58. Robinson, *God and the World of Signs*, 86.

affirmation in the Niceno-Constantinopolitan Creed that the Holy Spirit is both 'the Lord, the giver of life' and 'has spoken through the prophets.'"[59] In chapter six, I will show how Robinson engaged the traditional Christian Trinitarian thought within the framework of Peirce's metaphysical semiotics and uses it as a way of resolving problems associated with the traditional way of speaking of the relations within the Persons of the Trinity. In the meantime, we return to our exposition of ideas integral to Peirce's semiotics.

PRAGMATISM AS A METHOD OF ASCERTAINING TRUTH-CLAIMS

Pragmatism has been described as "America's home-grown philosophy."[60] The origin of this American philosophy goes back to the late 1860s and early 1870s when a discussion group known as the Metaphysical Club met with regularity in Cambridge, Massachusetts. The Metaphysical Club was a reading group comprising of eminent personalities, like Oliver Wendell Holmes, William James, Charles Sanders Peirce, John Fiske, Nicholas St. John Green, and Chauncey Wright. These men were, in their own rights, philosophers, mathematicians, scientists, and lawyers who found themselves at a critical juncture in the history of American intellectual life. They also happen to be "the first generation of philosophers to put some distance between philosophy and religion."[61] They tried to separate, in a systematic manner, the realm of religion from philosophy. These two realms had been mumbled together by the Protestant ministers who at the time taught philosophy in American colleges. According to Cheryl Misak, when The Metaphysical Club first began to meet, "the implications of Comte's positivism and Darwin's *On the Origin of Species* were hotly been debated in universities and in drawing rooms. Science seemed to entail the abandonment of the world-view that had God and religious absolutes at its center."[62]

Peirce, along with James and Wright, were three of the intellectual giants of The Metaphysical Club. Incidentally, all three also worked as scientists. Working as scientists, these three wanted to develop a philosophy of science because they wanted to have science inform philosophy.[63] In the 1860s, James and Peirce began developing, with varying degrees of success, philosophical position that will go under the name pragmatism. James's

59. Robinson, *God and the World of Signs*, 87.
60. Misak, *American Pragmatists*, ix.
61. Misak, *American Pragmatists*, ix.
62. Misak, *American Pragmatists*, ix.
63. Misak, *American Pragmatists*, ix.

Lowell lectures were actually published in 1907 as *Pragmatism: A New Name for Some Old Ways of Thinking*. At the heart of pragmatism is the basic fact that any domain of inquiry, whether science, religion, mathematics, or logic, is a human inquiry, and that our epistemological accounts of truth must acknowledge and take this fact as a starting point.[64] The overarching issue in pragmatism, according to Misak, pertains to how we can make sense of our standards of rationality, truth, and value as genuinely normative and binding while still mindful that they are profoundly human phenomena. "How do normativity and authority arise from within a world of human experience and practice?"[65] Misak suggests that among the members of the Club, Peirce was about the only one that answers these questions with utmost care and profundity.

Analytic philosophy today recognizes three different kinds of pragmatism: (1) There is the pragmatism of the British philosopher and mathematician, Frank Ramsey (1903–1930) and the pragmatism of the Austrian-British philosopher, Ludwig Wittgenstein (1889–1951), two intellectual giants of Cambridge, England, whose works on belief and truth were influenced by the pragmatism Peirce and James were developing in Cambridge, MA. (2) There is also the pragmatism of German-British philosopher, Ferdinand Canning Scott Schiller (1864–1937) and the pragmatism of the American philosopher, Richard Rorty (1931–2007). (3). The third is the pragmatism of Peirce (and the members of the Metaphysical Club). It is beyond the scope of this work to discuss the differences between these different brands of pragmatism. What is significant here, for our purpose, is that the pragmatism of Peirce helps us understand better how beliefs can both be the products of human inquiry and aim at the truth.[66] For Peirce provided and gave a guide to method of inquiry. Peirce himself writes that he understands pragmatism "to be a method of ascertaining the meanings, not of all ideas, but only of what I call 'intellectual concepts,' that is to say, of those upon the structure of which, arguments concerning objective fact may hinge."[67]

BACKGROUND OF PEIRCE'S SEMIOTICS

Semiotics is the study of signs. Interest in the nature of signs goes back to the ancients— when Greek physicians, like Hippocrates (c. 460–370 BCE),

---

64. Misak, *Cambridge Pragmatism*, ix.
65. Misak, *American Pragmatists*, xi.
66. Misak, *Cambridge Pragmatism*, x.
67. CP 5.467.

started the practice of relying heavily on the interpretation of signs in their medical practices. Semiotics possibly originated as one of the branches of Greek medicine.[68] Greek medical students were "taught that diagnosis depends on proper attention to the 'history,' examination, and special investigations, all of which consists of signs of various kinds."[69] The words spoken by patients, as well as their facial expressions, tone of voice, posture, etc., were considered signs to be interpreted by the physician.[70] Concisely, it was medicine that first provided a context for reflections on the nature of signs before it was broadened and extended to other fields by philosophers who saw in the concept of sign "a way of proceeding by inference from what is immediately given to the unperceived."[71] As understanding in the nature of signs evolved, Aristotle, the Stoics, the Epicureans, and even the Skeptics, began to connect the study of signs to logic and began to argue that both are inseparable.[72] Medieval philosophers and theologians developed the formula, which became a standard definition, that sign is *aliquid pro aliquot* (something that stands for, or serves in place of, something else).[73]

At the end of *Essay Concerning Human Understanding* (1690),[74] John Locke also hinted on the possibility of developing the doctrine of signs. As it turned out, however, it was the Swiss, Ferdinand the Saussure (1857–1913), and the American, Charles S. Peirce (1839–1914), the two founders of semiotics, who eventually took up Locke's challenge. Working independently of each other, they developed a doctrine of signs in a more systematic way. In spite of the similarities in the treatment of sign-theory in the works of these two men whose live span overlap, there are also significant differences. Saussure, a linguist interested in the study of natural language and cultural systems, developed socio-logical semiology and theory of relationship between signs. Peirce, a mathematician and logician interested in the theory of knowledge, developed a logico-scientific semiology or semeiotics and focused on theory of individual sign and its classifications.[75] Saussure developed a dyadic sign system—that the sign relation is between the signifier and the signified. He held that the

---

68. Robinson, *God and the World of Signs*, 16.
69. Robinson, *God and the World of Signs*, 16.
70. Robinson, *God and the World of Signs*, 16.
71. Robinson, *God and the World of Signs*, 17; quoting Sebeok, *Contributions to the Doctrine of Signs*, 47.
72. Robinson, *God and the World of Signs*, 17.
73. Robinson, *God and the World of Signs*, 17.
74. See Locke, *Essay Concerning Human Understanding*.
75. See Lagopoulos, "Meta-Theoretical Approach."

relation between the signifier and the signified in a sign system is arbitrary. Building on the groundwork of the Swiss master, Peirce replaced the dyadic conception of sign with a triadic one. He developed the idea that sign consists of relations between three elements: *representamen* (the sign itself, sometimes referred to as the sign-vehicle), the *object* (that which the sign represents), and the *interpretant* (the interpreting agent). A sign, for Peirce, mediates between the interpretant sign and its object.[76] In general, a sign is something which stands to somebody for something in some respect or capacity. It addresses somebody in that it creates in the mind of the person another sign (a more developed sign). This more developed sign, which is created in the mind of the addresser, is what Peirce calls interpretant. The interpretant is not necessarily a sign.[77] That which the sign stands for is the object. "The sign-vehicle does not signify anything in itself, but is able to signify something (an object) to the extent that its relation to the object is such that an interpreting entity or agent may make a purposeful response to the sign, where the fulfillment of that purpose depends on a certain relation between the sign-vehicle and the object."[78]

Since a sign consists of a relation of three connecting terms, i.e., sign-vehicle or representamen, object, and interpretant, the triadic relations are always suprasubjective and intersubjective.[79] The sign-vehicle can either be physical (material) or psychical mode of being.[80] The three elements in the sign relation, i.e., the *representamen* or sign-vehicle, object, and interpretant, for Peirce, are irreducible. The sign performs its task at the crossroad of nature and culture. In its proper being, the sign is native to neither realm.[81] Peirce is clear that "a sign is something by knowing which we know something more."[82] Hence, all our thoughts and knowledge are by signs.

Peirce's theory of signs contrasts with that of Saussure in many ways. For Saussure, sign depends on the presence of the conscious interpreter in whose mind the *signifier* and the *signified* are held together. For Peirce, sign does not depend on the presence of the conscious interpreter who may or may not be aware of the sign-vehicle. For Saussure the dyadic relations (signifier and signified) are arbitrarily related. For Peirce, the relations between the three elements in sign relation are not arbitrary. Rather they are dynamic and are

---

76. Peirce, "Two Letters to Lady Welby," 389.
77. Peirce, "Two Letters to Lady Welby," 389.
78. Lagopoulos, "Meta-Theoretical Approach," 18.
79. Deely, "Impact of Semiotics on Philosophy," 21.
80. Deely, "Beginning of Postmodern Times," 41.
81. Deely, "Impact of Semiotics on Philosophy," 14.
82. Peirce, "Two Letters to Lady Welby," 390.

involved in a continuous process of semiosis. Medieval thinkers jettisoned an argument when it slipped into an infinite process.[83] Aquinas highlighted medieval disgust for infinite regress in the cosmological argument where he made clear that one cannot regress into an infinite process. "By the fact of involving an infinite process, the argument was known to have skipped a cog in what was up for being explained, namely, some occurrence in the order and among the subjective structures of physical nature."[84] Peirce held a similar position with respect to avoiding regress to an infinite process. He accounts for how the sign relations cannot regress

Saussurean Theory of Signs	Peircean Theory of Signs
Dyadic theory of sign	Triadic theory of sign
Sign relation is between the signifier and the signified	Three elements in a sign relation: *representamen* (sign vehicle), object, interpretant
The two relations are arbitrary in that they are necessarily held together in the mind of the conscious sign user.	The three relations are irreducible; the signs do not depend on the presence of a conscious interpreter.

into an infinite process by devising a system of categories, the third of such systems in philosophy following Aristotle's great scheme of categories and Kant's.[85] "Peirce's categorical scheme is neither a scheme designed to express exclusively what is there in the objective world prior to it and independently of it, as Aristotle's was, nor is it a scheme designed to express exclusively necessary aspects of the mind's own working in developing discursively the content of experience, as Kant's was. Peirce's scheme is designed to express the mixture and interweave of mind-dependent and mind-independent relations which constitute human experience in its totality as a network of sign relations, a semiotic web (or semiosic web)."[86]

On their part, ancient Greek and medieval thinkers placed emphasis on the notion of being and offered a definition of human being as a rational animal. Retrieving and moving beyond this, Peirce shifts the focus from being to the action of signs. Being is knowable through experience. But experience is structured through the sign-relations. According to Peirce, All thought is through signs. "This means that all rational life is mediated through the action of signs, and "rational life" here embraces everything

---

83. Deely, "Beginning of Postmodern Times," 45.
84. Deely, "Beginning of Postmodern Times," 45.
85. Deely, "Beginning of Postmodern Times," 46.
86. Deely, "Beginning of Postmodern Times," 63.

that tends in any way to fix or unsettle belief."[87] With Peirce, the emphasis is no longer on the human being as a rational animal or a thinking thing, but human being as a semiotic animal—the animal that not only uses signs but also knows that there are signs.[88] A motorist comes to a red light and suddenly comes to a halt. The stopping of a car and a red in themselves have no relation, except that it has been determined by societal convention and will remain so as long as the convention is upheld. Similarly, the words and sounds we use point to something beyond themselves because they have been given special function by convention.[89] The point we are getting at is that if in mundane matters we employ signs and symbols to make headway, it becomes even more so in religious matters, for the language of faith is the language of symbols.[90]

DIVISION OF SIGN-VEHICLE

Peirce went to great length to show that a sign has two objects: its object as it is represented and the object in itself. Tillich, who also thought a symbol has two functions he termed the main and basic functions,[91] was probably hinting at this Peircean notion when he said symbols cannot be produced intentionally because they grow out of the individual or collective unconscious; they cannot function without being accepted by the collective unconscious of the group in which they appear.[92] Make no mistake—what Peirce calls sign is different from what Tillich means by symbol, but the correlation (no pun intended) in terms of their functions is everywhere evident. A sign, according to Peirce, has three interpretants: its interpretant as represented or meant to be understood, its interpretant as it is produced, and its interpretant in itself.[93] Tillich, for whom the main and basic function of symbol is to open up levels of reality which otherwise are hidden to us and cannot be grasped in any other way, again was probably hinting at this when he declared that symbols cannot be invented because, like a human being, symbols "grow when the situation is ripe for them, and they die when the situation changes."[94] That a sign has interpretants is important for the

---

87. Deely, "Beginning of Postmodern Times," 25.
88. Deely, "Impact of Semiotics on Philosophy," 22.
89. Tillich, *Dynamics of Faith*, 41.
90. Tillich, *Dynamics of Faith*, 45.
91. Tillich, "Religious Symbol and our Knowledge of God," 190–91.
92. Tillich, *Dynamics of Faith*, 43.
93. Peirce, "Two Letters to Lady Welby," 390.
94. Tillich, *Dynamics of Faith*, 43.

argument we shall be developing in chapter four regarding the risen Christ. Also, the Resurrection must have its object as represented and its object as it is in itself. It also has its interpretant as it is meant to be understood (remission of sin), its interpretant as it is produced (eliciting faith in the disciples and doubt in others, e.g., the proponents of hallucination hypothesis), and its interpretant in itself (God of infinite distance wanting to be a God of absolute closeness).

1. Peirce classifies signs according to the material nature of the sign-vehicle itself, giving rise to three distinctions: *qualisigns*, *sinsigns*, and *legisigns*. A *qualisign* is a sign-vehicle "that signifies by embodying the very quality it represents."[95] For example, color is embodied in whatever it signifies, like the color-sample of paint or cloth. This means that all qualisigns are icons, but not all icons are qualisigns. "A qualisign cannot signify without being somehow embodied, and in that sense there is some overlap with the category of sinsign (since a qualisign signifies only when embodied in actual instances). But its embodiment is not part of its character as a sign."[96] Its theological application, at least as far as Robinson and Southgate are concerned, is that since the person and life of Jesus of Nazareth embodied the very quality and being of God, Jesus is the iconic qualisign in that he embodied the quality of God's transforming presence.[97]

A *sinsign* (sin = simul or singular) is a sign that occurs simultaneously with what it represents.[98] In other words, it is "a singularly occurring sign, such as a leaf blown by the wind. As such, the leaf signifies the presence of a breeze, though not by any convention or rule; because the movement of the leaf signifies by virtue of the brute of its occurrence."[99] According to Peirce, a *Sinsign* is "an actual existent thing or event which is a sign. It can only be so through its qualities; so that it involves a qualisign, or rather, several qualisigns. But these qualisigns are of a peculiar kind and only form a sign through being actually embodied."[100] Theologically, my own hypothesis (which I develop in chapter four) is that the resurrection event of Christ is an iconic *Sinsign*. *Sinsign* is a singularly occurring event and does not follow a rule. Jesus performed many signs and wonders. He also commanded his disciples to do the same and laid guidelines for them to depart from their old ways and do some new things: "You have heard that it was said... but I

---

95. Robinson, *God and the World of Signs*, 39.
96. Robinson and Southgate, "Incarnation and Semiotics," 270.
97. Robinson and Southgate, "Incarnation and Semiotics," 271.
98. Peirce, "Two Letters to Lady Welby," 391.
99. Robinson, *God and the World of Signs*, 39–40.
100. CP 2.245.

say to you" (Matt 5:38–48). But the Resurrection-event was what Jesus did once and definitively. He did not admonish his followers to do the same. It was not something the disciples could replicate. Before his death, he went into the Temple and cleansed it. "Jesus' overturning of the traders' tables was a singular event. He did not repeat it himself, and did not suggest to his followers that they should do so in order to signify something."[101]

A *legisign* is a sign "replicated according to some rule for the purpose of signifying, as when a letter or word is written on a piece of paper or in some other medium."[102] Peirce writes that legisign is "usually made by men. Every conventional sign is a legisign, [but not conversely]. It is not a single object, but a general type which, it has been agreed, shall be significant. Every legisign signifies through an instance of its application, which may be termed a Replica of it . . . The Replica is a Sinsign. Thus every Legisign requires sinsigns."[103] Robinson and Southgate explain that a legisign is a sign signified by virtue of being a replica of a type. It is produced according to a rule, for the purpose of this signification. All symbols are legisigns, but not all legisigns are symbols.[104] How might one distinguish legisign from qualisign? Peirce writes,

> The difference between a legisign and a qualisign, neither of which is an individual thing, is that a legisign has a definite identity, though usually admitting a great variety of appearances. Thus, &, and, and the sound are all one word. The qualisign, on the other hand, has no identity. It is the mere quality of an appearance & is not exactly the same throughout a second. Instead of identity, it has great similarity, & cannot differ much without being called quite another qualisign.[105]

In theological terms, Robinson and Southgate think of the Eucharist as an iconic legisign. The Eucharistic "type" instituted by Jesus is replicated in individual instances of the celebration. Every Eucharistic celebration follows a pattern or "rule" instituted by Jesus in remembrance of the meal he shared with the disciples in the Upper room.[106]

2. Peirce also classifies signs according to the nature of the relationship between the sign-vehicle and the object. This relationship is dynamic and manifests in three ways: *icon, index, and symbol*. An *icon* is a sign "in which

---

101. Robinson, *God and the World of Signs*, 121.
102. Robinson, *God and the World of Signs*, 40.
103. CP 2.246.
104. Robinson and Southgate, "Incarnation and Semiotics," 269.
105. Peirce, "Two Letters to Lady Welby," 391.
106. Robinson and Southgate, "Incarnation and Semiotics," 269.

the sign-vehicle has some qualitative resemblance to the object."[107] An icon then may be any qualisign or even sinsign. Peirce example for this is a vision or sentiment generated in us when we hear a piece of music that represents what the composer intended.[108] An *index* is a sign "in which the sign-vehicle stands for the object by virtue of a direct connection."[109] If you remove the object the index loses the character that makes it a sign. Legisigns may be an index. Peirce's own example of an index is "the occurrence of a symptom of a disease (the Symptom itself is a legisign, a general type of a definite character. The occurrence in a particular case is a sinsign).[110] Peirce writes:

> No matter of fact can be stated without the use of some sign serving as an index. If A says to B, "There is a fire," B will ask, "Where?" Thereupon A is forced to resort to an index, even if he only means somewhere in the real universe, past and future. Otherwise, he has only said that there is such an idea as fire, which would give no information, since unless it were known already, the word "fire" would be unintelligible. If A points his finger to the fire, his finger is dynamically connected with the fire, as much as if a self-acting fire-alarm had directly turned it in that direction; while it also forces the eyes of B to turn that way, his attention to be riveted upon it, and his understanding to recognize that his question is answered. If A's reply is, "Within a thousand yards of here," the word "here" is an index; for it has precisely the same force as if he had pointed energetically to the ground between him and B.[111]

Peirce defines a symbol "as a sign which is determined by its dynamic object only in the sense that it will also be interpreted."[112] The interpretation "depends either upon a convention, a habit, or a natural disposition of its interpretant."[113] For Peirce, "every symbol is necessarily a legisign."[114]

3. Peirce further classifies signs according to how the sign-vehicle is presented to the interpretant. This distinction yields three relationships: *rheme, dicent, argument* (corresponding to the old distinction between Term, Proposition, and Argument). "A rheme is any sign that is not true

---

107. Robinson, *God and the World of Signs*, 38.
108. Peirce, "Two Letters to Lady Welby," 391.
109. Robinson, *God and the World of Signs*, 39.
110. Peirce, "Two Letters to Lady Welby," 391.
111. CP 2.305.
112. Peirce, "Two Letters to Lady Welby," 391.
113. Peirce, "Two Letters to Lady Welby," 391.
114. Peirce, "Two Letters to Lady Welby," 392.

nor false, like almost any single word except 'yes' and 'no.'"[115] A sign that can neither be true nor false is simply is.[116] A dicent is "not an assertion, but is a sign capable of being asserted."[117] A *dicent* then is like a term, which can be either true or false; it asserts something true or false.[118] An *argument* appeals to the reason of the interpreter for its interpretation. It therefore, as the name suggests, takes the form of an argument.[119] This last trichotomy of sign (rhemes, dicents, and arguments) is inconsequential to our argument.

In sum, Peirce's semiotics helps our attempt to understand "why and how the force of our experiential encounters with reality can be woven indexically into the net of our most sophisticated beliefs."[120] Robinson and Southgate have led the way in theologically appropriating Peirce's metaphysics of experience, suggesting that we have to reconstruct Christian theology in a way that engages contemporary philosophy of science.[121] Some traditional ways of doing Christology, very much like some ancient Christological debates, are fraught with conceptual logjams due to overreliance on ancient metaphysical categories. A careful attention to the Peircean derived metaphysics and its taxonomy of signs helps overcome many of these conceptual problems.[122] It can also open a new way of thinking about the Incarnation and redemption. Tillich was one of the leading theologians of the twentieth century who seemed to have grasped the import of symbols for theological reflection. Tillich was unapologetic about the place of symbols in his theological system. He writes: "The center of my theological doctrine is the concept of symbol."[123] For Tillich, "the direct object of theology is found only in religious symbols. . . [because] theology is the conceptual interpretation, explanation and criticism of the symbols in which a special encounter between God and man has found expression."[124] In fact, Tillich's main criticism of mainstream theology is that it lacks a systematic

---

115. Peirce, "Two Letters to Lady Welby," 392.

116. Robinson, *God and the World of Signs*, 40.

117. Peirce, "Two Letters to Lady Welby," 392.

118. Robinson, *God and the World of Signs*, 40.

119. Robinson, *God and the World of Signs*, 40.

120. Pape, "Searching for Traces," 22.

121. See Robinson and Southgate, "Semiotics as a Metaphysical Framework for Christian Theology," 689–712 and Robinson and Southgate, "Interpretation and the Origin of Life," 345–60.

122. Shults, "Transforming Theological Symbols," 728.

123. Tillich, "Reply to Interpretation and Criticism," 333.

124. Tillich, "Theology and Symbolism," 107–8.

presentation of the doctrine of symbolism and tries to fill this lacuna in his systematic theology.[125]

While Tillich may have grasped the import of symbol, he uses the term symbol in a way that is quite different from that of Peirce. A symbol, for Tillich, is something pointing beyond itself.[126] What Tillich calls symbol might perhaps be understood as a sign in the Peircean sense, especially in the light of Peirce's classification of the nature of the relationship between the sign-vehicle and the object, which Peirce says yields the dynamic icon-index-symbol. What Tillich does is reinforce Peirce's argument, theologically at least, by helping us to understand not only how symbols (sign in the Peircean sense) point beyond themselves to something else, but also how symbol participates in that in which it points, opens up levels of reality which are otherwise closed to us, and unlocks dimensions and elements in us which correspond to dimensions and elements of reality.[127] In theological terms, Tillich reinforces both the figurative and essential qualities of symbols. These make it more necessary to take seriously the suggestion that the doctrine of the Incarnation be understood "as a recognition that Jesus's life as a whole was an 'iconic qualisign' of the being and presence of God."[128] When you look at the life of the historical Jesus, the theme of the coming of the kingdom of God was central to his teaching. The first-century Jewish thought understood the kingdom of God not in terms of a distant heavenly realm, but in terms of a concrete expectation that Israel's God will reign on earth. Jesus saw his impending death and Resurrection as inaugurating that Kingdom on earth. Thus, Jesus performed a number of symbolic actions—the Temple cleansing, the Last Supper, and his journey to Jerusalem, and his whole life—to symbolize and personify the coming of God's Kingdom on earth.[129] Peircean semiotics and its evolutionary understanding of our world, as well the human person's place in it, can help deepen our understanding of the life and works of Jesus, particularly as this life and mission was embodied and signified in the resurrection event.

125. See Tillich, *Systematic Theology*.
126. Tillich, "Theology and Symbolism," 108.
127. Tillich, *Dynamics of Faith*, 43.
128. Robinson and Southgate, "Incarnation and Semiotics," 266.
129. See Robinson, *God and the World of Signs*, 115–17.

66   A SEMIOTIC CHRISTOLOGY

Classifications of Sign-Vehicle

Classification of Sign-Vehicle Itself. A sign is:	Classification of Sign-Object Relationship. A sign relates to its object by having the following:	Classification of the Relationship of the Sign-Vehicle to the Interpretant. A sign's interpretant represents it in the following ways:
Qualisign—a "mere quality." It is a sign that signifies by embodying the very quality it represents.	*Icon*—"some character in itself." An icon is a sign in which the sign-vehicle has some qualitative resemblance to the object.	*Rheme*—"possibility." A term that can neither be true or false. It simply is.
Sinsign—"an actual existent." It is a singularly occurring sign.	*Index*—"some existential relation to the object." An index is a sign in which the sign-vehicle stands for the object by direct connection.	*Dicent*—"fact." A term that can either be true or false.
Legisign—"a general law." It is a sign replicated by means of some rule.	*Symbol*—"some relation to the interpretant." A symbol is sign in which the sign-vehicle stands for the object by another resemblance	*Argument*—"reason." It appeals to the reason of the interpreter.

IMPLICATIONS OF PEIRCE'S METAPHYSICS OF EXPERIENCE FOR CHRISTOLOGY

Peirce went beyond his Kantian influence to invent his own signature categories. Kant was a transcendental idealist who held that ideas exist independent of the mind and that the human self—transcendental ego—can construct knowledge from sense impressions and align them with the universal concepts (categories) that impinge on them. On the basis of the Kantian idea, something is understood to be transcendental in so far as it brings to light the conditions of the possibility of knowing a thing or object as that thing or object can be known a priorily. Neo-Kantians, like the Belgian Jesuit Joseph Marechal (1878–1944) and the German Jesuit Karl Rahner (1904–84), have developed a metaphysical framework of knowledge following Kant's approach to philosophy. This has been termed a Transcendental method. Their transcendental analysis aims at making explicit "the a priori conditions of our speaking and thinking—more generally, of our reasonable activity."[130] Their transcendental analysis tries to show that "if a statement is shown by a transcendental analysis to be valid a priori, then the meaning of the statement must be understood exactly in terms of the operative definition used, in spite of the tendency to link it with familiar associations."[131] Thus, Rahner speaks of his own Christology as Transcendental Christology because his Christology examines the conditions for the possibility of faith in Jesus Christ and the conditions for believing that our human nature develops in response to God's grace.[132] In other words, Rahner's Christology is transcendental because "it shows how a specific event in history, the coming of Jesus Christ, can have a supra-historical significance. God has created human beings with a distinctive capacity. We have the capacity, in our choices and actions, to transcend ourselves and glimpse the mysterious God who has enabled us to make those choices."[133]

Although there is no one philosophy that encapsulates the general worldview arising out of the many revolutions in modern science that the twentieth-first century has thrust upon us, there must be a type of philosophy that evidence best supports. Everything from physics to psychology, points to the holistic character of reality and its fluidity and developmental trend.[134] It is to this type of thinking that philosophy must return, if it is to be consonant with contemporary science and accorded the epithet "scientific" it has long craved.[135] That philosophy, in my view, is the pragmatic philosophy of C. S. Peirce, whose metaphysics of presence we have argued, is best suited for Christology. In keeping with the scientific temper of our age, Peirce's metaphysics of presence, which is dialectical and semiotic, must be the point of departure, not the Teutonic or its allied philosophies of the twentieth century. In the previous chapter, we saw some of the basic issues and difficulties of Transcendental method. There is no point rehashing them again except to point out that there are those who do not accept Rahner's Transcendental Christology and find it inadequate for some of the reasons we mentioned in the previous chapter. One of such critics is Roger Haight who thought Rahner's Transcendental Christology is merely a response to extrincism—the thesis that "God's address to human existence in Jesus Christ comes entirely from the 'outside' and runs counter

---

130. Muck, "Logical Structure of Transcendental Method," 360.
131. Muck, "Logical Structure of Transcendental Method," 361.
132. See Rahner, *Foundations of Christian Faith*.
133. See Fischer, "Karl Rahner's Transcendental Christology."
134. Harris, *Foundations of Metaphysics in Science*, 451.
135. Harris, *Foundations of Metaphysics in Science*, 451.

to human interests and the inner exigencies of human freedom."[136] Haight prefers, rather, a Christology from below—Christology in the framework of the Antiochene School that highlights the duality of Jesus's humanity and divinity, highlighting theretofore Jesus's humanity.

What Peirce's metaphysics of experience does is offer an alternative to transcendental analysis. This alternative is sometimes called a theosemiotic analysis or theosemitism. Theosemiotic analysis can meet the kind of objection Haight raised with respect to Rahner's work. Haight had pointed out that the Logos Christology in Rahner's Transcendental Christology resembles the ancient Alexandrian Christology of enhypostatic union in which Jesus appears different from other human beings. Such a theology, for Haight, is no more than the textbook theology that was taught in the seminaries, a theology that is losing ground today.[137] Besides Haight's valid criticism, a theosemiotic analysis can help contemporary theology overcome any claims of extrincism. Before we attempt a theosemiotic analysis, we should perhaps draw attention to the different kinds of Christology and how they have been traditionally understood in the history of the Christian theology. This will help set the context for our own preferred theosemiotic analysis.

(a) Christology from Below vs. Christology from Above

Rahner distinguishes between "Christology from below" and "Christology from above" and referred to these as the two basic types of Christology.[138] The terms "from below" and "from above" refer to the distinctive quality of Christology being described. The term "Christology from below," for example, is used in epistemological sense, not ontological.[139] A Christology that develops from an examination of the birth, life, suffering, death, and resurrection of Jesus is what is designated as Christology from below. "From," as used in the phrase, represents a point of departure in the process of working out a Christology in which God's grace is mediated.[140] This is why Rahner referred to "Christology from below" as the "saving history type" (as opposed to the Christology from above he called "the metaphysical type.")[141] The three synoptics (Matthew, Mark, and Luke), as it were,

---

136. Fischer, "Karl Rahner's Transcendental Christology;" quoting Haight, *Jesus, Symbol of God*, 17.

137. Fischer, "Karl Rahner's Transcendental Christology."

138. See Rahner, "Two Basic Types of Christology," 213–23.

139. See Haight, *Future of Christology*, 33.

140. Haight, *Future of Christology*, 33.

141. Rahner, "Two Basic Types of Christology," 213–14.

present a Christology from below. They begin with an examination of the events in the life of Jesus and gradually walk us up to his divinity. Another term for this kind of Christology that begins with the humanity of Christ and culminates in his divinity is Ascending Christology. "Epistemologically, Christology is always ascending; it is always tied to human experience as to its starting point. It is always searching for transcendence. And when its conclusions are reached, they must always be explained on the basis of experience that generated them."[142]

The other kind of Christology, which is often distinguished from Christology from below, is Christology from above. This Christology begins by accepting as a fact the divinity of Jesus and walks us through to his humanity. The Christology of the Gospel of John, traditionally referred to as the Fourth Gospel, is a good example of Christology from above. It begins with the notion that Jesus is the pre-existent Logos or the Word of God that "became flesh and made his dwelling among us" (John 1:14). Another name for this kind of Christology is Descending Christology. In the history of controversies between the Alexandrian School of theology and the Antiochene School of theology, what we see essentially is one school showing preference for a particular style of Christology over the other. The Alexandrian School, with its emphasis on the pre-existent Logos, adopted Christology from above while the Antiochene School, which begins with the humanity of Jesus, adopted Christology from below. In so far as we understand that in speaking of Jesus we are employing analogical or symbolic terms, Christology from below should by no means be seen as something opposed to Christology from above. Rather, the two approaches are meant to complement each other. As Rahner pointed out, in the Christologies which have *de facto* been developed and transmitted to us, the two basic types (Christology from below and Christology from above) "figure for the most part in mixed form, so that it is extremely difficult to draw a clear and explicit distinction between the two."[143] Thus, a genuine Christology from above proceeds from the divinity of Jesus to his humanity, just as a genuine Christology from below begins with the humanity of Jesus and goes on to do justice to his divinity.[144] One of the consequences of approaching Christology "from below" is that Jesus's unity with God is substantiated, not by the resurrection of Jesus (as Christology "from above" tends to do), but by the claim to Jesus's authority in

---

142. Haight, *Future of Christology*, 34.
143. Rahner, "Two Basic Types of Christology," 213.
144. O'Collins, *Christology*, 17.

his proclamation and work—an authority that presupposes a nearness to God and solidarity with God that no one else has.[145]

According to Pannenberg, Christology from above was more common in the ancient church, particularly from the time of Ignatius of Antioch up to the period of the apologists in the second century. "It became determinative for the further history of Christology, particularly in the form of the Alexandrian Christology of Athanasius in the fourth century and of Cyril in the fifth century."[146] Impulse in the direction of Christology from below, can be found, according to Pannenberg, in the Middle Ages, particularly Martin Luther, who inquired about the relationship of Jesus to God.[147]

A note of caution here: Christology from above does not equal "high Christology," any more than Christology from below equals "low Christology." A "high Christology" may acknowledge the divinity of Christ, but it does not necessarily indicate how to incorporate his humanity in the larger picture. According to Pannenberg, one of the characteristics of "Christology from above" is that it presupposes the doctrine of the Trinity and in presupposing the Trinity raises the question: How has the Second Person of the Trinity assumed a human nature?[148] Christology from above presupposes the divinity of Jesus when the most important task of Christology is to present reasons why the early believers confessed Jesus as Lord.[149] Hans Kung, Edward Schillebeeckx, John Macquarie, and Wolfhart Pannenberg all agree that theology from above is not feasible—that theology must begin not from God above, but from below with the historical man Jesus. Nevertheless, what the two basic types of Christology and their mutual interrelationship do is help us understand that in present-day Christian theology pluralism of Christologies is both inevitable and legitimate.[150]

(b) High Christology vs. Low Christology

The central theme of Christology is to establish how the man Jesus, named *Christos* (messiah), is to be understood as God.[151] "This involves the legitimacy of the transformation in the understanding of Jesus that took place in the transition from the Jewish into the Gentile sphere of tradition."[152] This

---

145. Pannenberg, *Jesus—God and Man*, 53.
146. Pannenberg, *Jesus—God and Man*, 33.
147. Pannenberg, *Jesus—God and Man*, 36.
148. Pannenberg, *Jesus—God and Man*, 34.
149. Pannenberg, *Jesus—God and Man*, 34.
150. Rahner, "Two Basic Types of Christology," 223.
151. Pannenberg, *Jesus—God and Man*, 31.
152. Pannenberg, *Jesus—God and Man*, 31–32.

also involves a distinction of two kinds of Christology we alluded to earlier: "Christology from above"—a Christology that begins with the divinity of Jesus and has at its center the concept of incarnation and "Christology from below"—a Christology that begins with the historical man Jesus, beginning with his message and his brutal crucifixion and resurrection, and recognizes in the process his divinity. In Christology from below the concept of incarnation is arrived at only at the end.[153] According to Edward Oakes, the terminology of "high" and "low" Christology was coined by the German Lutheran theologian Wolfhart Pannenberg in *Jesus—God and Man* (1968).[154] The fact that the terms were formulated by Pannenberg does not mean that impulses in either direction does not predate Pannenberg. Pannenberg himself admits that he was not the first to employ the procedure of a Christology "from below" because impulses in this direction were already in existence in the ancient church, in the Middle Ages, and even by Luther.[155] The distinction Pannenberg makes between Christology "from below" and Christology "from above" is meant to be purely methodological: Does one begin the study of Jesus with his divinity (high Christology) or does one begin the study of Jesus with a consideration of his humanity (low Christology)?[156] High Christology traces the understanding of Jesus in terms that include an aspect of his divinity as contained in the titles ascribed to him: Lord, Son of God, and God. The Prologue of John (John 1:1–18) is a quintessential high Christology text. Low Christology traces the understanding of Jesus in terms that do not necessarily include his divinity: Messiah, Rabbi, Prophet, Priest, Savior, and Master.[157]

A "high Christology" does not always do justice to the humanity of Jesus because it begins with a supposition of the divinity of Jesus without adequately addressing how his divinity can be reconciled with his humanity. Similarly, a "low Christology" emphasizes the humanity of Jesus without doing justice to his divinity. Some scholars, in fact, do think that the distinction between "low Christology" and "high Christology" does violence to the New Testament data because it at times suggests wrongly that the New Testament account of the life of Jesus first began with "low" Christology and ended with "high" Christology.[158] But there is a caveat. All of Paul's epistles, for example, were written before the four Gospels (Matthew, Mark, Luke,

153. Pannenberg, *Jesus—God and Man*, 33.
154. Oakes, *Infinity Dwindled to Infancy*, 77.
155. Pannenberg, *Jesus—God and Man*, 36.
156. Oakes, *Infinity Dwindled to Infancy*, 77.
157. Brown, *Introduction to New Testament Christology*, 4.
158. Oakes, *Infinity Dwindled to Infancy*, 78.

and John) and the Acts of the Apostles. New Testament scholars are nearly unanimous that Mark exhibits a "low" Christology and that only John has "high" Christology. But they were all written after the Pauline epistles that "provide evidence for a 'high' Christology of unimpeachable pedigree."[159]

(c) Explicit Christology vs. Implicit Christology

The term "explicit Christology" refers to explicit statements of Jesus or claims by Jesus that are expressed in Christological titles. It refers largely to the kind of explicit statements about Jesus's life and works that we see in the Gospel of John for example. Some of the I-Am statements in John and other statements of high Christology, like Messiah (which though in Mark falls under Low Christology) and Lord, fall under the purview of explicit Christology. Implicit Christology is a term used to capture the Christological claims that Jesus makes about himself that are not explicitly stated. Implicit Christological claims about Jesus are usually found in the synoptic Gospels.[160] "To speak of an 'implicit' claim refers to the way in which the claim is expressed, and says nothing whatsoever about the 'lofty' or 'lowly' status of the claim. Exalted claims can also be expressed implicitly."[161] An example of implicit Christology is found in Jesus's answer to the emissaries sent by John the Baptist to inquire whether he was the Messiah. "Jesus replied, go and report to John what you hear and see: the blind receive their sight, the lame walk, the lepers are cleansed, the deaf hear, the dead are raised, and the good news is preached to the poor" (Matt 11:4).

(d) Ontological Christology vs. Functional Christology

An ontological Christology answers the question *Quid Sit* in reference to Jesus. It is reference to who or what Jesus is in himself. A functional Christology answers the question *An Sit* in reference to Jesus. It is a reference to why this is so, a reference to what the saving or redemptive activity of Jesus means for humanity and the world at large.[162]

---

159. Oakes, *Infinity Dwindled to Infancy*, 79.
160. See Frey, "Continuity and Discontinuity between 'Jesus' and 'Christ,'" 69–98.
161. O'Collins, *Christology*, 18.
162. O'Collins, *Christology*, 19.

Chapter Three

The Christological Titles

"THE CHRISTIAN CHURCH IS the community that results from the outer communication of Christ's message and from the inner gift of God's love."[1] At the heart of Christian theology is the Christian teaching about Jesus Christ. This affirmation involves primarily what Christians who affirm this faith in Jesus have to say about Jesus in contrast to what non-believers or non-Christians who provisionally abstain from a final, personal decision might think or say about Jesus.[2] A Christian is one who consciously knows Jesus's true significance and confesses him as Lord and Savior.[3] The Christian also knows what he or she believes, what he or she is to do to live out the Christian message, and what he or she is to do to become one like Christ. But how does the Christian know that his or her understanding of Jesus is true? From where does the Christian derive the data for speaking about Jesus as Lord and Savior? The data for speaking about the man Jesus who lived in Palestine at the time of the emperor Tiberius and who was crucified and died under the Roman procurator Pontius Pilate is found almost exclusively in the New Testament. Because the data for Christology can be found almost exclusively in the New Testament, the data of the New Testament can be meaningfully studied using the two approaches of study with origins in Linguistics that we discussed in the previous chapter: diachronic and synchronic approaches.[4] These approaches will lead to a fuller comprehension

---

1. Lonergan, *Method in Theology*, 333.
2. See Pannenberg, *Jesus—God and Man*, 19.
3. Pannenberg, *Jesus—God and Man*, 19.
4. See also Oakes, *Pattern of Redemption*, 26.

of the cognitive (what the Christian believes), constitutive (what the Christian is to do), and effective (what the Christian is to do to become one like Christ) meanings of the Christian message.

As discussed in the previous chapter, a diachronic approach to Linguistics investigates the etymology or origin of words. A diachronic approach to the New Testament will investigate which of the New Testament books were first and in what sequence.[5] A diachronic approach wants to know whether the epistles were written before the gospels and if so, which epistles were written first and why? It also investigates why the Gospels were written as narratives of the life of Jesus. Since the Gospels were written after the epistles, this approach probes the "extent the narrative progress of Christological doctrine inside the church of the first century itself affected the narratives about Jesus."[6] A synchronic approach to Linguistics, on the other hand, investigates variations of a standard language (dialects) and surveys their usage in contemporary society.[7] A synchronic approach to the New Testament will study "the whole range of the Christological teaching of the New Testament, irrespective of when each specific claim about Jesus was 'precipitated,' so to speak, in the New Testament."[8] A synchronic approach, like semantics (a branch of Linguistics) that is interested in the meaning of words, will investigate the meaning of terms or titles that the early church applied to Jesus. It will seek to know from where the primitive church derived those terms, irrespective of when they began applying those titles to Jesus.[9]

People unfamiliar with semiotics may question its relevance to Christology. One way of answering the objection is to show how the Christological titles given to Jesus by the early Church can benefit from a phenomenological and semiotic analysis. The early Christians did not just intuit descriptors or titles for Jesus. They derived them from their existing usage in the Jewish or Hellenistic world. That the early Christians worked these out of their lived experience of the man from Nazareth and scoured the Old Testament to see prefiguration in the man they called the Christ is in line with the thesis we have adopted here, following Peirce's metaphysics that shows how high grades of reality are grasped—that Christology has no place for privileged intuitive insight. The fact that some of the titles the early Christians ascribed to Jesus were derived from the Old Testament illustrates

---

5. Oakes, *Pattern of Redemption*, 27.
6. Oakes, *Pattern of Redemption*, 27.
7. Oakes, *Pattern of Redemption*, 26.
8. Oakes, *Pattern of Redemption*, 27.
9. Oakes, *Pattern of Redemption*, 27.

the important contribution of the Old Testament to the Christological message.[10] This further elucidates our argument that Christology has no place for deductivist logic based on the so-called necessary first principles and self-evident truth.

There are litany of titles that the early Christians applied to Jesus. These include, Logos (Word), Christ, High Priest, Second Adam, Wisdom, Prophet, Suffering Servant, Son of Man, Son of God, Lord, Rabbi (Teacher), Carpenter, Savior, and God. Edward Oakes has rightly cautioned against seeing these titles as mere honorifics. They are actually titles that refer to different aspects of Jesus's mission and identity.[11] These titles can be grouped under different schema or clusters. The schema adopted by the Swiss New Testament scholar, Oscar Cullmann, is quite helpful.[12] Cullmann classifies them under four rubrics, which is quite helpful because of its semiotic implications. The schema is consistent with the triadic logic in which understanding of a reality is not rigid, but fluid, and open to further and deeper understandings. The four clusters are as follows:

1. The Christological titles that refer to the earthly work of Jesus (Prophet, Suffering Servant, Rabbi, Carpenter, and High Priest).
2. The Christological titles that refer to the present work of Jesus (Second Adam, Lord, Prophet, and Savior).
3. The Christological titles that refer to the future work of Jesus (Messiah, and Son of Man, and High Priest).
4. The Christological titles that refer to the preexistence of Jesus (Logos/Word, Son of God, Wisdom, and God).[13]

One thing to keep in mind as we discuss these titles and try to get to the mind of the early Christians is that the early Christians did not always distinguish sharply between the titles as our analytic mind tends to do.[14] A detailed discussion of all these titles here will be too cumbersome. We will therefore discuss only a select few from each category. Our categorization of these titles is by no means rigid. The concepts themselves are fluid and can be placed in one or more clusters. The concept of "High Priest," for example, which we have placed in the cluster of Christological titles that relate primarily to the earthly work of Jesus, can also go under Christological titles that refer to the future work of Jesus. Similarly, the concept "Prophet" can

10. O'Collins, *Christology*, 24.
11. Oakes, *Infinity Dwindled to Infancy*, 28.
12. See Cullmann, *Christology of the New Testament*.
13. See Oakes, *Infinity Dwindled to Infancy*, 28.
14. Cullmann, *Christology of the New Testament*, 9.

find a home in either the Christological titles that refer to the earthly work of Jesus or the Christological titles that refer to the present work of Jesus. One of the benefits of schematization of these titles, as Cullmann whose cluster we are following pointed out, is that it prevents arbitrary determination of the sequence of the concepts. It also helps us work from within the New Testament itself, rather from an extra-biblical or later theological points of view.[15] In terms of metaphysics of experience, working from within the New Testament itself validates the caution to be wary of philosophical systems that derive knowledge a priorly. For, when the early Christians applied these titles to Jesus, it was based on an experiential testimony: "That which was from the beginning, which we have heard, which we have seen with our eyes, which we looked upon and have touched with our hands" (1 John 1:1).

CHRISTOLOGICAL TITLES THAT REFER TO THE EARTHLY WORK OF JESUS

1. Jesus as Prophet

Israelite prophets, particularly exilic prophets like Deutero-Isaiah and Ezekiel, proclaimed the exclusive divinity of Israel's God. But Jesus stood in sharp contrast to this parochial view and proclaimed the universal significance of Israel's God and signified by his resurrection the inclusion of the Gentiles into eschatological salvation.[16] This sharp contrast between Jesus and Israelite prophets has led some scholars to question whether the designation "Prophet" has a place in our Christological investigation: "Did not those who called Jesus a prophet simply want thereby to place him in a particular general human category of his time? Was he not in this way simply identified according to his purely human appearance?"[17] There is no denying that Jesus was called prophet in the same way he was called a teacher, as a way of specifying his humanity, not his divinity.[18] A biblical prophet was one who spoke to the people on God's behalf. They did not only convey God's message; ancient biblical prophets were also thought to be models of holiness. There were many prophets in Israel—Elijah, Elisha, Amos, Isaiah, Jeremiah, Ezekiel— and they all came from different works of life and backgrounds. In this regard, applying the generic title "prophet" to

---

15. Cullmann, *Christology of the New Testament*, 109.
16. Pannenberg, *Jesus—God and Man*, 70.
17. Cullmann, *Christology of the New Testament*, 13.
18. Cullmann, *Christology of the New Testament*, 13.

Jesus does not seem to convey anything unique about Jesus.[19] However, we should keep in mind that in the New Testament times prophecy as a profession or in the Israelite sense of spiritually attuned men who received divine message from God to speak for God was no longer in existence.[20] In fact, by the time of Jesus, the roles of prophets had changed and there was a shift in meaning following the death of classical prophets. So applying the title to Jesus at this time was not to place him in some human professional category, but to speak to his uniqueness.[21] More significant also is the fact that in most passages in which Jesus is called "prophet" in the New Testament, he assumes the persona of not just a mere prophet, but the final Prophet who would fulfil all Scriptural prophecies at the end of time.[22]

The reference to Jesus as Prophet in the eschatological sense makes it all the more necessary that we distinguish between the New Testament usage of the term "prophet" in the classical sense and "prophet" in the eschatological sense. Cullmann, to his credit, makes this point very well. He thinks we need to distinguish between passages in which Jesus is simply designated as a prophet and passages in which he is designated as an eschatological prophet. In many passages in the New Testament, John the Baptist is portrayed as an eschatological prophet, the new Elijah (Mark 9:11; Matt 17:10). But it is not clear whether John the Baptist was conscious of being the eschatological Prophet.[23] This uncertainty was given credence by his question to Jesus—whether Jesus is the one who is to come or whether they should look for another (Matt 11). The tone of uncertainty is evident in the way the question is formulated. What is clear, however, is that the Baptist knew and was expecting another sent from God, and mightier than himself.[24] This probably means that to be called a prophet at the time of Jesus implied expectation of a dawn of new era. For a long time the people held out hope of a new era to be restored. "Some of the prophets (Elijah primarily but not exclusively) were expected to return, coming down from heaven or at least reappearing in some mysterious way. This expectation then imbues the term 'prophet' at the time of Jesus with a certain eschatological hue."[25]

The Gospel writers explicitly made behavioral connections between Jesus and the prophets, like when Jesus went into the temple courts and

---

19. Oakes, *Infinity Dwindled to Infancy*, 29.
20. Cullmann, *Christology of the New Testament*, 13.
21. Oakes, *Infinity Dwindled to Infancy*, 29.
22. Cullmann, *Christology of the New Testament*, 13.
23. Cullmann, *Christology of the New Testament*, 25.
24. Cullmann, *Christology of the New Testament*, 26.
25. Oakes, *Infinity Dwindled to Infancy*, 29.

drove out all those who were buying and selling and cleansed the Temple of money changers (Matt 21:12). They saw his gesture as having been foreshadowed by prophet Jeremiah's protest inside the Temple precinct (Jer 25).[26] They also understood Jesus as aligning his own fate with the fate of the prophets when he came in confrontations with the priests and elders (Matt 23:37 and Luke 13:34).[27] In this wise, it would seem that the "application of the concept the Prophet to Jesus explains perfectly, then both his preaching activity and the unique authority of his eschatological vocation and appearance in the end time."[28]

In spite of the obvious advantages of conceiving Jesus as the Prophet, there are also disadvantages. Cullmann enumerates four of these. First, concerning the earthly work of Christ, the designation Prophet is inadequate for Jesus because it "emphasizes too strongly one side of Christ's earthly work, his preaching activity, and thus misplaces the emphasis."[29] Second, concerning the present and future work of Christ, the Jewish idea that the Prophet was one who was previously on earth does not recon with the idea that he has a further task to perform after the fulfillment of his eschatological work, which then makes the title, as applied to Jesus, inadequate.[30] Third, concerning the future work of Christ, the very nature of the role of the Prophet in Judaism requires that his role ceases where the kingdom of God begins. For this reason, it is difficult to apply the concept of the Prophet to the future eschatological phase, which the early church expected as the consummation of the work of Jesus.[31] Fourth, concerning the pre-existent being of Christ, the idea of Prophet does not answer the question of the pre-existent being of Christ. The idea of a Prophet was that of a person who was previously on earth and there is no prototype to suggest pre-existence.[32] Thus, the concept of eschatological prophet is too narrow and does not do justice to the early Christian faith in Jesus Christ. "The prophetic concept thus allows no room for the present work of Christ. For as early Christianity understands it, faith in the present Christ and the Christ who is coming again presupposes that New Testament perspective in which the decisive

---

26. Oakes, *Infinity Dwindled to Infancy*, 30.
27. Oakes, *Infinity Dwindled to Infancy*, 30.
28. Cullmann, *Christology of the New Testament*, 44.
29. Cullmann, *Christology of the New Testament*, 45.
30. Cullmann, *Christology of the New Testament*, 45.
31. Cullmann, *Christology of the New Testament*, 47.
32. Cullmann, *Christology of the New Testament*, 48.

thing has already happened in the incarnate Jesus, but the consummation is yet to come."[33]

2. Jesus as the Suffering Servant

The idea of the suffering servant is a Jewish concept. It is also a concept at the heart of the New Testament Christology.[34] We noted earlier that the term prophet in its generic application could refer to anyone in Israel who heard God's call and headed the call in so far as that person was specially called to speak for and on behalf of Yahweh to the people of Israel. "Suffering servant" is another ambiguous term in the Old Testament. It could be applied to any Israelite who fulfils a certain role that demands suffering and intimidation. But unlike the term "prophet" that has historical antecedents in ancient prophets, such as Amos or Elijah, the term "suffering servant" seems "not to have been historically instantiated by any known historical figure."[35] However, Isaiah the prophet remains a good example of one of the biblical prophets who appropriated the term "suffering servant."

The hymns of the Suffering Servant in Isaiah have been the subject of much speculation and study by scholars. There are four Servant Songs in the book of Isaiah and they all appear in what has traditionally been called Second or Deutero-Isaiah: Isa 42:1–9; Isa 49:1–13; Isa 50:4–11; and Isa 52:13–53:12.

> My servant grew up in the Lord's presence like a tender green shoot,
>   like a root in dry ground.
> There was nothing beautiful or majestic about his appearance,
>   nothing to attract us to him.
> He was despised and rejected—
>   a man of sorrows, acquainted with deepest grief.
> We turned our backs on him and looked the other way.
>   He was despised, and we did not care.
> Yet it was our weaknesses he carried;
>   it was our sorrows that weighed him down.
> And we thought his troubles were a punishment from God,
>   a punishment for his own sins!
> But he was pierced for our rebellion,
>   crushed for our sins.
> He was beaten so we could be whole.
>   He was whipped so we could be healed.

---

33. Cullmann, *Christology of the New Testament*, 49.
34. Cullmann, *Christology of the New Testament*, 51.
35. Oakes, *Infinity Dwindled to Infancy*, 31.

> All of us, like sheep, have strayed away.
>> We have left God's paths to follow our own.
> Yet the Lord laid on him
>> the sins of us all.
> He was oppressed and treated harshly,
>> yet he never said a word.
> He was led like a lamb to the slaughter.
>> And as a sheep is silent before the shearers,
>> he did not open his mouth.
> Unjustly condemned,
>> he was led away.
> No one cared that he died without descendants,
>> that his life was cut short in midstream.
> But he was struck down
>> for the rebellion of my people.
> He had done no wrong
>> and had never deceived anyone.
> But he was buried like a criminal;
>> he was put in a rich man's grave.
> But it was the Lord's good plan to crush him
>> and cause him grief.
> Yet when his life is made an offering for sin,
>> he will have many descendants.
> He will enjoy a long life,
>> and the Lord's good plan will prosper in his hands.
> When he sees all that is accomplished by his anguish,
>> he will be satisfied.
> And because of his experience,
>> my righteous servant will make it possible
> for many to be counted righteous,
>> for he will bear all their sins.
> I will give him the honors of a victorious soldier,
>> because he exposed himself to death.
> He was counted among the rebels.
>> He bore the sins of many and interceded for rebels (Isa 53:2–12)

The term "suffering servant is to Deutero-Isaiah what the "messianic secret" is to the Gospel of Mark. In other words, the term "Suffering Servant" could well be a scholarly invention that was used in reference to an anonymous figure that was sketched in the four hymns of the Suffering Servant in Deutero-Isaiah. This anonymous figure, as the hymn suggests, was characterized by his suffering.[36] Old Testament scholars are almost

---

36. Oakes, *Infinity Dwindled to Infancy*, 31; see note 10.

unanimous on the idea that the hymn of the suffering servant was intended to be a personalized description of the collective reality of the nation of Israel; its motif is vicarious suffering.[37] "The notion of vicarious suffering is the most distinctive semantic implication of the Suffering Servant Songs. In much of the rest of the Old Testament, suffering is seen as either just punishment inflicted upon Israel for its sins or as the inevitable, if regrettable, consequences of obedience to a call."[38] This vicarious suffering differed essentially from the suffering the prophets had to go through. The suffering of the prophets was not integral to their mission, but was only a by-product of their mission. Some of the prophets who bailed on their mission did so because they were not ready to accept the by-product of the mission, suffering.[39] "But the Suffering Servant suffers as the very essence of his mission."[40]

Deutero-Isaiah is not the only Jewish literature that identifies the servant of God and the messiah with vicarious suffering. There are other books, such as the Book of Enoch, the Apocalypse of Ezra, and the Apocalypse of Baruch, that identify the servant of God and the messiah with vicarious suffering.[41] Jesus must have been aware of the vicarious suffering of the messiah in all of these literature. We see him many times in the New Testament prophesying his own suffering and death and applying the Suffering Servant Song of 53:12 to himself. Following Peter's confession in Caesarea Philippi that he was the Messiah, Jesus echoed the Suffering Servant Song of Isa 53:12, prophesying that the Son of Man will suffer and be put to death (Mark 8:31; 9:31; 10:33). In the parable of the wicked tenants (Mark 12:1 ff.), he also alluded to his own suffering, echoing the Suffering Servant Song of Isa 53:12. Taken together, the Suffering Servant Songs in Christian interpretation describe the suffering and mission of the Messiah who as High Priest is a royal figure par excellence who atones for the sins of the people. The early Christian community saw in Jesus's passion a fulfillment of the hymn of the Suffering Servant. They also interpreted Jesus's attitude to his suffering as a vicarious suffering; that Jesus before his death "saw his suffering and death as a vicarious act meant to atone for the sins of 'the many,' an interpretation made even more solemn by its validation in the Eucharist itself."[42]

To return to our four clusters or rubrics, the Suffering Servant Song provides a clearer and desirable semiotic interpretation. The application of

37. Oakes, *Infinity Dwindled to Infancy*, 31.
38. Oakes, *Infinity Dwindled to Infancy*, 32.
39. Oakes, *Infinity Dwindled to Infancy*, 31.
40. Oakes, *Infinity Dwindled to Infancy*, 31.
41. Cullmann, *Christology of the New Testament*, 56.
42. Oakes, *Infinity Dwindled to Infancy*, 33.

the title to Jesus is not restrictive within one rubric. Rather, it shows the interpenetration of the earthly work of Jesus, the present work of Jesus, the future work of Jesus, and the pre-existence of Jesus. Concerning the earthly work of Jesus, the concept of the Suffering Servant, as Cullman points out, comprehends the central Christological event and does justice to the total witness of the New Testament, since Jesus understood his earthly work in terms of the Suffering Servant. "The atoning death of Jesus is not only the central act of his earthly life, but also the central act of the total history of salvation from the first creation at the beginning of time to the new creation at the end of time."[43] Concerning the present and future function of Jesus, the concept of the Suffering Servant "can very easily be connected with other concepts which emphasize the work of the present or returning or pre-existent Christ."[44]

3. Jesus the High Priest

The title of "high priest," which the New Testament applies to Jesus, is a variant of the concept of Suffering Servant in that they are closely related. The High Priest is fundamentally a Jewish concept.[45] The institution of priesthood in Judaism was connected to the Temple in Jerusalem, which was overseen by the High Priest.[46] There are traces of a connection in Judaism between the Messiah-King and the High Priest.[47] Genesis tells the story of Melchizedek who is described as a mysterious king who blessed Abraham (Gen 14:17ff). Abraham offered sacrifice through Melchizedek who will later be described as a type of Christ. The ideal high priest is conceived and understood to be according to the order of Melchizedek (Ps 110). Thus, "Judaism knew of an ideal priest who, as the one true priest, should fulfil in the last days all the elements of the Jewish priestly office. The Jewish conception of priest was bound sooner or later to lead to this expectation. Because of his office, the High Priest is the proper mediator between God and his people, and as such assumes from the very beginning a position of divine eminence."[48]

Jesus was not born into a priestly class. He does not come from the tribe of Levi, the priestly class of the Old Testament. There is also no evidence linking him to Aaron and the long the line of the Levitical priesthood

---

43. Cullmann, *Christology of the New Testament*, 80.
44. Cullmann, *Christology of the New Testament*, 81.
45. Cullmann, *Christology of the New Testament*, 83.
46. Oakes, *Infinity Dwindled to Infancy*, 33.
47. Cullmann, *Christology of the New Testament*, 83.
48. Cullmann, *Christology of the New Testament*, 86.

of the Old Testament. Ironically, it was the High Priest at the time of Jesus that colluded with the people to bring charges against Jesus, which ultimately led to his death.[49] So in what way was Jesus a High Priest? There are passages in the New Testament that show Jesus as expressly relating Psalm 110 to the messiah: "The Lord said to my Lord: 'Sit at my right hand until I make your enemies a footstool for your feet'" (see Mark 12:35–37; Mark 14:62). His critical stance towards the high priest notwithstanding, Jesus considered it his task to fulfil the priestly office.[50]

Jesus's attitude towards the priestly office, which he ascribed to himself, opened the door for later Christological interpretations of the title. First of all, the concept of priesthood in Judaism "entails a recognized need for a mediator, otherwise a society would not have recognized an institutional need for priesthood, which makes inevitable the linkage between High Priest and the mission of Jesus."[51] Second, in the new dispensation he was to inaugurate Jesus performed cultic duties and acted in priestly ways. Paul describes him as the "Paschal lamb" who has been sacrificed (1 Cor 5:7) for the remission of sins. His crucifixion coincided with the Jewish feast of Passover. He also instituted the Eucharist at the Passover. For these reasons, the first generation of Christians applied the Old Testament language of sacrifice to the death of Jesus.[52] Third, the Letter to the Hebrews describes Jesus as the great High Priest according to the order of Melchizedek (Heb 5:6). Hebrews lists two essential criteria for priesthood: divine appointment and solidarity with the people to whom the priest is sent to offer sacrifice (Heb 5:4).[53] Jesus meets these requirements because his was an eternal priesthood conferred on him before ages. He therefore does not have to belong to the Levitical priesthood in the flesh. In fact, his divine priesthood is far more superior and his sacrifice far more efficacious than the Levitical priesthood. This is attested to, not only by his divine identity and his direct appointment by God, but also by the perfect consistency between his life on earth and his cultic activity. All these helped to mediate the new covenant (Heb 6 20–10:18).[54]

As High Priest, the sacrifice Jesus offered is a "once and for all" event. He secured in the process our eternal redemption: "He did not enter by means of the blood of goats and calves; but he entered the Most Holy Place once

---

49. Oakes, *Infinity Dwindled to Infancy*, 33.
50. Cullmann, *Christology of the New Testament*, 89.
51. Oakes, *Infinity Dwindled to Infancy*, 34.
52. O'Collins, *Christology*, 29.
53. O'Collins, *Christology*, 30.
54. O'Collins, *Christology*, 30.

for all by his own blood, thus obtaining eternal redemption" (Heb 9:12). It is on the basis of the once-for-all-character of Jesus's atonement that the writer of Hebrews emphasizes strongly that as High Priest Jesus mediated a New Covenant with God.[55] "For this reason Christ is the mediator of a new covenant, that those who are called may receive the promised eternal inheritance—now that he has died as a ransom to set them free from the sins committed under the first covenant" (Heb 9:15). Hebrews also tells us that "Christ, having been offered once to bear the sins of many, will appear a second time, not to deal with sin but to save those who are eagerly waiting for him" (Heb 9:28). Many New Testament scholars doubt the adequacy of a literal interpretation of the second coming of Jesus in this Heb 9:28 text. But nothing stops us from interpreting it along the lines of eschatological hope that the author of Hebrews envisages. For the author of the letter to the Hebrews finds it pertinent to relate the concept of Jesus's high priesthood to the eschatological side of Christ's work. Even if the author of the letter to the Hebrews does not explain the particular meaning of the high priestly work of Jesus at the end of time, the author's allusion that the second coming is "not to deal with sin" lends itself to the interpretation of an eschatological hope of Jesus coming back to perfect us.[56]

The letter to the Hebrews is a significant New Testament writing for understanding the early Christian idea of the priesthood of Christ. It is the only New Testament writing with a detailed Christology of the High Priest. But that is not to say that the ideas are not implicit in other New Testament texts. The ideas developed in Hebrews are either slightly expressed or implied in many other New Testament writings.[57] In the Apocalypse of John, for example, we read that "among the lampstands was someone like a son of man dressed in a robe reaching down to his feet and with a golden sash around his chest" (Rev 1:13) This has an echo of the Son of Man in Daniel: "In my vision at night I looked, and there before me was one like a son of man, coming with the clouds of heaven. He approached the Ancient of Days and was led into his presence" (Dan 7:13). There is also the farewell discourse of John 17 where Jesus, in the fashion of a high priest who makes intercession on behalf of the people, prays for the disciples and all believers. "My prayer is not that you take them out of the world but that you protect them from the evil one. They are not of the world, even as I am not of it. Sanctify them by the truth; your word is truth" (John 17:16–17). Both the image of the Son of Man who appears in the midst of seven lampstands as High Priest

---

55. Cullmann, *Christology of the New Testament*, 100.
56. Cullmann, *Christology of the New Testament*, 103.
57. Cullmann, *Christology of the New Testament*, 104.

(Rev 1:13) and the lengthy high priestly prayer in the farewell discourse of John (John 17) are two good examples of a rich Christology of the High Priest found elsewhere in the New Testament. The Hebrew development of the concept of High Priest opens the door to a Christological development of the term that includes all the three fundamental aspects of Jesus's work: "his once-for-all earthly work, his present work as the exalted Lord, and his future work as the one coming again."[58] The High Priest concept describes more fully and adequately the New Testament understanding of Jesus.

CHRISTOLOGICAL TITLES THAT REFER TO THE PRESENT WORK OF JESUS

1. Jesus the Second Adam

Genesis describes the creation of Adam and Eve as the pinnacle of God's creation. The first human, Adam, was made in God's image and likeness. God gave him power and dominion to be steward over God's creation. The New Testament writers employed typological readings and interpretations of events in the Old Testament. They understood typology to be historical. Typology is different from allegory because it is grounded in history. Whereas allegorical interpretation has various levels of meaning that include tropological (moral) and anagogical understandings, it always tends to be exclusively spiritual, not historical. The New Testament writers also understood typology to be theological (as part of divine fulfillment) and divinely ordained.[59] Writing to the Corinthians, for example, Paul warns of idolatry and sexual immorality. He likens the Israelite crossing of the Red Sea to Christian baptism and also likens the rock that provided them water to Christ. He warns that idolaters will be like the Israelites whom God punished in the wilderness and whose bodies God scattered because they displeased God. "These things happened to them," he warns, "as examples and were written down as warnings for us, on whom the culmination of the ages has come" (see 1 Cor 10:1–11). Thus, in the Old Testament the New Testament writers found "types" whose "antitypes" are in the New Testament. A "type" is a mystery secretly placed in history by God to be fulfilled by the "antitype.[60] "The antitype fulfils the type yet exceeds it in some essential way."[61]

---

58. Cullmann, *Christology of the New Testament*, 103–4.
59. VanMaaren, "Adam-Christ Typology," 277.
60. VanMaaren, "Adam-Christ Typology," 277.
61. VanMaaren, "Adam-Christ Typology," 277.

In the Old Testament the New Testament writers found "types" of Christ that prefigure different aspects of Jesus's life and ministry, including his death and resurrection. In one of their typological interpretations of the Old Testament, the New Testament writers understood the person and work of Jesus (man-redeemer) through the person and work of the first man Adam (man-sinner).[62] There is also the Mary-Eve typology in which Mary becomes by her perfect obedience to God's command the antitype of Eve's disobedience. In their reading of Mary's obedience in Luke 1:39, the Church Fathers, Irenaeus especially, contrast Mary's perfect obedience with Eve's disobedience in Gen 3.[63] Regarding the salvific role of Jesus, the New Testament often presents a contrast between Jesus and Adam. The Adam of Genesis is often presented as foreshadowing a new or second Adam (messianic Jesus) who is to come at the end of time. The Adam of Genesis had a role to play in birthing sin in the world through his disobedience. Jesus the new or second Adam will play a role in expiating sin in the world by his perfect obedience to the will of God. Paul particularly develops this contrast between Adam and Christ in several of his letters (see 1 Cor 15:49; Rom 5:12–21). The New Testament refers to both Jesus and Adam as God's sons (Luke 3:38; Mark 1:1). Adam failed to perform his duties as representative of humanity before God, but Jesus succeeds. Because Jesus undid the harm done by Adam, the two have come to represent "antithetical orders of existence" (Rom 8:29; Col 1:15, 18).[64] "With the first Adam, son of God, creation dawned, and all those in him share in the results of his covenant failure. With the Second Adam, Son of God, new creation dawned, and all those in him share in the benefits of his covenant faithfulness."[65] In the Second Adam cosmic darkness (Gen 1) gives way to dawning of light (Mark 15). The creation-recreation motif of the Adam-Christ typology in the New Testament reaches its climax in the death and resurrection of Jesus.[66] Through his resurrection from the dead the fulfillment of human destiny was revealed in Jesus. "Jesus did not experience this event only for himself but for all men; Jesus' resurrection allowed the destiny of all men to a life in nearness to God, as Jesus proclaimed it, to appear to him."[67]

More explicit Adam-Jesus typology in the New Testament is found in the writings of Paul whose understanding of Adam is grounded in the

62. VanMaaren, "Adam-Christ Typology," 275–97.
63. VanMaaren, "Adam-Christ Typology," 283.
64. Ortlund and Beale, "Darkness Over the Whole Land," 226.
65. Ortlund and Beale, "Darkness Over the Whole Land," 226.
66. Ortlund and Beale, "Darkness Over the Whole Land," 229.
67. Pannenberg, *Jesus—God and Man*, 198.

Genesis 1–3 text.[68] Paul certainly was not the originator of Adam-Christ typology.[69] However, Adam-Christ typology is found in many places in his writings, particularly Rom 5:12–21 where Paul speaks of death, resulting from sin, as coming from one man,[70] and appealed to Christ's resurrection to argue for resurrection of believers. Also in 1 Cor 15, Paul defends bodily resurrection of believers.[71] In Adam all have died, but in Christ all will live. Paul also offers contrast between the First Adam and the Second Adam. The First Adam received life, the Second Adam is a life giver. The First Adam was made of flesh. The Second Adam is Spirit. The First Adam was from the dust of the earth, the Second Adam is from heaven (1 Cor 15:44–49). The contrast here that Christ is from heaven follows a long line of tradition in the New Testament Church in which Christ is understood as having preexistence.[72] Thus, the point of the Adam-Christ typology of Rom 5 and 1 Cor 15 is that Adam is a type of Christ because he prefigured Christ as one man whose one action (disobedience) had consequences (death) for the whole of humanity and Christ is the antitype by his obedience and resurrection.

In their application of the Adam-Christ typology, early Church Fathers, like Cyril of Alexandria (378 AD—444 AD), gradually shifted emphasis from Christ's resurrection that we see in Paul to his pre-existence. In Cyril's discourse of Jesus's baptism, for example, he argues that the advantage the Second Adam (Christ) had over the First Adam was that Christ was the heavenly man and therefore was able to resist sin where Adam could not. This emphasis on Christ's preexistence, though implicit in Paul, was not clearly brought out.[73] In terms of the earthly work of Jesus, the title Second Adam meets the Christological function of Jesus as humanity's representative before God. Unlike the First Adam, Jesus brings humanity's destiny to fulfillment by uniting them in his own person. This idea of representation also meets the Christological function of the present and future work of the Messiah. For the idea of representation "does not involve only—and not primarily—Jesus' death. It is already contained in Jesus' realization of man's destiny as such, in his simply becoming the representative of true humanity."[74]

---

68. VanMaaren, "Adam-Christ Typology," 278.
69. VanMaaren, "Adam-Christ Typology," 278.
70. Leithart, "Adam, Moses, and Jesus," 257–73.
71. VanMaaren, "Adam-Christ Typology," 278.
72. VanMaaren, "Adam-Christ Typology," 279.
73. VanMaaren, "Adam-Christ Typology," 296.
74. Pannenberg, *Jesus—God and Man*, 197.

2. Jesus *Kyrios* or Lord

The New Testament writers were unanimous that Christ had risen from the dead and that he is alive. They expressed this conviction in the confession that Jesus is *Kyrios* Lord.[75] Although the designation *Kyrios* developed into a Christological title in a Hellenistic context, Hellenistic Christians were fully aware of the meaning and implication of the title they were ascribing to Jesus. There are two senses of the Hellenistic usage of *Kyrios*, one secular or ordinary and the other religious. In the secular usage, the word was used to mean a "master" or "owner." It was used politely to address a superior or a master whose ownership of material goods is duly recognized. In the religious usage, it was used to denote submission to a superior being. The Hellenistic mind had no trouble applying the secular usage to deity, for deity was considered a divine *Kyrios*. It is not difficult to see "how the expression *Kyrios* could designate deity with respect to its absolute power or superiority, and how it actually became a name which emphasized divinity in a unique way."[76] There is, however, a development from the secular general meaning to the absolute religious meaning of *Kyrios* in the writings of early Christianity.[77] Thus, in confessing Jesus as Lord, the early Christian community "declared that he is not only a part of divine *Heilsgeschichte* in the past, nor just the object of future hope, but a living reality in the present—so alive that he can enter into fellowship with us now, so alive that the believer prays to him, and the Church appeals to him in worship, to bring their prayers before God the Father and make them effective."[78]

The name of God in Orthodox Judaism is the Tetragrammaton (the four consonants biblical name revealed to Moses) YHWH. The name of God is so holy that no one dares to vocalize it. It was gradually replaced, at least in synagogue worship, by another Hebrew name for God that can be vocalized, *Adonai* (Lord). The Septuagint (Greek translation of the Hebrew Bible designated by the Roman numerals LXX) translated it as *Kyrios* (Lord). But did Orthodox Judaism call the Messiah *Adonai* (Lord)? Cullmann argues (from the evidence of Mark 12:35 where Jesus states that David calls the Messiah Lord) that in Judaism the word "Lord," depending on how it is used, "could be given a special significance which makes possible a development from a secular meaning to the 'name which is above every name.'"[79] This leads to a further question: did Jesus call himself Lord? There is evidence in both the

---

75. Cullmann, *Christology of the New Testament*, 195.
76. Cullmann, *Christology of the New Testament*, 196–97.
77. Cullmann, *Christology of the New Testament*, 196.
78. Cullmann, *Christology of the New Testament*, 195.
79. Cullmann, *Christology of the New Testament*, 203.

synoptic Gospels and the Gospel of John that Jesus did call himself Lord. He also accepted reference to himself as Lord: "Why do you call me 'Lord, Lord" and do not do what I say?" (Luke 6:46) and "You call me 'Teacher' and 'Lord' and rightly so, for that is what I am" (John 13:13). Since Jesus called himself Lord, the other related question then is, in what sense did he use the word Lord? There is no doubt that the word "Lord" can mean different things, depending on the context. When Jesus was teaching in the temple courts, for example, he asked, "Why do the teachers of the law say that the Messiah is the son of David? David himself, speaking by the Holy Spirit, declared:

> "'The Lord said to my Lord:
>   "Sit at my right hand
> until I put your enemies
>   under your feet.'"
> David himself calls him 'Lord.' How then can he be his son?"
> The large crowd listened to him with delight (Mark 12:34–37).

In this passage that David calls the Messiah *Kyrios*, the passage is used to prove the superiority of the Messiah over David.[80] There is also the passage of Jesus's warning against false prophets in the Sermon on the Mount in which he stated "Not everyone who call me Lord, Lord, will enter the kingdom of heaven (Matt 7:21). Reference to "Lord" here can be interpreted in terms of Semitic form of polite address to a respected master or teacher.[81] Then there is Jesus's express statement: "You call me Teacher and Lord, and rightly so, for that is what I am" (John 13:13), which Cullmann interprets to mean "that the disciple-rabbi relationship can give the designation *Kyrios* in particular situations a significance which far exceeds the dignity of ordinary teacher."[82] So there are different ways of interpreting *Kyrios* in the New Testament texts. What one cannot simply say is that in all its occurrences in the New Testament *Kyrios* only means "teacher" as some New Testament scholars, particularly W. Bousset and Rudolph Bultmann have dismissively done.[83] A precise understanding of what is meant by Jesus's Lordship can be acquired only by attention to the whole of his earthly activity.[84]

There is the argument that Jesus could not have used the designation *Kyrios* in reference to himself, since the term was a post-Easter expression of faith on the part of the early Christians who declared how God "has made

---

80. Cullmann, *Christology of the New Testament*, 203.
81. Cullmann, *Christology of the New Testament*, 204.
82. Cullmann, *Christology of the New Testament*, 205.
83. See Bousset, *Kyrios Christos*.
84. Pannenberg, *Jesus—God and Man*, 365.

him both Lord and Christ" (Acts 2:36), bestowing on him the "name which is above every name" (Phil 2:9).[85] *Kyrios* was a title that developed naturally within the events of salvation history.[86] The pre-resurrection Jesus did not proclaim his Lordship over all the earth. He only proclaimed the coming of God's kingdom. In this way "his activity stands in the same line with the Old Testament and Jewish hopes of Yahweh's kingly rule on earth."[87] But the pre-resurrection Jesus also spoke of the dawn of God's Lordship in his work and mission. "This presence of God's future in Jesus' activity is rightly understood only when one has taken seriously the futurity of the Lordship of God whose imminence Jesus proclaimed."[88]

Finally, *Kyrios* is one of those Christological titles that can in principle be fitted into all four of our rubrics: Christological title that refer to the earthly work of Jesus, the present work of Jesus, the future work of Jesus, and the pre-existence of Jesus. One of the consequences of the application of the *Kyrios* title to Jesus, according to Cullmann, is that the New Testament can in principle apply to Jesus all the Old Testament passages that speak of God.[89] Tetragrammaton is strictly a Jewish concept based on the holiness of God. Although Christianity reveres the name of God as Orthodox Judaism does, it does not adhere by the Tetragrammaton code. There is no Christian equivalent of the Tetragrammaton. But assuming hypothetically there was one, *Kyrios* would play the role the Hebrew *Adonai* plays for Orthodox Judaism. In that sense, the application of the term *Kyrios* to Jesus is an affirmation of his pre-existence as One who "was with God in the beginning" (John 1:3). The early Christians understood *Kyrios* to be pre-existent—that if the resurrection prove that Christ is one with God, then he must have been united with God from the very beginning.[90]

3. Jesus the Savior

The Greek *soter* (savior) is one of the names for God in the Old Testament (Ps 24:5; 27:1; 79:9; Isa 12:2; 17:10; 43:3; Jer 14:8; Hab 3:18). At a much later time, the title was expanded and applied to people commissioned by God to deliver God's people, as in the case of Moses who "saved" the people of Israel.[91] The Old Testament connects *soter* with Messiah, implying that

---

85. Cullmann, *Christology of the New Testament*, 204.
86. Cullmann, *Christology of the New Testament*, 204.
87. Pannenberg, *Jesus—God and Man*, 365.
88. Pannenberg, *Jesus—God and Man*, 365–66.
89. Cullmann, *Christology of the New Testament*, 234.
90. Cullmann, *Christology of the New Testament*, 235.
91. Cullmann, *Christology of the New Testament*, 239.

the Messiah is the long awaited savior who will finally and permanently save Yahweh's people (Isa 19:20).[92] In the Hellenistic period, however, *soter* acquired a slightly different meaning. Whereas in Judaism *soter* is the savior of the people, in Hellenism the gods, heroes, and even rulers are called "saviors" because they deliver their people from distress, dangers, illness, infirmities, and uncertain existence.[93] In Greco-Roman sources, "savior" was used for gods, such as Zeus, Asclepius, Isis, and Serapis, and for philosophers and leaders of various ranks. In its imperial connotations, Roman rulers from Julius Cesar (whose rise to power began in 60 BC) to Publius Hadrian (who ruled from AD 117 to AD 138) and later emperors were all called "the savior of the world."[94]

One may be dismayed to find out that the honorific title "savior" was not one of the first central titles of honor for Jesus in the early Church, despite its widespread use in Hellenistic times.[95] Apart from one occurrence in Philippians: "But our citizenship is in heaven. And we eagerly await a Savior from there, the Lord Jesus Christ" (Phil 3:20), the title hardly occurs in most of the early Christian writings. It occurs relatively late in the Gospels of Luke and John.[96] Some New Testament scholars think that it was because of the bad connotation of *soter* in the Hellenistic world that the early Christians did not employ the term for Jesus.[97] But there are also others who think "that the real reason for the late appearance of the title Savior is connected precisely to the fact that the name *Kyrios* played such a predominant role in early Christianity. 'Savior,' an Old Testament attribute of God, was conferred upon Christ on the basis of faith in him as the risen Lord. But just because *Kyrios* was the 'name above every name,' it necessarily overshadowed and took precedence over all other titles which pointed in the same direction."[98] Those New Testament scholars who hold the latter view argue that when the title was finally employed in the New Testament, it was only as a supplement to *Kyrios* (Phil 3:20; 2 Pet 1:1; 11; 2:20; 3:2, 18).[99] Put differently, the early Christian application of "Soter" to Jesus is connected with the Jewish and Old Testament concept rather than the Hellenistic usage.[100] Nearly all the

92. Cullmann, *Christology of the New Testament*, 239.
93. Cullmann, *Christology of the New Testament*, 239–40.
94. Koester, "Savior of the World," 666.
95. Cullmann, *Christology of the New Testament*, 238.
96. Cullmann, *Christology of the New Testament*, 238.
97. See Taylor, *Names of Jesus*.
98. Cullmann, *Christology of the New Testament*, 238.
99. Cullmann, *Christology of the New Testament*, 238.
100. Cullmann, *Christology of the New Testament*, 241.

New Testament passages that call Jesus "Savior" have exclusive Christian motif,[101] i.e., that Jesus heals and delivers the people from sin and death.

The Pastoral Letters, such as the ones written to Timothy (1 and 2 Tim.) and Titus, not only contain injunctions to Christian leaders to whom they are addressed to guard the faith and maintain discipline in the church, but also maintains that one of the divine attributes is "savior." The Pastoral Letters also extend the same divine attribute "savior" to Jesus: "But when the kindness and love of God our Savior appeared, he saved us, not because of righteous things we had done, but because of his mercy. He saved us through the washing of rebirth and renewal by the Holy Spirit, whom he poured out on us generously through Jesus Christ our Savior" (Titus 3:4–6). There are at least six times in the Pastoral Letters God is referred to as 'savior." The letter to Timothy begins with the declaration: "Paul, an apostle of Christ Jesus by the command of God our Savior and of Christ Jesus our hope" (1Tim. 1:1; see also Titus 1:3; 2:20; 3:4). Cullmann argues that the application of the Old Testament name for God, i.e., "savior," to Jesus by the New Testament writers gives us more reasons to assume that the early Christian Church had very early appropriated an Old Testament title of honor for God and transferred it to Jesus. It also "confirms our assumption that the name 'Savior' (like all the divine attributes) was ascribed to Jesus in connection with his dignity as *Kyrios*."[102]

In all, the theological depth of *soter* emerges in reference to Christ's saving activity. John's Gospel provides a good example by juxtaposing the words "savior" and "salvation" in his narrative of the redemptive action of Jesus. The world that was created by God (John 1:3) has become estranged and hostile to God. God therefore sends his Son to the world to save the world (John 3:18). Hence, Jesus could say at the end of his public ministry, "I did not come to condemn the world, but to save the world (John 12:47).[103] Nowhere is this well buttressed than in the Fourth Gospel, in the story of the Samaritan woman (John 4) that culminates in a series of affirmations about the true identity of Jesus.[104] In the story of the Samaritan woman, the townspeople know that "salvation" is from the Jews, but not limited to the Jews (John 4:22). When they finally recognized Jesus and called him the "savior of the world" they used a title that was known in the Hellenistic

---

101. Cullmann, *Christology of the New Testament*, 241.
102. Cullmann, *Christology of the New Testament*, 238–39.
103. Koester, "Savior of the World," 668.
104. Koester, "Savior of the World," 667.

world. "They recognized that Jesus transcended national boundaries; like Cesar he was a figure of universal significance."[105]

CHRISTOLOGICAL TITLES THAT REFER TO THE PRE-EXISTENCE OF JESUS

1. Jesus as *Logos* or Word

We already noted in our discussion of the application of the title *Kyrios* to Jesus that it was on the basis of the affirmation that Jesus is *Kyrios* that the early Christians could apply all statements about God to Jesus. To affirm that Jesus is *Logos*, as the Fourth Gospel makes clear, is to "relate redemption and creation— the work of Christ who was incarnate, is still present, and will come again; and the work of the Christ who was the 'Word,' the pre-existent mediator of creation."[106] With this emerges the question of the essential relationship between God the Father and the pre-existent *Logos* Jesus.[107]

In employing the *Logos* concept, the Johannine writer was aware that they were making use of an extra-Christian concept that was widespread both before and contemporaneously with Christianity.[108] Recent studies have uncovered that the concept of *Logos* is "semantically flexible," with backgrounds in Jewish, Stoic, and Middle Platonism.[109] Stoicism was a philosophical system of the Greeks that was materialistic and pantheistic. As materialists, Stoics distinguished what they thought was passive unformed matter from the active dynamic reason or word or plan that forms and organizes the unformed matter.[110] This active dynamic reason or word or plan they termed Logos. The concept of *Logos* (plural = *Logoi*) was a ubiquitous concept that was very important in the Greek worldview or cosmology. They equated *Logos* with divine reason that gives shape or form to the cosmos. Similarly, a person's soul was understood to be a manifestation of the *Logos* within the human person, without which a person could not comprehend reality.[111]

The influence of Greek thought on Jewish thinking cannot be overstated. The Stoic concept of *Logos* is one of many Greek concepts that

---

105. Koester, "Savior of the World," 668.
106. Cullmann, *Christology of the New Testament*, 248.
107. Cullmann, *Christology of the New Testament*, 248.
108. Cullmann, *Christology of the New Testament*, 250.
109. See Gregersen, "God, Matter, and Information."
110. Robinson, *God and the World of Signs*, 64.
111. Robinson, *God and the World of Signs*, 64.

crept into Jewish thought and which significantly influenced Jewish ways of speaking about God. One of the famous Jewish thinkers in Alexandria, Philo of Alexandria (30 BC–AD 45), for example, found useful the Greek idea of *Logos*, which he used to explain how the transcendence of God can be reconciled with God's immanence. Philo identified *Logos* with Plato's ideal and unchanging Forms, suggesting that what this means in religious terms is that God is both transcendent and active in creation. Due largely to the influence of writers like Philo, the early Christians employed the concept of *Logos* to describe the relationship between Jesus of Nazareth and God the Father. If Jesus was pre-existent God, as the Christians thought, then Jesus must be the "principle of God active in the creation and the continuous structuring of the cosmos and in revealing the divine plan of salvation to man."[112] The Stoic contribution to *Logos* Christology, in a nutshell, was in their emphasis on the immanence of the *Logos* in the created world, while the Platonic contribution remains the emphasis on the transcendence of the *Logos*,[113] two dynamically related aspects that the early Christians harmonized to speak of the identity of Jesus.

The early Christian identification of Jesus with the *Logos* is more fully developed in the Gospel of John where the author of the Fourth Gospel sets up *Logos* Christology as antithesis to prevailing distortions of the true Person and mission of Jesus Christ. In fact, the Johannine writings are unique in the sense that the Fourth Gospel is the only New Testament writing in which the Christological title occurs. Even then it occurs only in a few passages, mainly the prologue to the Gospel of John, the first verse of 1 John: "That which was from the beginning, which we have heard, which we have seen with our eyes, which we have looked at and our hands have touched—this we proclaim concerning the Word of life" (1 John 1:1), and in Revelation: "He is dressed in a robe dipped in blood, and his name is the Word of God" (Rev 19:13).[114] The *Logos* designation does not dominate the Gospel of John as is sometimes erroneously believed, but "the point at which the author of John makes use of the *Logos* concept shows that the title is indispensable for him when he wishes to speak of the relationship between the divine revelation in the life of Jesus and the pre-existence of Jesus."[115]

Logos theology offered the New Testament writers endless Christological possibilities. Here I will follow the five outlines of Gerald O'Collins, which I find credible:

112. See "Logos" in the *Encyclopedia Britannica*.
113. Robinson, *God and the World of Signs*, 65; see n13.
114. Cullmann, *Christology of the New Testament*, 249.
115. Cullmann, *Christology of the New Testament*, 249.

i). Possibility of Identification and Distinction

For the author of the Fourth Gospel, the beginning of the history of Jesus does not begin with the appearance or introduction of Jesus by John the Baptist, as portrayed in the Synoptic Gospels, but rather that the beginning lies in the pre-existence of Jesus.[116] Although he directs our attention to the pre-existent beginning, the author of the Fourth Gospel is not interested in any speculations of pre-temporal existence of Jesus, but only that this same Person who was in the beginning with God is the center of divine revelation and salvation history.[117] Speculatively, how are we to understand the distinction between this *Logos* (Word) from the Father? A "word" proceeds from a speaker, can act as a kind of extension of the speaker, and can in some sense be identical with the speaker ("the Word was God"). A "word" uttered is also at the same time distinct from the speaker ("the Word was with God"). Christ is therefore identical and yet distinct from Yahweh.[118]

ii). Possibility of Eternal Pre-Existence of the Word.

The Word uttered by God opens up reflection on the personal, eternal pre-existence of the *Logos*-Son. Given that God has been uttering the divine Word from the beginning, the Word did not come to be, rather the Word was.[119] This incarnate *Logos* who is the center of salvation history cannot simply have appeared from nowhere. He was already active in creation before the beginning of time.[120] The author of the Gospel of John drives this point home by beginning with a parallel with the Genesis creation story: "In the beginning God created the heavens and the earth" (Gen 1:1); "In the beginning was the Word and the Word was with God and the Word was God" (John 1:1).[121]

iii). Possibility of the Word Revealing God

Words can and do reveal their speakers. The Old Testament uses the "word" to denote the revelation of God and divine will. For the New Testament writers, particularly John's Gospel, the Word was the Son who made the Father known (John 1:18).[122] The *Logos* Jesus, who in the flesh is definite

---

116. Cullmann, *Christology of the New Testament*, 249.
117. Cullmann, *Christology of the New Testament*, 249.
118. O'Collins, *Christology*, 40.
119. O'Collins, *Christology*, 40.
120. Cullmann, *Christology of the New Testament*, 250.
121. Cullmann, *Christology of the New Testament*, 250.
122. O'Collins, *Christology*, 40.

self-revelation of God, was at work in the history of Israel and will continue working in the Church after his death.[123] One of the advantages of the *Logos* Christology is that it helps to assert differentiation of Father and Son within the Godhead.[124]

iv). Possibility of Dialogue with Culture

The *Logos* Christology of John's Gospel opened the way for Christians to recognize how the *Logos* might dwell outside of Christianity, thus opening room for dialogue with non-Christians. "Those who endorsed Jewish, Platonic, and Stoic strands of thought the *Logos* could find a measure of common ground with Christians, who, nevertheless, remained distinctive with their claim that 'the *Logos* was made flesh.' The notion of 'the *Logos*' probably offered a more effective bridge to contemporary culture than that of 'wisdom.'"[125]

v). Possibility that Creation has a Christological Dimension

By expressing identity between divine wisdom and Christ, the New Testament writers were simply doing more than expressing the divine identity of Jesus. They were expressing the fact that Christology did not necessarily begin with the incarnation, but that Jesus as the Second or Last Adam (the pinnacle of God's creation) shows that creation from the very beginning had a Christological implication.[126]

2. Jesus the Wisdom of God

The *Logos* speculation is one strand of Hellenistic world's speculation of pre-existence. Another strand of pre-existence is associated with the Wisdom speculation (Prov 8:22ff).[127] In the Old Testament, particularly in the Sapiential or Wisdom literature, Wisdom is often personified and portrayed somewhat as a divine being. Whether this personification really implies that Wisdom is a real being distinct from God (the Father) or whether it is simply a literary device or a metaphor of speaking of God's own wisdom, it is difficult to ascertain. What is clear is that in the Old Testament there

---

123. Cullmann, *Christology of the New Testament*, 250.
124. Pannenberg, *Jesus—God and Man*, 160.
125. O'Collins, *Christology*, 41.
126. O'Collins, *Christology*, 41.
127. Pannenberg, *Jesus—God and Man*, 152.

is an extended theological interest in the notion of divine wisdom.[128] This passage from Proverbs helps to illustrate the point:

> "The Lord brought me forth as the first of his works,
>   before his deeds of old;
> I was formed long ages ago,
>   at the very beginning, when the world came to be.
> When there were no watery depths, I was given birth,
>   when there were no springs overflowing with water;
> before the mountains were settled in place,
>   before the hills, I was given birth,
> before he made the world or its fields
>   or any of the dust of the earth.
> I was there when he set the heavens in place,
>   when he marked out the horizon on the face of the deep,
> when he established the clouds above
>   and fixed securely the fountains of the deep,
> when he gave the sea its boundary
>   so the waters would not overstep his command,
> and when he marked out the foundations of the earth.
>   Then I was constantly[c] at his side.
> I was filled with delight day after day,
>   rejoicing always in his presence,
> rejoicing in his whole world
>   and delighting in mankind (Prov 8:22–31).

Whether or not the authors of the Wisdom literature meant to portray Wisdom as a being other than God, the conceptuality itself offered various possibilities to the first generation of Christians who drew on these Old Testament ideas about wisdom to reflect their experience of Jesus.[129] The possibilities the various accounts of Wisdom offered the New Testament writers in their understanding and interpretation of Jesus are endless. What the New Testament writers did was take strands from the Old Testament ideas about wisdom and alter them to fit their interpretation of Jesus. They not only ascribe wisdom roles to Christ, but also make explicit the equation "divine wisdom = Christ" (1 Cor 1:17–2:13).[130] Here are five good examples:

1. Like Wisdom, Christ pre-existed and dwelt with God (John 1:1–2) before all things were made.[131]

---

128. See Ormerod, *Trinitarian Primer*, 15
129. O'Collins, *Christology*, 35.
130. O'Collins, *Christology*, 37.
131. O'Collins, *Christology*, 36.

2. Like Wisdom who is the breadth of God and reflects divine glory, Christ is "the radiance of God's glory" (John 1:9), "the image of the invisible God" (1 Cor 4:4), and the "true light that gives light to everyone" (Col 1:15).[132]
3. Like Wisdom who acts as God's agent in the creation of the world, all things were made through Christ and without him there is nothing made that would have been made (see John 1:3 and 1 Cor 8:6).[133]
4. Like Wisdom which resides only in God, Christ is that wisdom of God that is "secret and hidden" (1 Cor 2:7) because it is defined by the Cross, which is folly to the so-called wise people of this world (1 Cor 1:18–25).[134]
5. Like Wisdom which needs to be learned and discovered, Christ is wisdom greater than Solomon (Matt 12:42) and teaches wisdom through his parables (Matt 25:1–12).[135]

Many of the Church Fathers, Gregory of Nazianzus especially, followed the New Testament tradition of equating Christ with Wisdom. In his *Orationes*, Gregory argued, regarding the knowledge of Christ, that Christ knew everything: "How can he be ignorant of anything that is, when he is Wisdom, the maker of the worlds, who brings all things to fulfillment and recreates all things, who is the end of all that has come into being?"[136]

THE CHRISTOLOGICAL TITLES THAT REFER TO THE FUTURE WORKS OF JESUS

1. Jesus as Christ or Messiah

"Messiah," rendered in Greek as "Christ" (meaning anointed one) is an eschatological concept. It has its origins in the Jewish hope for the future.[137] The term itself derives from the Old Testament. Its Jewish usage was not unambiguous. There were some Jewish conceptions of the coming messiah that contradicted other existing messiah types, although they were still under the common denominator "Messiah."[138] In all, Jewish messianic expectations had no hint of a suffering and martyred Messiah. "A crucified (and

---

132. O'Collins, *Christology*, 36.
133. O'Collins, *Christology*, 36–37.
134. O'Collins, *Christology*, 37.
135. O'Collins, *Christology*, 37.
136. O'Collins, *Christology*, 38.
137. Cullmann, *Christology of the New Testament*, 111.
138. Cullmann, *Christology of the New Testament*, 112.

resurrected) Christ was even more alien to Jewish messianic expectations. It was precisely over that point that the Christian proclamation of a crucified Messiah proved so new, strange, and scandalously offensive (1 Cor 1:23)."[139] Thus, the New Testament writers took over only Jewish Christological views that do not have to do with political Messiah, i.e., they "took over only certain important elements of the predominating picture of the Messiah, and did not apply to Jesus other quite essential aspects of the Jewish Messiah."[140]

In numerous passages in the New Testament, we see Jesus interpreting his mission messianically. At times he seems to show reservation accepting it as a description of his calling and person.[141] Since Jesus did not reject the title, the first generation of his followers did exactly the same, almost using the title "Christ" to speak of Jesus's other name as one would speak of a person's last (surname) name (1 Cor 15:3). Even the apostle Paul, who at times considered it necessary to argue to his audience that Jesus is the "Christ" for whom Israel had been longing, calls Jesus "Christ" in a way that suggests that the early followers of Jesus took this title for Jesus's identity and power for granted (1 Thess 1:1; 5:23, 28).[142]

To return to the origin of the term, "messiah" derives from the Hebrew *mashiah*, meaning "anointed one." It is rendered "Christ" in the Septuagint (Greek translation of the Old Testament). It was a common practice in the Old Testament to anoint kings at their investiture. Samuel anoints Saul King of Israel (1 Sam 9–10). He also anoints David to succeed Saul (1 Sam 16:1–13). The practice of anointing kings was later extended to priests, as in the example of the priests from the line of Aaron who were anointed.[143] Even prophets were thought to be anointed, even though there was no prescribed formal ritual rites for their anointing. Isaiah the prophet, for example, knew himself to be anointed when he proclaimed,

> The Spirit of the Lord God *is* upon Me,
> Because the Lord has anointed Me
> To preach good tidings to the poor;
> He has sent Me to heal the brokenhearted,
> To proclaim liberty to the captives,
> And the opening of the prison to *those who are* bound;
> To proclaim the acceptable year of the Lord,
> And the day of vengeance of our God;

---

139. O'Collins, *Christology*, 28–29.
140. Cullmann, *Christology of the New Testament*, 112.
141. Cullmann, *Christology of the New Testament*, 113.
142. O'Collins, *Christology*, 24.
143. O'Collins, *Christology*, 24.

To comfort all who mourn (Isa 61:1–2)

Messianic themes in the Old Testament were also associated with the Davidic dynasty (Isa 9:6). Even when David's dynasty fell in 587 BC, the Old Testament developed restoration themes and continued to associate the messiah with the line of David. Prophet Isaiah specifically notes that the messiah will be a "wonderful counsellor, mighty God, and prince of peace" (Isa 9:6). Since Jesus interpreted his person and actions messianically, his first generation of followers followed him in identifying him as the promised messiah.[144] While the Old Testament messianic expectation was one of kingly messiah who will deliver Israel from their enemies, Jesus was anything but kingly. Jesus's messiahship stands in contradistinction to royalty; his was one of servanthood (Luke 22:24–27). The first generation of Jesus's disciples, following Jesus's self-understanding of his identity and mission, will later apply the four Servant Songs of Second Isaiah (42:1–4; 49:1–6; 50:4–11; 52:13—53:12) to Jesus.[145] The followers of Jesus, who for the first time were called Christians (Messianites) in Antioch (Acts 11:26), chose to emphasize the title, albeit without completely rejecting "the fixed, nationalistically limited picture of the Messiah."[146] They emphasized that Jesus appeared on earth as the Son of David and that as King over the Church (the new Israel) to which all peoples are gathered, he will return again as Messiah at the end of time.[147]

2. Jesus the Son of Man

"The Son of Man" is the only title Jesus expressly applied to himself.[148] Except for two instances, i.e., Stephen's speech before the Sanhedrin when he saw "the heavens open and the Son Man standing at the right hand of God" (Acts 7:56) and John's vision in Revelation where he saw "someone like a Son of Man dressed in a robe reaching down to his feet and with a golden sash around his chest" (Rev 1:13), the title "Son of Man" was not a title others used in reference to Jesus; only Jesus used it in reference to himself. Even the Gospel writers did not employ the title to express their faith in Jesus. Their preference was more for the messianic designation "Christ."[149] So regarding these two terms (Son of Man and Messiah), we are faced with

---

144. O'Collins, *Christology*, 27.
145. O'Collins, *Christology*, 28.
146. Cullmann, *Christology of the New Testament*, 113.
147. Cullmann, *Christology of the New Testament*, 136.
148. Cullmann, *Christology of the New Testament*, 137.
149. Oakes, *Infinity Dwindled to Infancy*, 40.

a paradox: "Jesus regularly referred to himself as Son of Man, but the early Christians almost never so designated him by the title: Jesus largely deflects the title 'Christ' while the church calls him that constantly; but the term he uses for himself most of all, 'Son of Man,' almost never appears on the lips of Christians as a confessional term."[150]

In the Gospels there are many passages where Jesus refers to himself as the "Son of Man." For example, speaking of himself, Jesus is reported as saying "the Son of Man has no place to lay his head" (Matt 8:20). Based on the numerous references to the "Son of Man" in the Gospels, some scholars have suggested that this title was an invention of the evangelists based on the theology of the early church.[151] But there are some New Testament scholars who refute this thesis as too simplistic. They argue that the "Son of Man" was not a common title for Jesus in the early Church. Not only did the evangelists never used it for Jesus, they never report others using it in their dealings with Jesus.[152]

Linguistically, when used by a speaker of Aramaic, there are three possible semantic meanings of the "Son of Man." First, a male speaker of Aramaic could use the phrase "Son of Man" as a way of speaking in the third person to avoid sounding the egotistical connotation that comes from speaking too often in the first person.[153] Second, in Aramaic, the phrase "Son of Man" is a generic way of speaking of human beings.[154] Third, the phrase "Son of Man" is used to designate an eschatological figure from heaven who will be sent by God to bring an end to the world as we know it and inaugurate in a definitive way the reign of God. It is most likely in this third sense that the phrase "Son of Man" becomes a genuine Christological title.[155] The phrase the "Son of Man" actually derives from the Old Testament, the book of Daniel and Ezekiel especially. It was not a messianic title in the Old Testament. In Daniel where the phrase occurs with regularity, it is simply used to designate a "human being" or "someone" (the second semantic meaning of the word). It was also used in a way that suggests a speaker referring to self in the third person (the first semantic meaning of the word):

> In my vision at night I looked, and there before me was one like a son of man coming with the clouds of heaven. He approached the Ancient of Days and was led into his presence. He was given

---

150. Oakes, *Infinity Dwindled to Infancy*, 40.
151. Cullmann, *Christology of the New Testament*, 155.
152. Cullmann, *Christology of the New Testament*, 155.
153. Oakes, *Infinity Dwindled to Infancy*, 40–41.
154. Oakes, *Infinity Dwindled to Infancy*, 41.
155. Oakes, *Infinity Dwindled to Infancy*, 41.

> authority, glory and sovereign power; all nations and peoples of every language worshiped him. His dominion is an everlasting dominion that will not pass away, and his kingdom is one that will never be destroyed (Dan 7:13–14)

In the passage above, the phrase "Son of Man" has a double meaning and none of these meanings refers to an individual. It is specifically used to symbolize the angels, i.e., the heavenly figure who represents the people, as well as "the righteous and persecuted Jews who will be vindicated and given authority by God."[156] On the basis of these meanings, the phrase the "Son of Man" was never understood to be a title for the messiah that was to come. So it was somewhat surprising to see Jesus refer to himself as the Son of Man.

In the main, the phrase "Son of Man," as used by Jesus in the Synoptic Gospels, has three functions: first, Jesus uses it to refer to his earthly condition and his work on earth; second, Jesus uses it to refer to his impending suffering, death, and resurrection; and third, Jesus uses it to refer to his future coming in heavenly glory.[157] John's Gospel, on the other hand, uses the phrase somewhat differently from the synoptics. In John's Gospel the phrase is used to denote Jesus as a personally pre-existent being.[158] Later usage of the phrase, particularly in the writings of the Fathers of the Church, designates Jesus's humanity, as distinguished from his divinity (Son of God).[159]

Thus, since the phrase "Son of Man" did not function as a messianic title in the pre-Christian world and was not directly ascribed to Jesus in the Gospels by anyone other than Jesus himself, if Jesus did use the phrase "Son of Man" he could have imposed on it his own meanings.[160] For example, speaking of his impending return in glory, Jesus draws from the celestial figure of Daniel and speaks of the "Son of Man" coming in the clouds (Mark 14:62). This is well after he had stated that he, the Son of Man, will be rejected by the elders, scribes, and priests and that he will suffer and be killed, but will rise again on the third day (Mark 18:31–32). Here Jesus chooses to use the phrase "Son of Man" as a way of "signaling his acceptance of a divine vocation, one, moreover, that will transform God's relationship to history in a definitive way."[161] Jesus's passion and death and the end of the world are in some ways mysteriously linked.[162]

156. O'Collins, *Christology*, 62.
157. O'Collins, *Christology*, 63.
158. O'Collins, *Christology*, 63.
159. O'Collins, *Christology*, 64.
160. O'Collins, *Christology*, 63.
161. Oakes, *Infinity Dwindled to Infancy*, 44.
162. Oakes, *Infinity Dwindled to Infancy*, 44.

CONCLUSION

The Christological titles are a clear statement of the New Testament attitude towards the divinity of Jesus. They derive from the early Church's post-Easter understanding of Jesus's life and works, particularly his miracles, his attitude towards the Jewish Temple and the Sabbath observances, etc. The titles, in a nutshell, are "an index of the way in which the early Church confessed its understanding of what Jesus meant" for humanity.[163] "If Jesus presented himself as one in whose life God was active, he did so not primarily by the use of titles or by clear statements about what he was, but rather by the impact of his person and his life on those who followed him."[164] It is precisely because these are titles that the early Church applied to Jesus that we divided them under the four rubrics: the Christological tittles that refer to the earthly life of Jesus, the titles that refer to the future work of Jesus, the titles that refer to the present work of Jesus, and the titles that refer to Jesus's preexistence. The rubric itself suggests a semiotic understanding. The classifications, taken together, are meant to give us a fuller picture of who Jesus really is. Just like a sign vehicle can at one and the same time be an icon, an index, and a symbol and given that no single one of this triad is self-sufficient and no single one can exist without the other, in the same way no single one of the Christological titles is self-sufficient in itself as to encompass the infinite fullness of Christ. Our semiotic analysis reveals that each of the titles can be related to at least one or two other titles and can capture different functions of Jesus. The nature of the titles themselves reveal something about the early church and their understanding (or lack thereof) of who Jesus really is. "A mutual assimilation of meanings and connotations may have taken place in the consciousness of the first Christians, who often applied different titles to Jesus simultaneously."[165]

What also emerges from these titles is evolution of thought on the part of the disciples, the New Testament writers, and the early church as a whole. It is in grasping the meaning of the titles that the early Christians applied to Jesus that we also pay attention to "what basic event history, both of Jesus and the early church, and the documentary history, teach us about how each of these titles got applied to Jesus."[166] In other words, in our treatment of Christology, do we allow the Gospel writers' motifs and the New Testament's

---

163. Brown, *Jesus God and Man*, 2.
164. Brown, *Jesus God and Man*, 2.
165. Cullmann, *Christology of the New Testament*, 9.
166. Oakes, *Infinity Dwindled to Infancy*, 66.

own categories of understanding of Jesus and history to speak for itself?[167] One motif of the Gospel writers that is often overlooked in standard treatments of Christology is what Oakes calls the theme of the incomprehension of the disciples of Jesus when Jesus was with them in the flesh. "Not only did the disciples for the most part not 'get it,' they are described as not getting it."[168] If the disciples didn't get it when Jesus was with them in the flesh, then when did they start to get it?

The disciples not "getting it" coheres with the evolutionary perspective we have adopted in this work—the dynamic movement of the world in compliance with God's design, particularly in the Law of the Cross. The most fascinating aspect of the Gospel's strategy of the history of the disciples not getting it is, as Oakes said, to show that they still had a lot to learn.[169] What confirmed to the disciples that Jesus was really the Messiah was the resurrection. What the Gospel writers did was to write with "retrospective outlook" or what in common parlance we may say is "the benefit of hindsight."[170] Things that Jesus said and did began to make sense to the disciples after the resurrection event. The resurrection represents "a radical inbreaking and irruption of God's power into the course of history."[171] On the basis of the resurrection, therefore, the disciples could look back to the Old Testament and start interpreting things anew. Stated differently, "resurrection determines how the Old Testament is to be interpreted, rather than the Old Testament determining how resurrection is to be interpreted."[172] The same inner logic works with the titles applied to Jesus: "all the traditional titles of Jesus were reconstituted by the resurrection, and the Gospel writers wrote their narratives from that point of view."[173] The disciples who could not see and understand when Jesus was with them in the flesh were able to see and understand "retrospectively where, how, and why they continued to misunderstand him during his earthly ministry; and the evangelists, sharing that same benefit of hindsight, were able to apply that same benefit to the witness of the Old Testament."[174]

One final point on the New Testament's understanding of Jesus, the Gospels were written as narratives of the life of Jesus and with the sole goal

---

167. Oakes, *Infinity Dwindled to Infancy*, 69.
168. Oakes, *Infinity Dwindled to Infancy*, 69.
169. Oakes, *Infinity Dwindled to Infancy*, 70.
170. Oakes, *Infinity Dwindled to Infancy*, 70.
171. Oakes, *Infinity Dwindled to Infancy*, 72.
172. Oakes, *Infinity Dwindled to Infancy*, 72.
173. Oakes, *Infinity Dwindled to Infancy*, 72.
174. Oakes, *Infinity Dwindled to Infancy*, 72.

of eliciting faith. All of Paul's letters were written before the Gospels (and Acts of the Apostles) were composed. On the basis of the priority of Pauline letters, we need to take seriously Edward Oakes's point that "the essentials of the Christological thinking of the early church were already complete before the composition of the first Gospel. This is because the church was forced to think through the implications of the resurrection well before the narratives of the life of Jesus took shape in written form."[175]

---

175. Oakes, *Infinity Dwindled to Infancy*, 77.

Chapter Four

Resurrection—The *Sinsign* of Jesus's Identity and Mission

IN THE PREVIOUS CHAPTER, we examined the Christological titles that the early Church applied to Jesus and saw how these titles are themselves consequences of the faith of the disciples in the risen Christ. Jesus's claim that He is one with the Father is implicit in his message and life-long work. The claim itself precedes the faith of the disciples.[1] In fact, the disciples early on did not understand Jesus and asked whenever he made claims they considered outrageous, "What kind of man is this?" (Matt 8:27). Jesus's claim to authority alone cannot be the basis of Christology. That claim has to be validated and vindicated by the Father who raised him from the dead. We pointed out in the last chapter how the first generation of Jesus's followers interpreted his identity and mission through the lens of the messianic images of the Old Testament. It was following Jesus's brutal death on the cross that the resurrection became, for the disciples, the hermeneutical key for unlocking the identity and mission of Jesus. "If Christ had not been raised from the dead we are the most pitied of men," the apostle Paul stated (1 Cor 15:19). The event of the resurrection was not only a validation, but also an event continuous with the kerygma.

The episode of the resurrection divides opinion, even till this day. Biblical scholars are still polarized on the issue for different reasons. We need to stress that the very idea of resurrection is not new to Christianity. It was an idea that was already present in the ancient Hellenistic and Jewish

---

1. Pannenberg, *Jesus—God and Man*, 54.

conceptions of life after death. The burden of this chapter is to show how the ancient and Jewish notions enhance the Christian understanding of Jesus's raising from the dead. In semiotic terms, this entails applying indexical paradigm to both the ways we speak and understand resurrection. Ludwig Wittgenstein pointed out in *Philosophische Untersuchungen* that those things which are most important for us are often hidden from our sight by their simplicity and their everyday character and that the reason we don't notice them is because they are always before our eyes.[2] Indexical paradigm and the indexical use of thought, language, and representations are part of our everyday conscious activities,[3] regardless of whether we advert to them. If the "highest grade of reality," as Charles Sanders Peirce (1839–1914) says, "is only reached by signs,"[4] then the resurrection is that sublime reality that can be fully grasped with the aid of signs. Peirce designed indexical sign as a form of inquiry and urged that the empirical meaning of theoretical statements be determined by looking for indexical, experiential confrontation with the individual objects of the theory in question.[5] Following Peirce's theory of signs—a way of grasping the epistemic role of indexical relations in human conscious activities—[6] this chapter will show the biblical applicability of indexical signs. The suggestion here is that a proper application of indexical signs can help us appreciate what Christianity wants to convey by the biblical notion of resurrection of the body by the Man-Jesus.

INDEXICAL REPRESENTATION OF RAISING FROM THE DEAD

On three separate occasions that Jesus raised the dead: the raising of the widow's son (Luke 7:11–17), the raising of Lazarus (John 11), and the raising of Jairus's daughter (Mark 5:21–43; Matt 9:8–26; Luke 8:40–56), the Gospels referred to them as "signs" that the on-lookers saw, which elicited in them faith in Jesus. In the New Testament, the Fourth Gospel stands unique for its purposeful and strategic use of the term σημεῖα (sign) as apt description of the many miracles Jesus did in the presence of his disciples, which elicited in the disciples faith that Jesus is the Christ.[7] The sign-miracles σημεῖα capture the Fourth Gospel's central claim that Jesus is the promised Messiah that

2. As paraphrased by Pape, "Searching for Traces," 1–25.
3. Pape, "Searching for Traces," 1.
4. Peirce, "Two Letters to Lady Welby," 382.
5. Pape, "Searching for Traces," 5.
6. Pape, "Searching for Traces," 2.
7. Kim, "Significance of Jesus' First Sign-Miracle in John," 201.

the Old Testament prophets proclaimed would come. Σημεία is so central to the Fourth Gospel that some have considered it the key to interpreting the Gospel itself.[8] As used in this Gospel, σημεία has three possible meanings: (i) a sign by which something is known (ii) a sign wonder-miracle or a divine or demonic event contrary to the order of nature and (iii) a future or eschatological oriented sign.[9] The Fourth Gospel uses σημεία for the most part to demonstrate "significant truths through a miracle, as a sample of what is to take place in the future."[10]

The Fourth Gospel is also noted for its presentation of eight distinct "sign miracles," which in the view of the evangelist, reveal the divinity of Jesus. The sign miracles are a set of eight specific miracles performed by Jesus, demonstrating his power over creation, space, time, food, natural laws, physical laws, and death. The miracles all carry special significance and meanings beyond what the Fourth Gospel intends to convey:

1. The first sign-miracle occurs at the wedding at Cana where Jesus turned water into wine. (Jon 2:1–12).
2. There is the healing of the son of the high-ranking official who implored Jesus to come and heal his ailing son (John 4:43–54).
3. The healing of the man who had been lame for thirty-eight years at Bethesda (John 5:1–14).
4. The feeding of five thousand people with five loaves and two fish (John 6:1–14).
5. The fifth sign-miracle occurred when the disciples in a boat to Capernaum encountered storm and Jesus walked in water to calm the storm (John 6:16–24).
6. The sixth sign-miracle is the healing of the man who was born blind (John 9:1–12).
7. The seventh is the raising of Lazarus to life (John 11).
8. The eighth sign-miracle occurs after Jesus's resurrection when he appeared to Peter and the disciples who had gone fishing (John 21:1–14).

Notably, the resurrection of Jesus is not considered a sign-miracle in the Fourth Gospel.

If the purpose of the sign-miracles is to reveal "Jesus as the promised Messiah and the unique Son of God, and to affirm that those who believe in Him are promised eternal life,"[11] then an analysis of signs deeper than what

---

8. Kim, "Significance of Jesus' First Sign-Miracle in John," 202.
9. Kim, "Significance of Jesus' First Sign-Miracle in John," 202.
10. Kim, "Significance of Jesus' First Sign-Miracle in John," 202.
11. Kim, "Significance of Jesus' First Sign-Miracle in John," 215.

is presented in the Fourth Gospel is needed. Although the sign-miracles are central to the Fourth Gospel, John is not the only Gospel that makes extensive use of the miracle stories in his presentation of the ministry of Jesus. The Synoptics, Mark especially, also make use of σημεῖον (signs) and εργον (work), the latter being a more inclusive term that encompasses Jesus's whole ministry, including his miracles.[12] The purpose of "sign and works," in the synoptic Gospels and the Fourth Gospel put together, is to develop faith in those who experience them because these signs and works exemplify Jesus's unique authority over life and death, notwithstanding that it can also produce the contrary (lack of faith) in some others.[13]

Signs and symbols are by nature multivalent, "capable of more than one meaning, their referent unable to be fixed precisely."[14] Signs operate on two levels: the material and the spiritual, the ordinary and the extraordinary, and the present and yet to be. For this reason, signs and symbols generally require a second order or higher level of understanding for their meanings to emerge.[15] The resurrection of Jesus must have a role to play in the symbolic framework of the Gospels. What we gather in the Johannine and Synoptic use of sign, in relation to the miracles of Jesus, is that the early Church made some symbolic connections between the event of Jesus's ministry and the messages he proclaimed.[16] The miracles recorded in the Gospels are by no means exhaustive. The author of the Fourth Gospel was clear that if everything that Jesus said and did were to be recorded the world itself would not have enough books to record them (John 21:25). Precisely because the miracles recorded in the Gospels are not exhaustive, "they do not resolve the problem of evil nor remove altogether suffering, privation and pain but rather play a more representative role: as symbols either of reality that is still to come or of a relationship that can transform the present."[17] In all, the most noteworthy thing about the miracles is that they possess the capacity for symbolic extension.[18]

It is not my intention to interrogate why the resurrection is not considered one of the sign-miracles of the Fourth Gospel. That is a problem for biblical scholarship. My goal, rather, is to further or deepen, as it were, our understanding of the miracles, the bodily resurrection of Jesus being the

---

12. Lee, "Signs and Works," 90.
13. Lee, "Signs and Works," 90–91.
14. Lee, "Signs and Works," 93.
15. Lee, "Signs and Works," 93.
16. Lee, "Signs and Works," 93.
17. Lee, "Signs and Works," 100.
18. Lee, "Signs and Works," 100.

miracle of miracles. I shall use Peirce derived categories to show the capacity for symbolic extension that the miracles possess. Because Jesus's whole life and works embody the presence of God, they include moments that can be interpreted iconically (symbolically), like the temple action and the last supper.[19] Peirce's semiotics, at least, gives us the paradigm for this symbolic extension. When the religious authorities asked for a "sign" of his authority, Jesus simply said, "Destroy this temple and in three days I will raise it up." To which the religious authorities retorted, "It took forty-six years to build this temple, and will You raise it up in three days?" In reporting this exchange between Jesus and the authorities, the author of the Fourth Gospel was convinced that the religious authorities missed the point because Jesus was actually speaking of the temple of his body, not the physical place of worship (John 2:18–22). In other words, the "sign" that Jesus would give was his own resurrection. Herein lies my hypothesis for the chapter: the resurrection of Christ is the hermeneutical key for understanding the whole of the New Testament and this resurrection can be conceived as a *Sinsign*. What Peirce calls a *Sinsign* refers to actual existents.[20] The ancient Jewish and Hellenistic notions about the raising of dead are actual existents. Jesus asserting "I Am the resurrection and the life" (John 11:25) by so doing embodies what the ancients thought they knew about the raising of the dead in a unique way— a *Sinsign*. Now I show how the resurrection of Jesus —*Sinsign*— sheds light on what the early Christians hoped to achieve by proclaiming the kerygma.

Ancient and Jewish Notion of Resurrection

In the *Odyssey* (Books 10 and 11), Homer presents an account of life after death as it was perceived in the Homeric times and beyond. What Homer presents in the Odyssey regarding the underworld is actually both the Greek and pre-Greek (ancient) views of the subject. Since Homer's was the first actual formal written account of the subject, his view of the underworld draws from a long history of oral stories that were current in the ancient world. These stories of the ancients set a dichotomy between what happens in life and what happens in death. The New Testament scholar, N.T. Wright, recons that the ancient worldview about life after death was largely shaped by Homer's depiction in the *Odyssey* of a pretty bleak place. Hades, the abode of the dead, was a place of shadows and wrath.[21]

---

19. Shults, "Transforming Theological Symbols," 728.
20. CP 2.243.
21. Wright, "Jesus' Resurrection and Christian Origins," 41.

Plato and the Pythagoreans differed a lit bit and presented alternatives to the Homeric viewpoint by offering "the chance of a blissful afterlife at least for some."[22] They also speculated about reincarnation and transmigration of the soul, even though they did not offer a clear picture of how the souls emerged and the criteria for transmigration. There were also other viewpoints, like those of the Stoics who taught that the world would be destroyed by fire and reborn.[23] But the common thread in all these differing viewpoints of the ancients is that there was no such thing as belief in bodily resurrection. "Homer does not imagine that there is a way back; Plato does not suppose anyone in their right mind would want one. There may or may not be various forms of life after death, but the one thing there isn't is resurrection."[24] Even when the language of resurrection was used in Egypt in connection with the world that exists after death "it did not involve actual bodily return to the present world."[25] Similarly, when ancient kingdoms developed the notion of apotheosis (deification of their leaders and heroes), those who were exalted and accorded divine or quasi-divine status were said to have been alive alongside gods (like Jupiter and Apollo in the case of the Romans), not alive in this bodily realm.

The same fluidity we see in the ancient conception of life after death is also present in ancient Jewish idea of life after death. Wright writes that "the Hebrew Sheol, the place of the dead, is not very different from Homer's Hades. People are asleep there; they can sometimes be woken up, as with Saul and Samuel, but to do so is dangerous and forbidden."[26] The Psalms (cf. Ps 73), however, speak glowingly about life beyond the grave, though these are predicated not "on the existence of an immortal soul which will automatically have a future life, but on the love and faithfulness of YHWH in the present, which must...continue into the future."[27] But we see a different discourse in Isaiah where there is a hint of Jewish belief in embodied life after death:

> But your dead will live, Lord;
>   their bodies will rise—
> let those who dwell in the dust
>   wake up and shout for joy—
> your dew is like the dew of the morning;
>   the earth will give birth to her dead (Isa 26:19)

22. Wright, "Jesus' Resurrection and Christian Origins," 41.
23. Wright, "Jesus' Resurrection and Christian Origins," 41.
24. Wright, "Jesus' Resurrection and Christian Origins," 41.
25. Wright, "Jesus' Resurrection and Christian Origins," 41.
26. Wright, "Jesus' Resurrection and Christian Origins," 42.
27. Wright, "Jesus' Resurrection and Christian Origins," 42.

Prophet Ezekiel also hints at the same idea of a resurrected embodied life after death:

> Then he said to me, "Prophesy to these bones and say to them, 'Dry bones, hear the word of the Lord! This is what the Sovereign Lord says to these bones: I will make breath enter you, and you will come to life. I will attach tendons to you and make flesh come upon you and cover you with skin; I will put breath in you, and you will come to life. Then you will know that I am the Lord.'" So I prophesied as I was commanded. And as I was prophesying, there was a noise, a rattling sound, and the bones came together, bone to bone. I looked, and tendons and flesh appeared on them and skin covered them, but there was no breath in them (Ezek 37:4–8).

In all, the notion of afterlife is, at best, ambiguous in Judaism. The religion presents a wide range of views that veers between a future world to be anticipated as the ultimate reward of the pious Jew who devotes self to the Torah, transmigration of the soul developed by Jewish mystics in the Middle Ages, and the biblical notion of resurrected body. Isaiah 25–26 is a classic example of the latter. There is also the text of Daniel: "Multitudes who sleep in the dust of the earth will awake: some to everlasting life, others to shame and everlasting contempt (Dan 12:2). Another extant reference to the resurrection of the dead appears in Second Maccabees— in reference to self-sacrificing death. In Second Maccabees, self-sacrificial death was intertwined with the promise of afterlife.[28] There is the story of the torture and death of Eleazer (2 Macc 6:18–31), the story of the death of a mother and her seven sons under the foreign ruler Antiochus (2 Macc 7:1–41) and the story of Razis's death (2 Macc 14:37–46). In the story of the torture of the mother and her seven sons, "the last son is exhorted to his death by his mother, who urges him to die rather than perform a sacrifice under the king's auspices."[29]

Wright cautions against a straightjacket understanding of Jewish conception of resurrected body. He argues that "resurrection" is not a general word for life after death in Judaism, but a term for a particular belief.[30] Judaism also espouses belief in an intermediate state in between death and resurrection. In the apocryphal book of Enoch, we are told of a peaceful garden or paradise where the souls of the just rested before their

---

28. Janowitz, "Rereading Sacrifice," 202.
29. Janowitz, "Rereading Sacrifice," 203.
30. Wright, "Jesus' Resurrection and Christian Origins," 42.

newly bodily life begins (1 Enoch 37–70).³¹ Thus, resurrection can mean, "being given back one's body, or perhaps God creating a new similar body, sometime after death. It is in fact, life after 'life after death.'"³² Resurrection, in other words, amounts to "conquest of death and its effects."³³ The book of Wisdom expresses this very well:

> The souls of the righteous are in the hand of God,
> and no torment shall touch them.
> They seemed, in the view of the foolish, to be dead;
> and their passing away was thought an affliction
> and their going forth from us, utter destruction.
> But they are in peace.
> For if to others, indeed, they seem punished,
> yet is their hope full of immortality (Wis 3:1–4).

On the flip side, within Judaism there is also the other extreme of denying resurrection entirely, as the Sadducees did. As N.T. Wright points out, the whole spectrum of beliefs in the resurrection, ranging from the Sadducees who deny belief in the resurrection of the dead and the Pharisees who believe in the resurrection, shows that belief in resurrection was for the Jews an explicitly political doctrine. The Pharisees adhered strictly to the Torah (written law) and the *Mishnah* (oral law). In this respect they were strongly related to the Scribes. The Sadducees, on the other hand, had more connection to the High Priest and the Temple. They were more interested in maintaining their social and political status in the society. "The Pharisees belief in the resurrection was part of their generally revolutionary ideology; as in Daniel and Maccabees, resurrection was an incentive to martyrdom."³⁴ Thus, those Jewish groups that believed in the resurrection also believed in the coming of the messiah. They believed that the coming of the messiah would signal Yahweh's time to defeat their enemies, rebuild their temple, and establish Yahweh's rule over the world. Like the belief in resurrection, which has a political undertone, belief in the coming messiah was also as political as it is theological.³⁵ According to Wright, it "was from within one such prophetic and messianic renewal movement that the early Christians emerged, saying two things in particular: Jesus was and is the Messiah, and this proved because he has been raised from the dead."³⁶

31. Wright, "Jesus' Resurrection and Christian Origins," 42.
32. Wright, "Jesus' Resurrection and Christian Origins," 42.
33. Wright, "Jesus' Resurrection and Christian Origins," 42.
34. Wright, "Jesus' Resurrection and Christian Origins," 43.
35. Wright, "Jesus' Resurrection and Christian Origins," 43.
36. Wright, "Jesus' Resurrection and Christian Origins," 43.

We turn next to Christian understanding of resurrection, a concept for which the Jewish notion provides a background. Even in its Jewish understanding, the concept of resurrection, in so far as it is a thought and imagery, is indexical. Imagery, though figurative, is significative, whether verbal or nonverbal.[37] A sign, as we have pointed out repeatedly, is grounded in an object. This grounding in turn determines the interpretant. Whatever the human signifier thinks they are conveying is the meaning of the sign to them, and everything the receivers assimilate or get from it is their own understanding of the meaning of the sign.[38]

KERYGMA OF THE RESURRECTED CHRIST

Christian idea of life after death derives, not from the pagan notion, but from the Biblical Jewish belief, though with some significant modifications. To state it differently, the early Christian understanding of what it means for Jesus to be raised from the dead did not emerge in a vacuum. It is an understanding that has a socio-cultural context. The Jews had long believed in the resurrection of the body, at least as far back as the Maccabean period in the second century BC. This idea can be found in Daniel and in the subsequent intertestamental literature.[39] The hope that the early Christians placed in the resurrection was never in doubt (see 2 Tim 2:18). Even if some saw Jesus's resurrection from the dead as unexpectedly premature, for many, it was a sign of the eschaton.[40] We shall return later to this Christian anticipatory hope of resurrection after a discussion of Christ's own resurrection from the dead.

Our earliest accounts of the New Testament writings come from Paul. His writings contain the creedal summaries of the early Christian beliefs and practices. Paul was not a witness to the raising of Christ from the dead three days after he had been put to death, but a witness to the post-resurrection appearances in which he encountered the risen Christ (Acts 9:1–22; Gal 1:11–24). Paul, like other apostolic witnesses to the resurrection, saw his task as that of furthering Christ's own mission by testifying to the resurrection and contributing to the establishment of the Church.[41] Paul inherited

---

37. Smith, *Arguing with Lacan*.
38. Tejera, "Has Eco Understood Peirce?" 255
39. Smith, *Sense of Presence*, 26.
40. Smith, *Sense of Presence*, 26.
41. O'Collins, *Christology*, 91.

from the early church a four-part formula or kerygmatic tradition: Christ's death, burial, resurrection, and post-resurrection appearances.[42]

> For what I received I passed on to you as of first importance: that Christ died for our sins according to the Scriptures, that he was buried, that he was raised on the third day according to the Scriptures, and that he appeared to Cephas, and then to the Twelve (1 Cor 15:3–5).

There are questions regarding the nature of resurrection Paul had in mind in 1 Cor 15—whether he envisioned a revival and transformed body or whether he thought of the resurrection as involving a bestowal of a new non-material body discontinuous with the body one had here on earth. Even more, did he even envision "an ethereally material body composed not of flesh but of a heavenly pneumatic substance?"[43] Although Gnostic interpreters, like Valentinus (c. AD 100–160), read 1 Cor 15 as implying resurrection discontinuous with one's earthly body, Patristic writers, Irenaeus, Tertullian, Jerome, and Augustine in particular, interpreted Paul as identifying resurrected body with earthly body in a transformed and imperishable shape.[44] The patristic teaching helped to shape Christian understanding of resurrection as "the reconstitution and glorious transformation of the present mortal body, a transformation involving 'enhancement of what is, not metamorphosis into what is not.'"[45]

The argument for the bodily resurrection of Jesus was based on a sign, albeit an ambiguous one, the empty tomb. But the validation of the sign came with confirmation of the appearances by the risen Christ. Paul does not mention the empty tomb in 1 Cor 15. Scholars have speculated on what could be the reason for this. Some think that the empty tomb tradition is post-Pauline—that it was developed as a natural consequence of the appearance tradition that Paul inherited. Their argument goes like this: If Jesus was bodily alive and was seen by the more than five hundred people that Paul listed, then he could still not be in the tomb.[46] Others suggest that Paul could have omitted the empty tomb on the logic that if Jesus had been buried (1 Cor 15:4), and had been seen alive by the multitude of disciples, including Paul himself, then the empty tomb was obvious and hardly needs mentioning. In addition, Paul's main concern in 1 Corinthians has to do

---

42. O'Collins, *Christology*, 83.
43. Ware, "Paul's Understanding of the Resurrection," 809–35.
44. Ware, "Paul's Understanding of the Resurrection," 810.
45. Ware, "Paul's Understanding of the Resurrection," 811.
46. Smith, *Sense of Presence*, 89.

with the implication of the many appearances of the risen Christ, not the empty tomb, and therefore has no reason to mention it.[47]

The Empty Tomb

The historicity of the empty tomb is an established fact. Even the opponents of Christianity do not dispute that there was an empty tomb. What they disputed was not whether the tomb was empty, but why it was empty.[48] In itself, an empty tomb story does not necessarily imply resurrection. There are various possible explanations for why there was an empty tomb. It could perhaps be that the disciples had visited the wrong tomb and the body was elsewhere. Or perhaps that someone had stolen and hidden the body elsewhere.[49] Or even perhaps, as some have wrongly claimed, because of Roman hostility against the Jews the body was not taken down from the cross and given a proper Jewish burial; it was either left hanging on the cross or was cast into the ditch.[50] But if Jesus's disciples knew for sure the site where he was buried and returned later and found the tomb empty, their proclamation that Jesus had been raised from the dead becomes more intelligible.[51] This latter point the enemies of the Christian church did not want to see. So let us conclude here, at least tentatively, that the disciples knew for sure the site where Jesus was buried and returned there to find it empty because he had been raised from the dead. For, if Jesus had not risen from the dead, "it makes sense that those who opposed the teaching of Jesus' resurrection would have found it, or produced it had they stolen it, to the derision and embarrassment of the disciples. If the body had indeed been taken by Jesus' disciples or they had gone to the wrong tomb, the reality of Jesus' body itself would have come to light and the location of his dead body would have put an end to the claims of resurrection."[52]

However, we cannot deny that there is variety of scholarly opinions on the issue of the empty tomb. At the same time, the historical truth of the empty tomb, is not something to be subjected to a democratic vote.[53]

---

47. Smith, *Sense of Presence*, 89.
48. O'Collins, *Christology*, 100.
49. See Martens, "Empty Tomb," 39.
50. See Evans, "Jewish Burial Traditions and the Resurrection of Jesus," 233. See also Crossan, *Who Killed Jesus?* 160–88.
51. Evans, "Jewish Burial Traditions and the Resurrection of Jesus," 233.
52. Martens, "Empty Tomb," 39.
53. See Davis et al., *Resurrection*.

It is not something to be decided on the basis of majority opinion.[54] The empty tomb was not vacuous; it was a sign of the resurrected Christ who had left the tomb. He was seen by Mary Magdalene (John 20:11–18; Mark 16:9) and other women (Matt 28:8–10). He appeared to Peter (Luke 24:34), to the disciples on the road to Emmaus (Luke 24:34; Mark 16:12), to ten of the apostles, i.e., minus Judas and Thomas who was not present at the time (Luke 24:36–43; John 29:19–29), and thereafter to the eleven apostles, i.e., including the doubting Thomas (John 20:24–29). He also appeared to seven disciples by the Sea of Tiberias (John 21:1–23). We also know that he appeared to five hundred disciples (1 Cor 15:6), to James (1 Cor 15:17), to the eleven apostles before the ascension (Acts 1:3–12), and finally he was seen by Paul (Acts 9:38; 1 Cor 15:18) and by John the revelator (Rev 1:12–18)

One of the reasons why the historical truth of the empty tomb cannot be subjected to democratic opinion is because of the new trend in New Testament studies. Spearheaded by the likes of the Swiss theologian, Hans Kung (1928–), the trend claims that majority of critical biblical exegetes conclude that the stories of the empty tomb are legendary elaborations of post-resurrection appearances. But the argument has been dismissed as nothing "more than an unsubstantiated rhetorical ploy, rather than simply the reporting of a documented state of affairs."[55] There is, according to O'Collins, solidly probable conclusion to believe that the core of the story of the empty tomb is historically factual.[56] One reason why some critical discussions of the Christian resurrection story seem to be all over the place is because some critics are not well acquainted with Jewish traditions of death and burial, particularly with respect to executed criminals and those who were put to death in a dishonorable manner. Some critics also suffer from the wrong inferences they draw from archeological and historical records.[57]

It is not unusual for Roman authorities to deny burial for people who are executed or die dishonorably. Objections against the burial of Jesus rests primarily on this practice that the victim of Roman crucifixion was normally not buried, but left hanging on the cross to be devoured by birds and animals.[58] But the assumption that this was a normal Roman practice in Jewish Palestine has been challenged. In Jewish Palestine "leaving the

54. O'Collins, "Resurrection Revisited," 171.
55. O'Collins, "Resurrection Revisited," 171.
56. O'Collins, "Resurrection Revisited," 172.
57. Evans, "Jewish Burial Traditions and the Resurrection of Jesus," 233.
58. Evans, "Jewish Burial Traditions and the Resurrection of Jesus," 239. See also Hengel, *Crucifixion*, 22–32.

bodies of the executed unburied was exceptional, not typical."[59] In the case of Jesus, it was probable he was buried in keeping with Jewish customs or Mosaic Law—that the dead (righteous or unrighteous) be buried (cf. Gen 23:4–19) and avoid defilement of the land (cf. Gen 50:22–26; Josh 24:32).[60] He was neither left hanging on the cross nor cast into the ditch or exposed to animals.[61] It is also very probable "that some of Jesus' followers (such as the women mentioned in the Gospel accounts) knew where Jesus' body had been placed and intended to mark the location, perfume his body, and mourn, in keeping with Jewish customs."[62]

The Gospels were intent on showing that the empty tomb signifies bodily resurrection.[63] The Gospel of Mark does not have any description of the appearances of the risen Jesus. The absence of post-resurrection appearances in Mark led some to suggest that the empty tomb story was "created by Mark primarily in reaction to traditions of the appearances of the risen Jesus."[64] It would seem reasonable to assume that Mark did not narrate post-resurrection appearances because his source did not contain any—because the empty tomb story he inherited was a disappearance story.[65] Mark's own commitment to the tradition he inherited was to use it to show that Jesus, the Son of Man who suffered violent death, had been vindicated by bodily resurrection and had returned to the heavenly glory. The opponents of the early disciples of Jesus taught the empty tomb was a case of theft by the disciples who came to steal the body in the dead of the night while the guards were fast asleep (Matt 28:13). The disciples taught it was a case of Jesus fulfilling a promise he made before his death: "Destroy this temple and in three days I will raise it up again" (John 2:19).

The historical reliability of the empty tomb is not unconnected to the central role played by the first women witnesses, like Mary Magdalene (John 20:1–2), who were the first to discover the empty tomb. Paul's account in 1 Cor 15, however, does not include a list of witnesses by women. Was this a case of misogyny on Paul's part? Or was it a case that he did not know of the list of women witnesses? Or was it the fact that under Jewish law women were discounted as credible witnesses and had he included list of women witnesses

---

59. Evans, "Jewish Burial Traditions and the Resurrection of Jesus," 239.
60. Evans, "Jewish Burial Traditions and the Resurrection of Jesus," 234 and 236.
61. Evans, "Jewish Burial Traditions and the Resurrection of Jesus," 239.
62. Evans, "Jewish Burial Traditions and the Resurrection of Jesus," 247.
63. Smith, "Revisiting the Empty Tomb," 135.
64. Smith, "Revisiting the Empty Tomb," 132.
65. Smith, "Revisiting the Empty Tomb," 134.

he would not have been taken seriously by his Jewish audience?[66] Perhaps including the list of women witnesses would not have served Paul's purposes at this time.[67] But the point remains that if the story of the empty tomb had been legends created by the early disciples, "they would have attributed the discovery of the empty tomb to male disciples, given that in first century Palestine women were, for all intents and purposes, disqualified as valid witnesses. Legend makers do not normally invent positively unhelpful material."[68]

O'Collins points out six key determining factors of the resurrection appearances, whether to individuals, like Paul, or to groups, like the two disciples on the road to Emmaus (Luke 24:13–35) that is worthy of note, particularly in the light of the Hallucination hypothesis that will be discussed in the next section:

1. The encounters between the risen Jesus and the apostolic witnesses came on the initiative of Jesus who "appeared" and allowed himself to be seen.[69]
2. Apart from the one exception of Paul's episode on the road to Damascus where he was struck by a light from heaven (Acts 26:13), these encounters do not take place during ecstasy. They also do not occur in dreams or at night, but during normal circumstances (Mark 9:2–8; Matt 28:3–4).[70]
3. These appearances were episodes of revelation, which called the witnesses to faith (John 20:29).[71]
4. For those disciples who had been with the earthly Jesus from the beginning, these experiences were special in the sense that they were unique experiences that could not be duplicated.[72]
5. For those disciples who had been with the earthly Jesus from the beginning, these experiences furthered their sense of mission and ministry entrusted to them from the beginning by the earthly Jesus. As the apostle Peter stated: "God raised this Jesus; of this we are all witnesses. Exalted at the right hand of God, he received the promise of the Holy Spirit from the Father and poured it forth, as you [both] see and hear" (Acts 2:32- 33).

---

66. Smith, *Sense of Presence*, 89.
67. Smith, *Sense of Presence*, 89.
68. O'Collins, *Christology*, 100.
69. O'Collins, *Christology*, 90.
70. O'Collins, *Christology*, 91.
71. O'Collins, *Christology*, 91.
72. O'Collins, *Christology*, 91.

6. These experiences had something visually perceptible about them.[73] Although the New Testament often speaks of intellectual perception, the post-Resurrection appearances privilege corporeal sight: Jesus actually "appeared" and the disciples did "see" him (1 Cor 15:5–8; Luke 24:34; 1 Cor 9:1). "One can 'see' truth in a purely interior, non-corporeal way. But, with the Easter encounters we are dealing with a claim about a bodily resurrected person appearing to other persons who exist within our space-time world and see him."[74]

Hallucination Hypothesis or Hallucination of Group Hypothesis

Christianity stands or falls on the episode of the resurrection. Critics of Christianity have attempted to discredit the resurrection story for this very reason. Some have gone as far as developing a hypothesis that the witnesses to the risen Christ were victims of hallucination. An early version of this theory was formulated by the second century Greek philosopher of the Middle Platonist school and opponent of Christianity, Celsus, who recorded in *True Discourse* (published c. AD 170), "that the alleged witnesses to the risen Christ were either hysterical and hallucinated or else ambitious liars."[75] The second century Church Father, Origen (died c. AD 254), who like Celsus was a Middle Platonist and who must have shared with Celsus many of the same common presuppositions of Middle Platonism (like the *Logos* doctrine and its implications for ethical conduct), the exception being that Origen saw God as a personal God who intervenes in human history, but Celsus did not, reported that Celsus also dismissed the witnesses of the women who discovered Jesus's empty tomb as lacking credibility. Celsus described them as "hysteric female" whose hallucination stemmed from some mistaken notion.[76]

Celsus's hallucination theory was revived in the nineteenth century by the German liberal Protestant theologian and naturalistic thinker, David Straus (1808–1874). Strauss argued that what the hallucination suffered by the so-called witnesses to the risen Christ did was to restore their hitherto lost faith in Jesus.[77] But Strauss was caught in his own logic, which made it difficult for him to accept the idea of a bodily resurrection. According to Strauss's logic, "The proposition: a dead man has returned to life, is composed of two

---

73. O'Collins, *Christology*, 91.
74. O'Collins, *Christology*, 92.
75. O'Collins, *Christology*, 93.
76. See Chadwick, *Origen*, 109; cited in Bergeron, "Resurrection of Jesus."
77. See Bergeron, "Resurrection of Jesus;" see also Strauss, *New Life of Jesus*.

such contradictory elements, that whenever it is attempted to maintain the one, the other threatens to disappear. If he has really returned to life, it is natural to conclude that he was not wholly dead; if he was really dead, it is difficult to believe that he has really become living."[78] In spite of the difficulties of Strauss's argument, his hallucination theory did not completely die off. It was revived in the twentieth century, particularly in the light of modern scientific rejection of corporeal resurrection as unscientific, i.e., untestable and unverifiable.

a). Gerd Ludemann and Michael Goulder

The hallucination hypothesis was popularized in the twentieth century by the German New Testament scholar, Gerd Ludemann (1946–) and the British Michael Goulder (1927–2010) who both think that what the first generation of Jesus's disciples called resurrection was nothing but hallucinatory experiences induced by guilt-complexes in Peter and Paul. Ludemann's historical research suggested that Jesus was not raised from the dead.[79] Ludemann reduced the post-resurrection appearances to psychological events in the minds of the so-called witnesses and concluded that Christianity is nothing but "a worldwide hoax."[80] Ludemann, on his part, reduces the Apostle Peter's claim that he saw the risen the Lord to a guilt complex. Ludemann claims that Peter did not see the risen Lord, but that Peter had a vision and that this vision was as a result of Peter's own denial of Jesus before his crucifixion. According to Ludemann, it was Peter's vision that sparked a series of visions by other disciples who claimed to have seen the risen Lord. Here Ludemann is referring to 1 Corinthians 15 where the apostle Paul gives a list of witnesses that Jesus appeared to, including "more than five hundred of the brothers and sisters at the same time" (1 Cor 15:6). Ludemann thinks this "appearance of Christ [to the multitude] can be explained as mass psychoses (or mass hysteria)."[81]

Goulder's view is similar to that of Ludemann. The former surmises that the bases of Christian belief in the resurrection of Christ are the Empty Tomb that was first reported by Mark and the post-Resurrection appearances that were reported by Paul. He thinks that "there are excellent reasons for being skeptical about both of these two bases of belief."[82] With respect to the post-resurrection appearances, he thinks it can be easily explained

78. Strauss, *Life of Jesus*, 359.
79. Ludemann, *Resurrection of Christ*, 190.
80. Ludemann, *Resurrection of Christ*, 190.
81. Ludemann, *What Really Happened to Jesus*, 130.
82. Goulder, "Baseless Fabric of a Vision," 48.

psychologically. With respect to the empty tomb, he thinks the story of the empty tomb was "the creation of the Marcan church" to settle a dispute within the ranks of Christians in the middle of AD 50, particularly the "Jewish Christians who said there was no physical resurrection—neither for the dead generally, nor, we must suppose, for Jesus in particular."[83] Goulder argues that the stress of the passion and death of Jesus, particularly the shame of the denial of Christ at the most trying period of his life, induced in Peter a "Jesus hallucination." Peter's hallucination then became the basis for the mass hysteria (similar to the distressing symptoms, paralysis, tremors, anesthesia that the Middle Ages ascribed to demons).[84] Rather than name it for what it is, Goulder argues, "the early Church took a supernatural explanation for its visions of Jesus, being the only explanation on offer."[85]

Like Ludemann, Goulder abandons the Church's supernatural explanation and opts for a naturalistic-psychological explanation for the post-resurrection appearances. Goulder thinks Peter and the first followers of Jesus may have had a "conversion experience." What Goulder means by 'conversion experience' is by no means religious, but wholly mental. What he calls conversion experience is, according to him, "the result of events that undermine the self-image and bring all the emotional forces of our psyche into play. They often find expression in some outward form, such as seeing visions, hearing voices, moments of insight and so on; and these give the impression of coming from outside and of being in revelations."[86] Goulder's conversion experience happens when people experience a combination of traumatic events with an emotional temperament. They claim to have conversion visions. Conversion vision, according to Goulder, "seem usually to involve a series of traumatic experiences to people who have committed themselves to a cause in which it is no longer possible to believe."[87] Goulder concludes that the Resurrection tradition of the New Testament have only natural (not supernatural) explanations and that the Gospel preached by Peter and Paul was necessitated by their conversion-visions.

To set the records straight, first, Ludemann and Goulder, who both share the view that a great deal of post-Resurrection appearances are based on mass hysteria that was sparked by Simon Peter's hallucination, wrongly assume that Peter was the first of Jesus's followers to see the resurrected Jesus. The Gospel accounts (Matt 28 and John 20) list the testimonies of women who first saw

83. Goulder, "Baseless Fabric of a Vision," 55.
84. Goulder, "Baseless Fabric of a Vision," 54.
85. Goulder, "Baseless Fabric of a Vision," 55.
86. Also Goulder, "Explanatory Power of Conversion-Visions," 93 and 87.
87. Goulder, "Explanatory Power of Conversion-Visions," 96.

Jesus. The point has been made time and time again that the testimony of women could not have been fabricated by the Gospel writers because women in the first century Palestine were not credible witnesses. So had the Gospel writers concocted the story, rather than help their cause, it would have had the opposite effect.[88] Second, the argument of mass hysteria is unsustainable. According to psychiatric definition of hallucination, for hallucination to occur, (i) "an individual seer must perceive an auditory or visual stimulus (or both), and believe that this stimulus really exists (i.e., that it is not imaginary or only in one's head) and (ii) a third party must be unable to detect a stimulus of any sort that corresponds to the seers' perception."[89] Accordingly, this definition makes it clear that hallucination is different from vision for two good reasons: (i) unlike in hallucination where a third party must not be able to detect a stimulus, in visions there are stimuli that the third party can observe and (ii) hallucinations, by definition, are intensely private. We know it is a historical fact that the women first saw Jesus before Peter did. "So, if the women first saw Christ, and only later did Peter see him, we have an example of three different persons having exactly the same hallucinations. There was no time for mass hysteria to develop since Peter saw the resurrected Lord very shortly after the women did."[90] Given the cultural world of first century Palestine, the accounts of the women who first saw Jesus were not taken seriously (see Luke 24:10–11), therefore, they could not have created an atmosphere for mass hysteria.[91] "Given the fact that three different persons all saw the resurrected Lord, it is hard to discount the three sightings as hallucinations, since hallucinations are very much individual affairs."[92]

b). Maurice Casey

Ludemann and Goulder were not alone in challenging the resurrection story. Numerous scholarships today attempt to exploit perceived weaknesses in the Gospel evidence for the resurrection of Jesus.[93] The British scholar of the New Testament, Maurice Casey (1942–2014), represents a modern restatement of the hallucination hypothesis. In fact, it can be misleading to suggest that Casey calls the post-Resurrection appearances "hallucinations" because he did not. Rather, he steered a middle road between excessive denunciation of the disciples' experiences as hallucination and blind acceptance of the

88. Johnson, "Were the Resurrection Appearances Hallucinations?" 228.
89. Johnson, "Were the Resurrection Appearances Hallucinations?" 229.
90. Johnson, "Were the Resurrection Appearances Hallucinations?" 230.
91. Johnson, "Were the Resurrection Appearances Hallucinations?" 230.
92. Johnson, "Were the Resurrection Appearances Hallucinations?" 230.
93. See Price and Lowder, *Empty Tomb*.

traditional Christian doctrinal formulation of these appearances as God's vindication of Jesus. Casey proposes "that the resurrection appearances may reasonably be called 'appearances,' because that is how those people who saw them interpreted them, and so did the early tradition about them. They may reasonably be called 'vision,' because this fits everything which we know about them, in a culture in which visions were normal, and considered to be perfectly real."[94] He thinks the term "hallucination" should be dropped because it is a term that belongs to our culture, not the culture of the first century disciples of Jesus. Also, the pejorative implications of the term "hallucination have been almost invariably used to confuse the major issue because it is a loaded term and belongs to our culture. While Casey does not dismiss the substance of the argument of those who think what Peter and the mass of people who claimed to have "seen" the risen Lord experienced was a sort of mass hysteria, the product of emotional contagion, or that the disciples were victims of their over luxuriant imaginations, Casey thinks "none of these is helpful in understanding the Resurrection appearances, and most of it is quite misleading."[95] Casey does not doubt that "the first followers of Jesus had genuine visions of him after his death, and that they interpreted these as appearances of the risen Lord,"[96] but that their experiences "fit into what is generally known of the experiences of bereaved people."[97]

Bereavement experiences, according to Casey, are relevant for understanding the resurrection appearances. W. Dewi Rees (1929–2018), the Welsh general practitioner is known as the pioneer of bereavement hallucination. Rees carried out an experiment that was published by the *British Medical Journal* in 1971. Rees summarized his experiment as follows:

> 227 widows and 66 widowers were interviewed to determine the extent to which they had hallucinatory experiences of their dead spouse. The people interviewed formed 80. 7% of all widowed people resident within a defined area, in mid-Wales, and 94.2% of those suitable, through the absence of incapacitating illness, for interview. Almost half the people interviewed had hallucinations or illusions of the dead spouse. The proportion of men and women who had these experiences was similar. The hallucinations often lasted many years but were most common during the first 10 years of widowhood. Social isolation did not affect the incidence of hallucination,

94. Casey, *Jesus of Nazareth*, 488.
95. Casey, *Jesus of Nazareth*, 493.
96. Casey, *Jesus of Nazareth*, 498.
97. Casey, *Jesus of Nazareth*, 497.

nor was it related to the incidence of known depressive illness. There was no variation within cultural groups and there was no variation with place of residence, whether this was within town, country, or village, or within England and Wales. Young people were less likely to be hallucinated than those widowed after the age of 40. The incidence of hallucination increased with length of marriage and was particularly associated with a happy marriage and parenthood. Members of the "professional and managerial" group were particularly likely to be hallucinated, while widows of "non-manual and sales workers" were the ones least likely to be hallucinated. The incidence was greater with hysteroid than obsessoid people. It was unusual for the hallucinations to have been disclosed, even to close friends or relatives. These hallucinations are considered to be normal and helpful accompaniments of widowhood.[98]

Rees's experiment has led to a distinction of five species of hallucinations:

1. Feels presence of the deceased—39.2 percent of Rees's patients claimed to have seen their dead spouse.
2. Sees deceased—14 percent of Rees's patients claimed to have seen their dead spouse.
3. Hears deceased—13.3 percent of Rees's patients claimed to have heard their dead spouse with whom they conversed.
4. Speaks to deceased—11.6 percent in Rees's experiment who heard their deceased spouse claimed to converse with them.
5. Touched by deceased—2.7 percent in Rees's experiment claimed to have been touched by their deceased spouse.[99]

In all, nearly half of Rees's patients claimed to have had either one or a combination of some of these hallucination experiences. About 37 percent reported that these experiences lasted for years.[100] Following Rees's pioneering work, subsequent experiments in different countries more or less replicated Rees's findings.[101]

Modern scholars now speak of bereavement hallucination as a sub-specie of hallucination—that appearance of the dead are part of cross cultural experiences that we need to understand without reading too much into the Gospel account of post-resurrection appearances of Jesus.[102] As

---

98. Rees, "Hallucinations of Widowhood," 37.
99. Rees, "Hallucinations of Widowhood," 38.
100. See Goulder, "Explanatory Power of Conversion-Visions," 93.
101. O'Collins, "Resurrection and Bereavement Experiences," 225.
102. Casey, *Jesus of Nazareth*, 490.

Casey notes, all the resurrection appearances, except for Paul's vision on the road to Damascus, "were to recently bereaved followers of Jesus."[103] These protagonists think "bereavement experiences are relevant for understanding the Resurrection appearances."[104] They argue that in ordinary lives of regular people, "there are regular reports of apparitions in which departed people are 'both seen and heard,' though 'they tend to say little;' 'are seen now by one person and later by another;' 'are seen by more than one percipient at the same time;' 'are sometimes seen by some but not all present;' 'create doubt in some percipients;' 'give guidance and make requests or issue imperatives.'"[105]

The suggestion here is that the first followers of Jesus must have suffered bereavement hallucination—that Peter and Paul and the over 500 people reported in 1 Cor 15:6 to have witnessed the post-resurrection appearances suffered collective delusions stemming from one or combinations of Rees's bereavement hallucinations. It was on this basis that Casey offers a natural explanation to the claims of Jesus's followers who saw him after he rose from the dead and warns "that we should not blindly accept the traditional Christian view that the Resurrection of Jesus was God's vindication of him."[106]

Were the disciples of Jesus motivated by deceit, as Ludemann, Goulder, and Casey claim? Were they motivated by a desire to make Jesus's claim come true that they invented the resurrection? Was there even the possibility that the disciples were hallucinated and therefore mistook the events taking place in their deranged mind for reality? O'Collins provides a credible refutation of these claims. First, the evidence provided by the synoptics and the Gospel of John "does not support any picture of Jesus' disciples excitedly expecting to meet him risen from the dead. Instead of persuading themselves into thinking that they saw him, they had to be persuaded that he was gloriously alive again (Matt 28:16–18; Luke 24:36–43)."[107] Second, the New Testament reports that post-resurrection appearances occurred over a period of time and to different individuals and groups of people. "The thesis of an ecstatic group hallucination might be more feasible if the New Testament had reported only one appearance and that to a particular group on a particular day,"[108] which certainly was not the case. Third, the only ecstatic group experience that the New Testament reports was the Pentecost event, but the episode involves receiving the gift of the Holy Spirit by

---

103. Casey, *Jesus of Nazareth*, 490.
104. Casey, *Jesus of Nazareth*, 490.
105. Casey, *Jesus of Nazareth*, 491; summarizing Allison, *Resurrecting Jesus*, 278–82.
106. Casey, *Jesus of Nazareth*, 498.
107. O'Collins, *Christology*, 94.
108. O'Collins, *Christology*, 94.

a group of early Christian believers and not meeting or seeing the risen Christ.[109] Fourth, the hypothesis of group hallucination falls apart in the case of Paul who was persecuting the early Christians and was not hoping to meet the risen Christ. "His encounter with Christ took place at a later time and in a different place from the other Easter appearances (see 1 Cor 15:8; Gal 1:11–24).”[110] It is therefore reasonable to conclude that the resurrection of Jesus from the dead was a special event that happened to Jesus alone,[111] which leads to the thesis I develop next that this singularly occurring event should be conceived as a *sinsign*.

The Resurrection of Jesus as a Sinsign

The resurrection understanding, no doubt, has its roots in Jewish apocalypticism. But the thesis here is that the resurrection of Jesus be viewed as a *sinsign*. A *sinsign* in Peirce's semiotics is a singularly occurring event. The resurrection is a unique singularly occurring event that took place once and for all in Jesus the Christ. Lonergan, following patristic understanding, affirms that there are certain things that properly belong to Christ.[112] Some of those things that properly belong to Christ are the virgin birth, the Incarnation, the hypostatic union, and the resurrection. These are all events that occur only once in Christianity. To the extent that these singularly occurring events simultaneously reveal the being of God, they are *sinsigns* of God's activity in the cosmos. One of the reasons the Second Person of the Blessed Trinity became man is, as the Church Fathers taught, that in assuming what is ours (humanity) he might share with us what is his.

Although he does not use the term *sinsign*, in the way he enumerates what properly belongs to Christ, Lonergan was one who understood and elaborated on how Christ, to use this Peircean term, is the *sinsign* of God's activity in the cosmos. In *The Incarnate Word*, Lonergan developed several theses with respect to Christ. In one these theses, he states: "The human nature of Christ is adorned by habitual grace, together with the virtues and gifts in singular fullness."[113] Fleshing out this thesis that goes back to Thomas Aquinas, Lonergan develops the argument that there is something, which Christ possesses singularly and in fullness. This notion that there is something which Christ possesses singularly and in fullness (the virgin

---

109. O'Collins, *Christology*, 94.
110. O'Collins, *Christology*, 94.
111. Pannenberg, *Jesus—God and Man*, 66.
112. See Lonergan, *Incarnate Word*, 541ff.
113. Lonergan, *Incarnate Word*, 541ff.

birth, the Incarnation, the hypostatic union, and the resurrection) meets the Peircean criteria of a *sinsign* and should, therefore, be understood as *sinsign* of God's activity in the universe.

To return to Lonergan's argument, Christ's grace is different from ours because Christ had no sin at all. Christ as man not only did not sin but was also absolutely incapable of sin.[114] Lonergan's position derives from the teaching of the Fathers who held "that in Christ the spark of sin was not only dampened but also extinct. For there was no original sin in him, and in him there was fullness of grace; and although a lesser grace does not rule out concupiscence, the fullness of grace does."[115] Christ does not need the grace (remission of sin or justification of the wicked) that heals our fallen human nature. As man, Christ had a singular fullness of grace.[116] When Lonergan says Christ had fullness of grace, he is referring to the hypostatic union:

> What is substantial is not so designated in terms of more or less. Something either is or is not God, either is or is not an angel, either is or is not a man, either is or is not a horse, and so forth. And what is not designated in terms of more or less either fully is, or else is not at all. Now the grace of union was substantial; necessarily, then it meets the definition of fullness. And since nobody else has the grace of union, this fullness is singular.[117]

Another reason why Christ singularly possessed the fullness of grace, according to Lonergan, is that Christ had this fullness of grace on the basis of sanctifying grace (the special love he shares with the Father). "For the Father's love for his eternal Son was full and singular."[118] Christ also had supernatural operations and infused virtues that lead to eternal life and he exercised those virtues here on earth.[119] One of such supernatural operation is his resurrection. On the basis of the resurrection and the supernatural significance of this event, it is adequate to speak of every grace as the grace of Christ. Lonergan writes:

> Essentially, every grace is Christ's grace. Of itself, grace does not belong to God, who needs nothing created; it belongs to no creature, for grace is disproportionate to creatures; it belongs to Christ the man, to a divine person subsisting in a created nature,

114. See Thesis 13 in Lonergan, *Incarnate Word*, 715.
115. Lonergan, *Incarnate Word*, 725.
116. Lonergan, *Incarnate Word*, 559.
117. Lonergan, *Incarnate Word*, 559.
118. Lonergan, *Incarnate Word*, 559.
119. Lonergan, *Incarnate Word*, 553.

for grace confers on that nature what befits a divine person subsisting in such a nature, so that he may be united to God on the basis of full friendship. And it is possible to understand on that basis the Father's saying: 'Christ assumed what is ours that he might give us what is his.' Actually, every grace is Christ's grace in the redeemed, who have grace only through the mediator, our Lord Jesus Christ.[120]

Resurrection and Eschatological Hope

Our hypothesis is that the resurrection of Jesus is a *Sinsign* in the Peircean understanding of signs. In this case, the sign happens to be a special event in God's offer of an eschatological hope to a forlorn world. Peirce urged that every abstractly expressed proposition be translated into its precise meaning in reference to an individual experience.[121] The ancient or Jewish concept of resurrection was an abstract proposition. Although belief in resurrection of the body was part of Jewish thought since the Maccabean period (second century BC), to Daniel (c. 164 BC), and to the intertestamental literature (four hundred year period between the close of the Old Testament and the beginning of the New Testament), it was always a future-oriented event. The bodily resurrection of Jesus that the early Christians witnessed was a concrete experience that gave precise meaning to the abstract ancient concept of the eschaton. N. T. Wright points out that the early Christian belief in resurrection had a much more precise shape and content than that of Judaism. For the early Christians, particularly Paul, "resurrection will be an act of new creation accomplished by the Holy Spirit, and the body which is to be already planned by God."[122] Far from return to an old body, resurrection involves a transformation of an old body to a new one. Wright juxtaposes the Jewish idea of resurrection in Daniel 12 with the Christian idea (Matt 13:43) and concludes that the Christian hope of resurrection "is much more sharply focused than its Jewish equivalent."[123]

The Christian hope of resurrection is longing for a new identity (see Rev 21)—a *Sinsign* as it relates to us. Let me explain it. A major difference between the Christian hope of resurrection and that of Judaism (Second Temple Judaism especially), is found in Paul's statement that the resurrection of the dead is a single event that takes place in two phases: first, the

120. Lonergan, *Incarnate Word*, 561–63.
121. CP 2.315.
122. Wright, "Jesus' Resurrection and Christian Origins," 44.
123. Wright, "Jesus' Resurrection and Christian Origins," 44.

Messiah, then at his return, all his people.[124] Where Jews spoke about an intermittent phase of paradise where the dead reside before they are resurrected, the early Christians used a slightly different language, speaking instead of those people who are "asleep in Christ" (1 Cor 15:18) who will be resurrected.[125] Finally, there is the most important difference. Where Jews were still longing for the messiah, the early Christians spoke of this Jewish hope as already realized in Jesus who was and is the Messiah. Jesus had not done what the Jewish Messiah was supposed to do: he had not won a political battle over Israel's enemies and he had not brought God's justice to bear in the sense of dealing a heavy blow on Israel's enemies, yet he is for Christians the Christos (anointed one).[126] The *sinsign*— resurrection event— is evident in its inherent significance. Five of this significance (i.e., what it indexes or points to) has been outlined clearly by Pannenberg:

1. The Resurrection of Jesus signifies the beginning of the end of the world:

Jesus's resurrection shows that the universal resurrection of the dead and the judgment of the world is imminent.[127] Paul speaks to this nearness of the end in many texts, speaking of Christ as "the first born among many brethren" (Rom 8:29) who has been raised as the first fruits of those who have fallen asleep (1 Cor 15:20). The early Christians understood the eschatological significance of the resurrection to mean that the same Spirit of God by which Jesus has been raised dwells among Christians.[128]

2. The Resurrection of Jesus means that God has confirmed the pre-Easter activity of Jesus:

The pre-Easter Jesus made many statements and claims that the Jews considered blasphemous. He was put to death on account of what the Roman authorities considered blasphemous and treasonous. If Jesus really has been raised, then his claims have "been visibly and unambiguously confirmed by the God of Israel, who was allegedly blasphemed by Jesus."[129] Peter's address in Acts that "God has made this Jesus whom you crucified both Lord and

---

124. Wright, "Jesus' Resurrection and Christian Origins," 44.
125. Wright, "Jesus' Resurrection and Christian Origins," 44.
126. Wright, "Jesus' Resurrection and Christian Origins," 44.
127. Pannenberg, *Jesus—God and Man*, 67.
128. Pannenberg, *Jesus—God and Man*, 67.
129. Pannenberg, *Jesus—God and Man*, 67.

Messiah (Acts 2:36) shows the early Christian belief that the resurrection from the dead is a confirmation of Jesus's pre-Easter claims.[130]

3. The Resurrection of Jesus indicates that Jesus is the Son of Man who will come again:

The pre-Easter Jesus claimed himself to be the Son of Man. He preached a correspondence in function between his attitude toward the people and that of the coming of the Son of Man at the end of time. "The distinction between these two figures consists only in the fact that the pre-Easter Jesus walked visibly on the earth, whereas the Son of Man was to come only in the future on the clouds of heaven and was expected as a heavenly being. This difference disappeared, however, with Jesus's resurrection. As one who has been taken away to God, Jesus is a heavenly being."[131] Jesus's coming from heaven as the heavenly Son of Man has been initiated by the Easter appearances. His resurrection "will bring on the universal resurrection of the dead and judgment, just as the apocalyptic tradition had predicted of the appearance of the Son of Man on the clouds of heaven."[132] Thus, Jesus is no longer distinguished from the Son of Man. He is the Son of Man whose coming was expected in future because his resurrection makes it meaningless to expect a second figure in addition to him and with the same function.[133]

4. The Resurrection of Jesus shows that God has been ultimately revealed in Jesus:

The apocalyptic expectation is that God will be revealed at the end of time as the end of all things. In Jesus's resurrection, the end of all things, including those that are yet to happen, has taken place. In this way, it can be said that in Jesus "the ultimate already is present in him, and so also that God himself, his glory, had made its appearance in Jesus in a way that cannot be surpassed."[134] In so far as the end of the world is already present in Jesus's resurrection we can say that God is revealed in him; in Jesus God has appeared on earth.[135]

---

130. Pannenberg, *Jesus—God and Man*, 67–68.
131. Pannenberg, *Jesus—God and Man*, 68–69.
132. Pannenberg, *Jesus—God and Man*, 69.
133. Pannenberg, *Jesus—God and Man*, 69.
134. Pannenberg, *Jesus—God and Man*, 69.
135. Pannenberg, *Jesus—God and Man*, 69.

5. The Resurrection of Jesus has opened the Church to all Nations:

In contrast to the narrow and exclusive conception of God by Jewish prophets, particularly post-exilic ones like Deutero-Isaiah and Ezekiel, Jesus's resurrection has opened the door for all nations to claim membership in God's kingdom. "A Gentile mission seems to have arisen for the first time as a result of the conviction that the resurrected Jesus has now already been exalted to Lordship in heaven and consequently the news of his Lordship is to be carried to all nations."[136]

CONCLUSION

Traditional Christian theology, particularly Christology and the Trinitarian Godhead, have often been framed in categories derived from the Aristotelian-Thomistic metaphysics. In the light of the findings of modern science, the Aristotelian-Thomistic categories need to be interrogated and transposed and the traditional Christian doctrinal symbols reinvigorated. The ancient framework not only needs to be refreshed, "it needs to be radically criticized and many of its central features (for example, dualistic metaphysics and hermeneutics) rejected as no longer live (or enlivening) options in contemporary public theology."[137] This means that our way of engaging Christian symbols, like the Incarnation, Christology, Trinity, Resurrection, and eschatology, etc., "will need to be transformed if they are to function generatively in late modernity."[138] Re-interpreting these is not to be done just for the sake of transforming people, for symbols themselves "must be transformed or they decay into triviality."[139]

Following those scholars committed to challenging theology's excessive reliance on the categories of ancient metaphysical schemes, and using Peircean philosophy to challenge the ways of asking theological questions that were forged within those ancient schemes,[140] I have attempted a fresh look at the Christian doctrine of the resurrection of Christ. This Christian event has its antecedents, though not clearly defined, in Jewish tradition. The Jewish notion of resurrection is a sign (in the Peircean sense). It provided the basis on which the Christian notion can be grasped. In his essay "On the Foundations of Mathematics," Peirce writes that "All that we know

---

136. Pannenberg, *Jesus—God and Man*, 71.
137. Shults, "Transforming Theological Symbols," 714.
138. Shults, "Transforming Theological Symbols," 714.
139. Shults, "Transforming Theological Symbols," 719.
140. Shults, "Transforming Theological Symbols," 726.

or think we know is known or thought by signs, and our knowledge itself is a sign."[141] Peirce's theory of sign assumes that the primary function of sign-use is knowledge acquisition about whatever may count as a real object of thought and attention.[142] "Signs are what people use to learn about one another and the rest of the world. Consequently, the task of indexical signs and expressions in a learning process is an empirical one: to make individual objects, persons and events accessible for present verifying experience of what is represented in other ways (symbolically, iconically)."[143] Peirce also demonstrates in his trichotomy of signs that one kind of sign often involves other signs as well.[144] Because signs are pervasive, Peirce's semiotic analysis allows us to see that all indexical signs have a common grammar.[145] "Although everything, regardless of whether we have access to it because of its material, mental, social or cultural properties, may become an index, it will always and in other respects have properties and relations that differ from those used indexically."[146] Elsewhere Peirce writes, "Anything which startles us is an index, in so far as it marks the junction between two portions of experience."[147] Resurrection, in its ancient and Christian understandings, were startling experiences, indexing something other than themselves nonetheless. One of the essential characteristics of an index or sign is its ability to establish a connection between the object and "the senses or memory of the person for whom it serves as a sign."[148]

In sum, we must see the bodily resurrection of Jesus as a different kind of sign, a *sinsign* that can never be replicated. It is the hermeneutical key for understanding Jesus's identity and mission. The weight of the argument for the resurrection is predicated on the empty tomb and post-resurrection appearances of the risen Lord. Since not too many saw the risen Lord, but hardly anyone could dispute there was an empty tomb, the empty tomb historically becomes for Christians a sign of the resurrection. Signs, in the Peircean sense, do not depend on the presence of the conscious interpreter who may or may not be aware of the sign-vehicle. Some of the arguments against the historical reliability of the empty tomb are premised on a wrong notion of sign, i.e., one in which there must be conscious interpreter. The problem is, most of the skeptics have refused to be conscious.

141. As cited in Colapietro, *Peirce's Approach to the Self*, 12.
142. Pape, "Searching for Traces," 17.
143. Pape, "Searching for Traces," 17.
144. Weber, "Proper Names and Persons," 349
145. Pape, "Searching for Traces," 21.
146. Pape, "Searching for Traces," 21.
147. CP 2.285.
148. CP 2.305.

Chapter Five

Towards an Evolutionary Christology

IN THE PREVIOUS CHAPTER, we used semiotic language to speak of the Resurrection of Jesus because we are convinced that the radical and exhaustive analysis of sign that Charles Sanders Peirce puts forward can be a theoretical basis for a phenomenological investigation,[1] including Christology. A fundamental aspect of Peirce's phenomenology is semiotics, i.e., the representation of sign—an object represented by a sign creates in the mind of the interpreter another sign. This, at least, means that the object and the sign are not the same, but two different realities. The two realities exhibit continuity (what Peirce terms synechism). Implicit in this semiosis (action of signs) is an evolutionary process. The sign relations are closely related in such a way that a person cannot understand one in isolation from the other. The interpretant cannot be understood apart from the sign-vehicle or the object of the sign. In terms of evolution of thought, this means that ideas are always evolving and always developing. One idea begets another, which in turn begets other ideas. The three categories Peirce terms Firstness, Secondness, and Thirdness refer to the elementary modes of relation in a semiotic processes and furthers evolution of thought. The categories "comprise all that is possible, actual, and intelligible in human experience. They also describe a continuously evolving universe, whose admixtures of chance, necessity, and mediation are made intelligible to human perceivers through objectively verifiable hypotheses."[2]

---

1. See Guinard, "Critical Analysis of Peirce's Semiotics and an Ontological Justification of the Concept of the Impressional."
2. See Slater's review of *God and the World of Sign*, 86.

Since Peirce's theory of evolution involves understanding the development of triadic structure of signs that are grounded in the categories and their meanings, then his evolutionary understanding of the world process stands in opposition to any materialist presupposition of science. This understanding suggests rather a psychosocial approach to reality, i.e., one that emphasizes subjectivity/contingency vis-à-vis objectivity/necessity within the cosmic process.[3] Is it possible to construct a Christology consistent with an evolutionary view of the universe? The new approach to the theological reflection on evolution and Christology, which Peirce's taxonomy of signs and categories suggest, is already implicit, though not well developed, in the evolutionary Christology of the Jesuit Karl Rahner (1904–84). Thus, the task of this chapter is to examine this evolutionary Christology of Rahner, with a view to connecting contemporary understandings of biological evolution to God. As will be fleshed out later in the next chapter, contrary to what Richard Dawkins[4] and Daniel Dennett[5] would make us believe, biological processes are not reducible to genetic self-promulgation, but rather include a range of final and efficient causes that Peirce's categories help illuminate.[6] Rahner attempted to explain, in his reconciliation of immanent and economic Trinity, albeit with partial success, the meaning of the triune God in relation to humanity in an ever-evolving world. To his credit, Rahner stands in an exclusive line of contemporary theologians who have attempted to use the relationality intrinsic to the Incarnation as a way of connecting science with Christology and Trinitarian theology. John Polkinghorne states, regarding this relationality: "Just as physicists in their own domain have found relationality to be more extensive and more surprising in its character than prior expectation would have led them to anticipate, so philosophers and theologians should be open to the possibility of unexpected discovery and counterintuitive insight."[7]

EVOLUTION AND CHRISTOLOGY

Rahner wrote that the Chalcedonian definition of the Person and two natures of Christ should be seen more as a beginning, not an end of Christology.[8]

3. See Bracken, "Feeling Our Way Forward," 319–31.
4. See Dawkins, *River Out of Eden*; *Blind Watchmaker*; *Ancestors Tale*; *Devil's Chaplain*; *God Delusion*; and *Greatest Show on Earth*.
5. Dennett, *Breaking the Spell*; *Darwin's Dangerous Idea*; and *Science and Religion*.
6. See Slater's review of *God and the World of Sign*, 88.
7. Polkinghorne, *Trinity and an Entangled World*, x.
8. See Rahner, "Currents Problems in Christology," 149.

This cryptic remark can equally be extended to the first seven Ecumenical Councils that attempted to resolve and clarify Christological disputes. The definitions of these ecumenical councils are the beginning, not an end of Christology. The councils established some regulatory linguistic code for speaking about the nature of Christ. But while dogma may be permanent, linguistic codes are not final, but open to further refinements and developments. The contemporary understanding of "person," for instance, is quite different from the Chalcedonian or medieval understanding. Without a nuanced understanding, the contemporary notion can confuse what Chalcedon means when it says the human and divine qualities come together in one person, Jesus Christ. The Chalcedonian formulation of the doctrine of the Trinity and Christology were constructed with the best available metaphysical and philosophical systems at the time. Legitimate questions are now been raised as to what will happen to Christology when that metaphysical superstructure of the Chalcedonian world is no longer in place and the ontology of substance that gives it logical consistency is consigned to the philosophical dustbin.[9] Thus, the question of how to articulate the Christological doctrine in the face of shifting metaphysical presuppositions or even skepticism is a question that every generation and epoch has to answer because of shifting situational circumstances.

Christology needs a paradigm shift. The shift must be one that is attentive to the evolutionary view of the world. The American physicist and philosopher of science, Thomas Kuhn (1922–96), developed the notion of paradigm shift. Working out of the field of astronomy, physics, and chemistry, Kuhn argued that a paradigm shift occurs as a result of crisis. In Kuhn's technical term, "crisis" occurs when an old theory that is well entrenched becomes difficult to sustain and must be replaced with a newer and more intellectually satisfying one.[10] "Crisis" or conflict occurs regularly in scientific discourse. It is through conflicts that new theories are born and old ones are discarded, though it may take decades for the transition to actually take place.[11] The field of evolutionary science is one such arena where conflicts take place, old theories are declared dead, and new theories emerge. The year 1859 was a year of "revolution" in the Kuhn's sense of the term. It was the year Charles Darwin (1809–1882) published *The Origin of Species* and attempted to explain the origin and appearance of new and higher forms of life. Darwin developed the idea of evolution by natural selection—that in their struggle for existence the species able to adapt the most evolve and

---

9. Robinson, *God and the World of Signs*, 133–34.
10. See Kuhn, *Structure of Scientific Revolutions*.
11. Peterson, "Whose Evolution?" 222.

survive ("survival of the fittest" as Herbert Spencer later explains it). Christian reaction to Darwin's theory of evolution has been mixed. Some see the theory as antithetical to the Christian creation story in Genesis and therefore oppose it. Others embrace it—that a nuanced view of Darwin's theory can shed light on the Genesis creation story. In Christian theology today, Darwin's theory still divides opinion because of the various ways it has been applied to other fields of investigation.

One of those who have publicly taken up the mantle of Neo-Darwinism in the twenty-first century is the English ethologist and atheist Richard Dawkins (1941–) and the American cognitive scientist and atheist Daniel Dennett (1942–). There is also a second group representing alternative theories to Neo-Darwinism, sometimes called non-Darwinian evolution. The American biologist and paleontologist, Niles Eldridge (1943–), and the American paleontologist and evolutionary biologist, Stephen Jay Gould (1941–2002), are two good representatives of the non-Darwinian evolution. Eldridge and Gould made famous the theory of Punctuated Equilibrium (PE) in a paper they jointly published in 1972.[12] Darwin had understood evolution as a slow and gradual process in which species evolve and accumulate small variations over a long period of time until new species are born. Niles and Eldridge add to it that species are generally stable for millions of years until the leisurely pace is "punctuated" by a rapid burst of change of new species that leave fossils behind. PE was first advanced to account for development of differences among species and was seen as a radical idea at the time. Today PE has gradually been accepted as one of the useful models of evolutionary change.

The atheistic Neo-Darwinists and the alternative theories of Neo-Darwinism disagree on the mode and tempo of evolution, as well as the interpretation and pattern of evolution. In spite of their differences, both groups accept the fact of evolution. They accept that the earth is very old and that a variety of species have evolved and flourished and perished over time and that pattern of evolution, chronologically, is that later organisms evolve from some of the earlier ones.[13] Neither one of these two groups is content to limit their theories of evolution to science alone. Both groups have at various times extended their musings to the theological arena, even to the point of making normative ethical claims.[14] Dawkins replaces the Judeo-Christian God with the blind watchmaker of natural selection and Gould emphasizes the improbability of human existence and the spiritual

---

12. Eldridge and Gould, "Punctuated Equilibria," 82–115.
13. Peterson, "Whose Evolution?" 224–24.
14. Peterson, "Whose Evolution?" 222.

revolution provided by evolution.[15] In short, there are at least four central claims of the Neo-Darwinists put together: (i) that evolution is a gradual process that occurs in geologic time; (ii) evolution occurs in random, modest mutations; (iii) the unit of selection is individualistic (individual gene in the case of Dawkins and individual organism itself for others); (iv) selection is primarily a process of local optimization and the ones that survive in a given generation are the ones that best adapt to their environment and who then pass on their genes to the next generation.[16] Dawkins's own position with respect to these matters is more stark. Not only does he see the process of evolution as rationally understandable, he thinks it is a largely adaptive goal-oriented phenomenon. He thinks evolution is primarily about design and natural selection and that to understand evolution is to understand the law-like character of the evolutionary process. By the law-like character of the evolutionary process, he means predictability, i.e., the law-like character of the evolutionary process predictably produces adaptations that are functionally advantageous to the organisms that possess them.[17] Therefore, when Dawkins says we have to speak scientifically about evolution, he means that the science of evolution is incompatible with the idea of God because evolution is about laws, fit, design, and progress. His thinks Neo-Darwinism is incompatible with God because Neo-Darwinism offers a better and superior explanation of laws and design.[18] Taking Dawkins's argument a step further, his colleague Dennett posits the existence of what he calls "natural algorithms" to explain both design and the engineered quality of biological organisms.[19]

Atheistic evolutionary scientists, in the mold of Dawkins and Dennett, think that evolutionary science has put the God-question to bed—that since evolution proceeds from the simple to the complex, it is inconceivable to speak of a giant universal mind. Therefore, "natural selection obviates the need for any designer."[20] Christian fundamentalists who hold on to strict literal interpretation of six day creation story in Genesis reject evolution because their religious commitment to the belief that God created the earth in a six day span makes such rejection necessary.[21] But others who work out of historical criticism and whose critical method does not admit of a literal

---

15. Peterson, "Whose Evolution?" 222–23.
16. Peterson, "Whose Evolution?" 225.
17. Peterson, "Whose Evolution?" 228.
18. Peterson, "Whose Evolution?" 228.
19. Peterson, "Whose Evolution?" 228.
20. Peterson, "Whose Evolution?" 223.
21. Peterson, "Whose Evolution?" 223.

understanding welcome and embrace evolution. In the view of the latter, "because human beings are themselves products of evolution and natural selection, it follows that evolutionary theory has a potentially significant contribution to make to concepts of human nature, a subject about which theology is profoundly concerned."[22]

What we are saying, in a nutshell, is that evolution matters to theology. One contemporary scholar who has vigorously reinforced this fact is Gregory Peterson. He argues that the only way to escape the conclusion that evolution matters to theology "is to deny the significance of origins and historicity."[23] Evolutionary theory, Peterson explains, touches all facets of human existence. It affects the concepts of the origin of life (creation), the questions of human origins and questions of original sin. It affects questions of human nature, human behavior and human destiny. It affects questions of human uniqueness and our understanding of human beings as persons made in the image and likeness of God; it even affects the formation and evolution of religious belief itself; and "because soteriology and Christology are based partly on these prior theological claims, they are affected as well."[24]

Theologians tend to interpret the design argument in terms of God's grander design, suggesting that "the divine intent is seen not specifically in the design of the eye but rather in the laws governing evolution that allow such wonderfully complex and beautiful organs to develop."[25] One such theologian and one who embraced Darwin's theory of 1859 is the French Jesuit philosopher, Teilhard de Chardin (1881–1955), Teilhard applied the theory of evolution to creation, anthropology, and Christology and developed the schemes of cosmogenesis, anthropogenesis, and Christogenesis. His essential thesis was that humanity and the universe as a whole are moving towards a final consummation he calls the Omega Point, which is Christ. According to Chardin, Christ is the intrinsic goal and purpose of the evolutionary process. For Chardin, "God's design is woven through the general progressive pattern he saw implied in the evolutionary process."[26] Rahner adopts a teleological view of evolution similar to Teilhard's. Like Chardin, Rahner does not see evolution as an aimless series of random adaptions, but as systematic and tailored progress toward God, the final goal.[27]

22. Peterson, "Whose Evolution?" 223.
23. Peterson, "Whose Evolution?" 224.
24. Peterson, "Whose Evolution?" 224.
25. Peterson, "Whose Evolution?" 229.
26. Peterson, "Whose Evolution?" 229.
27. Corduan, "Hegel in Rahner," 293.

Karl Rahner: Background Information

Karl Rahner (1904–84) was one of the twentieth century theologians to embrace the door opened by the Second Vatican Council (1962–65) for a fresh way of thinking about the Church and Catholic Christian theology. As a Jesuit, Rahner was trained in Neo-Scholastic theology. Neo-Scholasticism was a theological system and method of probing theological topics that emerged after 1840 out of medieval Scholasticism, which itself was a system of inquiry built around Aristotelian logic and metaphysics.[28] As a theological system, Neo-Scholasticism emerged as part of the larger "effort to retrieve the medieval synthesis to overcome the severe challenges posed to Christianity by the Enlightenment."[29] By the time of Vatican II, this theological system that had a lot of promise had become "somewhat rigid and unimaginative."[30] Apart from its oversimplification of the rich diversity of Christian theology, Neo-Scholasticism in its extreme form can be unhistorical. It is also "ill-equipped to deal with the modern turn to the subject," not to mention that it is "out of touch with modern science, and overly focused on lifeless concepts as opposed to experience."[31] Needless to say, Rahner was of the early twentieth century Catholic theologians who began moving away from the Neo-Scholastic way of thinking and approaching major theological themes.[32]

Rahner was also one of the early twentieth century theologians to embrace and respond adequately to the challenges posed by Darwinism. Rahner took upon himself the task of making theology intellectually respectable in the face of this challenge. His other related task was to make theology relevant to the larger concerns of Christian faith and life.[33] He saw these tasks (the life of faith and the life of the intellect) as two sides of the same pole that must be done together to avoid the two extremes of naïve realism (false intellectualism) and fideism (uncritical faith) that bedeviled theology at the dawn of modernity. Thus, in light of these challenges, Rahner put forward a Christology that attempts to answer questions posed by Neo-Darwinism. He develops in the process a theology of the symbol that is built on the belief that Christians know God directly when they reflect on their experiences,

---

28. See Rahner, *Trinity* (1999), vii.
29. Rahner, *Trinity* (1999), vii.
30. Rahner, *Trinity* (1999), vii.
31. Rahner, *Trinity* (1999), vii–viii.
32. Rahner, *Trinity* (1999), viii.
33. See Dych, "Theology in a New Key," 2.

especially their experiences of the "nameless" being.³⁴ In the main, Rahner's Christology cannot be understood apart from his metaphysics and his analysis of the natural-supernatural and symbolic relations. Given that Rahner's philosophical presuppositions of the symbolic nature of reality determines his overall approach to theology,³⁵ an analysis of his Christology will not be complete without an attempt to explain these fundamental presuppositions.

Rahner's Philosophical and Methodological Presuppositions

One cannot properly understand Rahner's Christology without understanding his methodological and philosophical presuppositions. For this reason, I begin with a brief expose of some key terms that may be tangential to our discussion, but nonetheless important for understanding Rahner's Christology. Rahner's Christological insight, rests upon his philosophical and theological anthropology. It rests, on the one hand, on his philosophical anthropology because he understands human nature in terms of the human capacity to transcend self (self transcendence). It rests, on the other hand, on his theological anthropology because "he sees the term of this transcendence, which is realized perfectly on in the case of Jesus, as hypostatic union with the divine Son."³⁶ With respect to his philosophical anthropology, Rahner is perhaps one of the most recognized contemporary theologians to grapple with the problem of how we can know God from human experience. In chapter one I offered a critique of Transcendental Thomism that derived from Joseph Marechal and furthered by Karl Rahner, pointing out some of the counter-positions in the method. Here I will draw attention only to a few poignant problems in Rahner's transcendental method, without however undercutting the essential argument of this chapter, which is that Rahner offers a unique Christology that attempts an answer to questions posed by Neo-Darwinism. To do this effectively, I begin with a brief survey of Rahner's philosophical anthropology.

Rahner structures his philosophy around principles he and Marechal derived from Immanuel Kant's (1724–1804) transcendental method. He suggests that out of these principles arise approaches one can employ on three levels: epistemology, anthropology, and Christology, each level laying the foundation for the subsequent one.³⁷ Building on the landmark work of Isaac Newton (1643–1727), Kant was thought to have initiated a Copernican

---

34. Molnar, "Can We Know God Directly?" 231.
35. Molnar, "Can We Know God Directly?" 231.
36. Coffey, "'Incarnation' of the Holy Spirit in Christ," 467.
37. Corduan, "Hegel in Rahner," 285.

revolution in philosophy. He was thought to have placed philosophy at par with the sciences. Kant also realized that the essence of science does not lie in mere recording of facts that are objectively perceived, but in the assimilation of theoretical scheme provided by scientists.[38] Having understood that what the scientist provides is the certainty of knowledge, not the nature of it, Kant then offered the hypothesis that in philosophy the certainty of knowledge is also due to what the knowing subject contributes to the stock of knowledge. Thus, Kant thought that the way of uncovering this knowledge is the essence of the transcendental method.[39] Rather than construct new knowledge, Kant's transcendental method assumes that whatever we know is true and certain, thereby posing the question: how is it that we have this knowledge?[40]

Before Kant, scholastics and traditional Catholic Christology had relied on metaphysics for the norm of the doctrine of God. Rahner adopts instead the Kantian method, opting for possibility of knowledge we have at the level of human experience—that whether or not we advert to it, we all have an unthematic experience of God.[41] Rahner's basic presupposition of religion is that there is a transcendental reality, which people may identify by different names, but most call God. He insists that God cannot be the starting point of theology for the following reasons: first, for some people God is an unnecessary or at best an unverifiable hypothesis;[42] second, for others the very idea of God is a "projection" or an "illusion;"[43] third, still for others, God cannot be known by the canons of scientific method.[44] On these bases, Rahner concludes that for the modern inquirer, God is not an answer but a problem and therefore cannot be the starting point or the presupposition of theology.[45] If God cannot be the starting point of theology, what about Jesus? Rahner argues that Jesus Christ can also not be the starting point of theology because for people of no faith (and even for some people of faith as well) Jesus Christ is not a verifiable hypothesis. The Christian Scriptures have not been able to give an accurate account of the life of Jesus as to make Him the starting point of theology.

---

38. Corduan, "Hegel in Rahner," 286.
39. Corduan, "Hegel in Rahner," 286.
40. Corduan, "Hegel in Rahner," 286.
41. Molnar, "Can We Know God Directly?" 228–29.
42. Dych, "Theology in a New Key," 2.
43. Dych, "Theology in a New Key," 3.
44. Dych, "Theology in a New Key," 3.
45. Dych, "Theology in a New Key," 3.

Rahner thinks that by not making God or Jesus Christ the starting point of theology he is preserving God's freedom and revelation. He also thinks he is helping us avoid the temptation of collapsing these two together. Rahner wants to avoid "extrincism" in the way we conceive of the relations between the God and the cosmos.[46] For this reason, he makes human experience, not metaphysics, the norm of the doctrine of God.[47] If ever there is an aspect of human life in which believers and non-believers, educated and non-educated, can come to some reasonable agreement, it is on the matter of our shared human existence or experience. Rahner makes our shared human existence and experience the starting point of theology because these shared existence and experience are what touches us all to the core and that to which we all have immediate and direct access.[48] Rahner argues that human existence and our experience of it can be analyzed in such a way that we can discover from it categories with which we can speak intelligently about a nameless being religious believers call "God." The crucial question, for Rahner, "is not whether this experience of the 'nameless' is an experience of the true God; rather, it is a question of whether we interpret this experience correctly, thus explicating our implicit, though unobjectified, knowledge of the true God."[49] It is from this analysis of human existence, in Rahner's view, that we can then discover a framework for understanding the history of Jesus, and make sense of what history of Christian tradition has said about him.[50]

In the light of what we have said about human existence—that it is not a thing that we possess or an object to be observed, but a process which we do and are,[51] we have to admit that one must first be in existence before one can reflect on it.[52] Since Rahner's philosophical and methodological assumption are that human existence should be the starting point of theological reflection because knowledge of God's revelation cannot contradict knowledge gained from metaphysical reflections about God and the world,[53] it makes sense then briefly to consider some key elements of these assumptions.

---

46. Rahner, *Theological Investigations* 1, 298.

47. See Rahner, "Observations on the Doctrine of God in Catholic Dogmatics," 127–44.

48. Dych, "Theology in a New Key," 3.

49. Molnar, "Can We Know God Directly?" 230–31.

50. Dych, "Theology in a New Key," 3.

51. Dych, "Theology in a New Key," 4.

52. Dych, "Theology in a New Key," 3.

53. Molnar, "Can We Know God Directly?" 232.

a). Preconceptual or Unthematic Knowledge:

A key feature of Rahner's theory is that God's grace is available to everyone, at least as an offer, and that the unthematic and implicit presence of God is available to everyone, including those who deny God's existence.[54] This stems from Rahner's assumption that there is a kind of knowledge everyone experiences by the mere fact of being in existence. This knowledge is not conveyed to us from outside, but from within. It is knowledge that comes from one's own experience. To use the example of my own existence: that I exist is not something that is conveyed to me by someone other than myself. I know it from within me. This is an instance of what Rahner calls "experiential knowledge." Experiential knowledge is not like the knowledge of the galaxies that is conveyed to us through external forces, say by words and concepts. Since experiential knowledge is knowledge that does not derive from outside and is a knowledge that is not conveyed by words or concepts, Rahner calls it preconceptual or "unthematic knowledge."[55] Knowledge on the first level of experience is the unthematic experience of God Rahner insists everyone has.[56]

b). Original Knowledge

The fact of our existence is not an object to be stared upon, rather it is what we are. In our experiential knowledge, i.e., knowledge on the first level of experience, we know we are mortal humans in a network of beings and relationships, i.e., we are related to other persons and things in a complex world. The knowledge of this fact Rahner calls original knowledge. "It is 'original' not in the sense that no one had it before, but in the sense that it wells up from the origins or depths of our own selves in our lived interaction with the world."[57]

c). Thematic Knowledge

If we admit the fact of our intersubjective relations — that we are social beings who live out our lives in a system or network of relationships with other people and things — then we must also admit that we have the need to reflect, express, and communicate our experiential knowledge to others with whom we are involved in a complex network of relationships. To communicate our experiential knowledge, we have to objectify and embody it

---

54. Rahner, "One Christ and the Universality of Salvation," 217.
55. Dych, "Theology in a New Key," 4.
56. See Rahner, *Hearers of the Word*, 171.
57. Dych, "Theology in a New Key," 4.

in words and concepts that are easily understandable to those to whom we are communicating. This knowledge, when made explicit, Rahner calls thematic knowledge.[58] Thematic knowledge is knowledge on the second level of reflection.

d). Two-Directional Relationships of First and Second Level of Reflection.

We use words and concepts to capture or symbolize our objectified experiences. But we are sooner or later faced with the stark reality that the words and concepts we use do not always capture exactly the experience we wish to convey. This means that we will constantly need to reflect on our experience (knowledge on the first level of reflection) and clarify what we intend to communicate (knowledge on the second level of reflection). What does this mean for Rahner? He says this means then that there is a two-directional relationship between knowledge on the first level of reflection and knowledge on the second level of reflection.[59]

Key Elements of Rahner's Theological Anthropology

Experiential Knowledge	Knowledge that one knows by the fact of one's existence.	It is neither conveyed from outside nor is it conveyed by words or concepts. Rahner calls it "preconceptual" or "unthematic" knowledge.	Experiential knowledge is knowledge on the first level of experience.
Original Knowledge	We know from experiential knowledge that we are one among many beings.	We know we are related to other beings in a network of relationships.	Rahner calls this knowledge "original knowledge."
Thematic Knowledge	Experiential knowledge has to be objectified and embodied in words and concepts in other for us to communicate them to others.	Rahner calls this thematic knowledge.	Thematic knowledge is knowledge on the second level of experience.

---

58. Dych, "Theology in a New Key," 4.
59. Dych, "Theology in a New Key," 5.

146   A Semiotic Christology

Two Directional Relationships	Because words and concepts do not always capture exactly what we mean to convey, we constantly reflect on our experience to clarify what we mean to convey.	We reflect on knowledge of first level of experience to clarify what we intend to convey on the second level of experience.	There is a two-directional movement between knowledge on the first level of experience and knowledge on the second level of experience.
Transcendental Experience	Because knowledge is two-directional, both the subject and object are known.	Rahner calls his own method Transcendental.	Transcendental method examines the necessary conditions for the possibility of knowledge and action on the part of the subject.
Existentials	Philosophy needs to help theology discover the general structures of human experience.	The structures philosophy reveals are valid for all times and for all places. The structures revealed include "self-presence," "freedom," and "transcendence."	Rahner calls these three "existentials."
Supernatural Existential	The three existentials which philosophy reveals are the philosophical suppositions of what Christians call Grace.		Rahner's preferred term for Grace is Supernatural Existential.

e). Transcendental Experience

Rahner calls his own method transcendental in that it examines "the necessary conditions given by the possibility of knowledge and action on the part of the subject."[60] This means that in the knowing process both the subject and the object are known because knowledge is two-directional. Once it is established that knowledge is two-directional because we have to reflect on our experience before we can express and communicate it in words and concepts, Rahner argues that we must then admit that in reflecting on our

---

60. Rahner, "Theology and Anthropology," 29.

experience we become aware of ourselves as experiencing and reflecting. Self-awareness is an essential ingredient in knowledge. Self-awareness, which is our capacity to be present to ourselves, is the basic characteristic that makes human existence spiritual.[61] In experiencing our subjectivity, we also become aware that although we exist in the world as free and conscious subjects, we are not confined or determined by the world. In experiencing our subjectivity, we also go beyond it because the more we know, the more we realize that we do not know and then desire to know even more. This going beyond self to seek "more" is what Rahner calls transcendental experience. It is this transcendental experience that he says is the starting point of theology.[62] Theology claims to be an interpretation of all human existence (which is universally valid), it is therefore the task of theology to present the Christian interpretation of the human situation.[63] Rahner would therefore use his transcendental investigation to identify the existential structures of human existence, hoping by so doing to demonstrate the intrinsic relationship between being human and being Christian.[64]

f). Existentials

Rahner relies on philosophy to help theology discover the general structures of human experience. The relationship between philosophy and theology will provide the background for Rahner's later development of the supernatural existential. Just as there is no such thing as pure philosophy which stands independent of theology, Rahner reasons, there is no such thing as grace independent of the full revelation of God to be made in Jesus Christ. The general structures of human experience that philosophy reveals are valid for all places and times. The general structure that philosophy can discover includes "self-presence," "freedom," and "transcendence." Rahner calls these three "existentials." He suggests that the three existentials are the philosophical presuppositions of what Christians call grace, but he chooses to call it "supernatural existential." Grace or supernatural existential will be, for Rahner, a fourth important existential.[65] What Rahner tries to do in stressing the unity of our lives as Christians and our ordinary human life is to show that we are "involved in a circle in which these two dimensions inescapably presuppose one another. Human life itself, understood through

---

61. Dych, "Theology in a New Key," 5.
62. Dych, "Theology in a New Key," 6.
63. Dych, "Theology in a New Key," 6.
64. Skiba, *Transcendental Christology of Karl Rahner*, 77.
65. Dych, "Theology in a New Key," 7.

a philosophical anthropology, opens out toward the fulfillment of which the gospel speaks."[66]

g). Supernatural Existential

Rahner develops a transcendental theology of grace to express the universal nature of grace, salvation, and revelation of God in Christ Jesus,[67] This is what he calls the supernatural existential. He reasons that in the same way "self-presence," "freedom," and "transcendence" are universally valid and universally applicable, grace is also universally open to everyone. His other term for this human openness to God's saving will is *potential obedientialis*.

It is good to note here that there are three-pronged ingredients in what Rahner technically calls the supernatural existential: first, God communicates God's self to human beings; second, this self-communication of God to creature is gratuitous (free and unmerited); third, God can reveal only what the human person is able to hear. What he calls the supernatural existential is therefore "supernatural" because it is a manifestation of the free and unmerited gift of God for spiritual creatures. It is also "existential" because human beings are constituted in a way that leaves them open to the self-communication of God.[68] This is how Rahner tried to bring anthropology and theology together. "As soon as man is understood as the being who is absolutely transcendent in respect of God," he writes, "'anthropocentricity' and 'theocentricity' in theology are not opposites but strictly one and the same thing, seen from two sides."[69] In another essay where he clarified the relationship of anthropology to Christology, Rahner writes: "How can a Christian speak appropriately of God unless at the same time he also speaks of man? The word made flesh is and remains the eternal and unlimited man. We cannot know God as he is without at the same time thinking of him as the God made man. Consequently we cannot have a complete theology without considering its anthropological aspects. If we want to talk of God properly, we have to talk of human beings."[70]

In sum, Rahner has been lauded as one of the few contemporary theologians who attempted to distinguish conceptually how God is transcendent and at the same time involved in creation without collapsing

---

66. Skiba, *Transcendental Christology of Karl Rahner*, 77; quoting Carr, "Starting with the Human," 18.

67. Dych, "Theology in a New Key," 13.

68. Robinson, *God and the World of Signs*, 139.

69. Rahner, "Theology and Anthropology," 28.

70. As cited in Skiba, *Transcendental Christology of Karl Rahner*, 79; see also Rahner, *Karl Rahner in Dialogue*, 267–68.

God into human or creation. But his position is not without some serious logical and theological difficulties.[71] Rahner's former student and disciple, Johan Baptist Metz (1928–), thinks Rahner's theology is too embedded in abstract German idealism.[72] Some have also questioned his inability to demonstrate "that his concept of God's transcendence corresponds with anything other than the concept of man's experience of the absolute, conceived philosophically."[73]

If what Rahner is trying to do is show that theology is a religion in search of a metaphysics, I am on board. No one can truly deny that as human beings we are always encountering the mystery of being or the mystery of God. But Rahner's overreliance on Transcendental Thomism complicates his argument somewhat. In chapter one, I stressed how it is a mistaken assumption to think that the transcendental method gives one a privileged access to the dynamic structure of the human spirit. Rahner, as it were, interprets the dynamic structure of the human spirit in categories he derived from faculty psychology. I also drew attention to Donald Gelpi's suggestion that rather than locate the openness to mystery in the power of the spirit or the intellectual apprehension of Being as Rahner does, it might be more fruitful, or at least more psychologically plausible, to locate it, not in the intellect, "but in imaginative and appreciative forms of knowing."[74] There is no denying that Rahner's philosophical presupposition lends itself to the theory of supernatural existential, which he articulates so well. But the theory, as Gelpi points out, "rests on an inadequate logic, on a false and inflated belief in the virtual infinity of the human mind, and on a contradictory and unverifiable account of human cognition."[75] Gelpi, it is good to recall, began his intellectual career as a devotee of Rahner's before he abandoned it. Gelpi abandoned Rahner's theory when he realized that the theory may resonate with cradle Christians, but not with the unbelievers with whom he worked in his pastoral practice:

> I find it entirely understandable when cradle Christians resonate with Rahner's theory of the supernatural existential. In some ways, the idea of unthematized grace waiting for thematization by an adult act of faith interprets the adult conversion experience of those raised in an atmosphere of faith. Allow me to explain what I mean. I noted above that the converts from

---

71. Molnar, "Can We Know God Directly?" 228.
72. See Metz, *Faith in History*.
73. Molnar, "Can We Know God Directly?" 228.
74. See Gelpi, *Grace as Transmuted Experience and Social Process*, 77.
75. Gelpi, *Turn to Experience in Contemporary Theology*, 103.

unbelief to belief with whom I dealt pastorally could make little sense of Rahner's theology of unthematic grace. It makes more sense to cradle Christians, however, because cradle Christians convert differently than unbelievers. Unbelievers pass from no faith to faith; cradle Christians pass from infantile faith to childish faith to adolescent faith and then, hopefully to adult faith.

There is also a related criticism that Rahner's Transcendental Thomism is actually an attempt to reduce theology to philosophy—that Rahner makes God indistinguishable from human experience by assuming, "that God is 'dimly known,' not as an object of knowledge but as the infinite horizon within which every finite object is apprehended."[76] Thus, critics question whether it is possible to reach God first via metaphysics and only then by revelation without reducing revelation to a metaphysical assumption.[77] According to Molnar, "by assuming that everyone has an unthematic experience of God and that natural theology is an inner factor in a general doctrine of being, Rahner does in fact reduce the triune God to his naturally known God. The result of this thinking is Rahner's inability to see that the answer to the truth question can only be a theological and not a philosophical answer."[78] My own position is that Peirce's metaphysics of experience offers a better way of apprehending what Rahner has been at pain to describe. Peirce's phenomenology can properly describe spatio-temporal realities as well as those realities that transcend space and time in a way that avoids the dualism of matter and spirit which Transcendental Thomism and faculty psychology inherited from classical Greek philosophy.[79] Where Rahner takes a leap forward, in my view, is in his evolutionary Christology, which I discuss next.

HOW RAHNER DEVELOPED EVOLUTIONARY CHRISTOLOGY

Fundamental Presupposition 1: Rahner takes the evolutionary view of the world as a given—posing the question whether Christology can be compatible with such an evolutionary worldview?[80] Rahner's goal is

---

76. Molnar, "Can We Know God Directly?" 228. See also Tripole, "Philosophy and Theology—Are They Compatible?" 25–74.
77. Molnar, "Can We Know God Directly?" 229.
78. Molnar, "Can We Know God Directly?" 229.
79. Gelpi, *Turn to Experience in Contemporary Theology*, 103.
80. Rahner, *Foundations of Christian Faith*, 178.

to make the Christian faith intelligible and credible in the light of an evolutionary view of the world.

Fundamental Presupposition 2: Rahner takes as a given the unity of matter and spirit ("hypostatic union") because of the transcendental experience of human beings who can reach to and grasp what is beyond them. The human person is "the existent in whom the basic tendency of matter to discover itself in spirit through self-transcendence reaches its definitive breakthrough."[81]

Fundamental Presupposition 3: God has a universal salvific will to save humanity (uncreated grace) and this universal salvific will to communicate God's self to creature is irrevocable. God does not merely communicate things *about* God to creature, but God actually communicates God's-self.

Fundamental Presupposition 4: Human beings (following presupposition 2 and 3) have the capacity to hear and respond to God. "The creature is endowed, by virtue of its inmost essence and constitution, with the possibility of being assumed, of becoming the material of a possible history of God. God's creative act always drafts the creature as the paradigm of a possible utterance of himself."[82]

Fundamental Presupposition 5: Following presupposition 3, 4, and 5, all grace is Christ's grace. The world was made for Christ, a purpose that was achieved in the incarnation. Rahner accepts the Scotist idea that Christ is the end of creation; that the incarnation is not God's afterthought or "belated mechanism after the fall,"[83] but part of the plan from the beginning.

Fundamental Presupposition 6: Following presupposition 3, the divine self-communication of God finds concrete historical concretization and expression in Jesus Christ.

Fundamental Presupposition 7: Following presupposition 5, the resources for speaking about Jesus must be Scripture, Tradition, Human Reason, and Reflection.

The human person is a being who stands in openness to God because of the supernatural existential. Rahner employs the Scholastic expression *potential obedientialis* (obediential or supernatural potency) to drive home the point that this human capacity for transcendence is not a purely natural

---

81. Rahner, *Foundations of Christian Faith*, 181.
82. Rahner, "On the Theology of the Incarnation," 111.
83. Siebenrock, "Christology," 113.

potency of the human person, but something actualized only under the power of grace.[84] The implication of this for our understanding of God's activity in creation is that this openness to God, which is the fundamental essence of a person, is realized perfectly in the God-man, Jesus. "What does it mean to say that human nature has the possibility of being assumed by the person of the Word of God? Correctly understood, it means that this potential is not one potentiality along with other possibilities in the constituent elements of human nature; it is objectively identical with the essence of man."[85]

Rahner presupposes that both a priori and a posteriori the human person is a being oriented towards an "absolute savior. It is God's prior elevation of our essence as human beings by supernatural grace that enables us to understand who and what Christ is.[86] What is distinctive about Christianity is Jesus Christ. The supernatural existential is available not to Christians alone, but to everyone—Christians and non-Christians alike. The supernatural existential is the grace of Christ. Anyone who does not have contact with the Church can still be saved because of the supernatural existential, which is available to everyone, at least as an offer. Rahner calls non-Christians who accept God's offer of grace (which is actually the grace of Christ) "anonymous Christians."[87] Rahner writes, "Since the transcendental self-communication of God as an offer to man's freedom is an existential of every person, and since it is a moment in the self-communication of God to the world which reaches its goal and its climax in Jesus Christ, we can speak of 'anonymous Christians.'"[88] Non-Christians— African Traditional Religions (ATRs), Hindu, Muslims, and Buddhists— may accept, at least intellectually, some of the teachings of Christianity without explicitly professing the Christian faith. Anyone can accept and respond to God's call to self-transcendence without knowing it. Such people Rahner calls Anonymous Christians. But those who respond explicitly to this call by membership in the Church through baptism he calls Christians.

---

84. Coffey, "'Incarnation' of the Holy Spirit in Christ," 467.

85. Rahner, "On the Theology of the Incarnation," 105–20.

86. Molnar, "Can We Know God Directly?" 246; see also Rahner, "Theology and Anthropology," 28–45.

87. See Rahner, "Anonymous Christian" and "Anonymous Christianity and the Missionary Task of the Church."

88. Rahner, *Foundations of Christian Faith*, 176.

HISTORICAL AND ESSENTIAL CHRISTOLOGY

Rahner distinguishes between what he sees as the two approaches in the history of Christology and characterizes them as Historical Christology and Essential Christology. The Historical Approach probes the historical records dealing with the life, death, and resurrection of Jesus as found in the Scriptures and Tradition.[89] What Rahner calls the Historical approach is the same as what we have identified in an earlier chapter as the Christology from Below or Ascending Christology (as distinguished from Christology from Above or Descending Theology). On the other hand, the Essential Approach "examines the necessary conditions in the human person which makes possible a genuine capacity to hear and respond to the historical message of Jesus Christ."[90] The Essential and Historical approaches are not mutually exclusive; they are mutually dependent. The two approaches reveal Rahner's overarching Christological concern, which is to reconcile the claims of classical Christology (like the dogmas of the first seven ecumenical councils) with the challenges of modern science, particularly the evolutionary view of the world. They also reveal Rahner's awareness that we live in a multi-religious and multi-cultural world and Jesus Christ must have something to say (grace of Jesus Christ) in all religions.[91]

TRANSCENDENTAL CHRISTOLOGY

After several reformulations, with respect to the Incarnation, the Thomistic notion that the human person is the only being in of all creation with *capax Dei* (capable of God) reached its zenith of development in the transcendental Christology of Rahner.[92] Rahner's transcendental Christology places the mystery of Christ within the evolutionary view of the world.[93] He responds to the scientific evolutionary view of world order by developing a Christology that is cosmological and historical. We pointed out already that Rahner takes the fact of evolution as a given. Rahner's term for human evolution is "active self-transcendence." As human beings we are called by God to evolve and transcend ourselves. We know ourselves as persons who are part of the material universe. However, we also know that we are spirit and not mere

---

89. Schineller, "Discovering Jesus Christ," 93.
90. Schineller, "Discovering Jesus Christ," 93.
91. Siebenrock, "Christology," 114.
92. Coffey, "'Incarnation' of the Holy Spirit in Christ," 467.
93. See Rahner, "Jesus Christus."

matter. For this reason, we are always reaching out to our spiritual vocation. As Sprit, we know and accept Jesus Christ as the absolute savior.

"Active self-transcendence," Rahner's preferred term for evolution, is a principle of two movements— creation is moving towards Christ and Christ himself active in creation. The historically developing creation reaches its apex and goal in the human person who is free and self-conscious.[94] Thus, there is unity between creation and soteriology (of Christ). For Rahner, creation and Incarnation are not two different and disparate acts of God, but "two moments and two phases of the one process of God's self-giving and self-expression, although it is an intrinsically differentiated process."[95] Human beings evolve and transcend themselves in their quest to respond to God's own invitation to divinize humanity. God wants to save humanity, but does not want to do it from a distance. God prefers to save humanity from a close proximity, hence the incarnation.

Transcendental Christology begins by attempting to understand "the a priori possibilities in man which make the coming of the message of Christ possible."[96] Rahner reckons that transcendental Christology was not part of traditional Christian theology and thinks this is unfortunate. He says that the lack of transcendental Christology in traditional Christology is what at times makes statements about Christ in traditional theology seem "mythological (in a pejorative sense)."[97] Hence, he argues that the starting point of transcendental Christology must be an anthropology that takes seriously the human experience—a person "who in every categorical act of knowledge and of freedom always transcends himself and the categorical object towards the incomprehensible mystery by which the act and the object are opened and borne, the mystery which we call God."[98]

HYPOSTATIC UNION

Rahner loosely calls the unity of matter and spirit (human person) a "hypostatic union." It is this unity or hypostatic union that enables a person to live a life of self-transcendence. This hypostatic union (unity of matter and spirit) reached its sublime or final and irrevocable stage in the God-Man Jesus Christ. "The incarnation of God," Rahner writes, "is therefore the unique, supreme, case of the total actualization of human reality, which consists

---

94. Siebenrock, "Christology," 119.
95. Rahner, *Foundations of Christian Faith*, 197.
96. Rahner, *Foundations of Christian Faith*, 207.
97. Rahner, *Foundations of Christian Faith*, 207.
98. Rahner, *Foundations of Christian Faith*, 209.

of the fact that man is in so far as he gives up himself."⁹⁹ Rahner accepts the Chalcedonian definition of the two natures of Christ, which according to the Council are unmixed, unchanged, undivided, and inseparable, as decisive for both the faith of the Church and Christology. Contemporary Christology, he argues, cannot be a simple rejection of fifteen hundred years of classical Christology. It can also not be a mere repetition of the Chalcedonian formula.[100] One of the weaknesses of classical Christology, in Rahner's view, is that it tends to idealize the humanity of Jesus Christ, to the point of (unintentionally) lapsing into monophysitism.[101] He insists, therefore, that we not see the two natures of Christ as polar opposites. In Rahner's dynamic and relational way of framing it, what we can say is that in the incarnation, humanity whose essential nature is to seek oneness with God, has realized this union with God.[102] This means "that Rahner understands the human being as obediential potency for hypostatic union with the Son of God, and Jesus Christ as the only man in whom this fullness of being human has been actualized."[103]

In restating the Chalcedonian definition of the union of two natures in terms of the divine nature coming to the most perfect expression of which humanity is capable in the man-Jesus,[104] Rahner shows that humanity's evolutionary history culminates in Christ. The hypostatic union already has its antecedent in the unity of matter and spirit—a union that moves matter towards its goal. "Though matter possesses no interiority of its own, being only a passive potentiality, like spirit it has its source in God, and it is the pre-step and instrument open to the life that serves as the unifying principle of the universe and is grounded dynamically in God who attracts as the goal of the movement."[105] What the hypostatic union shows is that the self-communication of God, which God gives to the human person as an offer, as well as the human person's acceptance of this offer, is irreversible.[106] God is, and has been, at the root of evolution, which God moves to its goal. Evolution has all along been moving to the human person as the possible

---

99. Rahner, "On the Theology of the Incarnation," 110.

100. See Skiba, *Transcendental Christology of Karl Rahner*, 140.

101. Skiba, *Transcendental Christology of Karl Rahner*, 141. See also Rahner, "Christology Today?" 29.

102. Corduan, "Hegel in Rahner," 296.

103. Coffey, "'Incarnation' of the Holy Spirit in Christ," 467.

104. Coffey, "'Incarnation' of the Holy Spirit in Christ," 467.

105. McDermott, "Christologies of Karl Rahner," 110.

106. McDermott, "Christologies of Karl Rahner," 110.

self-revelation of God. In Christ evolution attains its goal irreversibly.[107] "Christ comprises the high point of human history, the attainment of mankind's goal of union with God, his divinization as the highest achievement of self-transcendence under grace."[108]

For Rahner, the hypostatic union is not so much something that distinguishes Jesus from us, but something that must occur once and only once when the world begins to enter upon its final phase.[109] Once it occurred, the hypostatic union of the God-Man Jesus becomes "the necessary and permanent beginning of the divinization of the world as a whole."[110] Rahner also says that the hypostatic union has a history—a history attested to by "Christ's awareness of his immediate relationship to God."[111] The idea that the hypostatic union has a history raises anew the age-old question of *communication idiomatum*, i.e., communication of idioms or interchange of attributes from the divine to the human in Christ and vice versa on the basis of the unity of these two natures in Christ.[112] Traditional Christology debated whether Christ had one will or two wills and whether or not his human nature existed as a person before it was assumed by the eternal Word. The Third Council of Constantinople (AD 681) settled the monothelite controversy, decreeing that Christ has two wills: human and divine. At the heart of the monothelite controversy is the debate regarding the two natures—how can two competing things (human nature and divine nature) coexist without one subsuming the other?[113] Rahner helps us to see how, at its deepest sense, *communicatio* is identical with the incarnation itself. "If divine being or subsistence can be received in a human way such that human being truly becomes divine being, the Incarnation becomes the most radical possible instance of the communication of the divine to the human, and as such the basis of any other communication that might take place in Christ. We can go on to say that whatever is communicated from God to man in the Incarnation is bestowed in a divine way but received in a human way."[114]

The argument regarding the evolution of the universe and its culmination in Christ raises for Rahner the question regarding how Jesus effects

---

107. McDermott, "Christologies of Karl Rahner," 111.
108. McDermott, "Christologies of Karl Rahner," 111.
109. Rahner, *Foundations of Christian Faith*, 181.
110. Rahner, *Foundations of Christian Faith*, 181.
111. Seibenrock, "Christology," 120.
112. Coffey, "'Incarnation' of the Holy Spirit," 468.
113. Robinson, *God and the World of Signs*, 130.
114. Coffey, "'Incarnation' of the Holy Spirit," 469.

the salvation of the human person.[115] Anselm of Canterbury (1033–1109) propounded a satisfaction theory in *Cur Deus Homo?* (Why the God-Man?) —that the death of Jesus was a substitute for human sinfulness and that the infinite merit won by Christ was what "satisfied" God's wrath. Simply put, for Anselm, it was necessary for the justice of God for the atonement to take place. Rahner rejects this Anselm's theory of atonement as insufficient. Against the Anselmian theory that God did a turn around because of the death of Christ on the cross, Rahner emphasizes instead the unity of human history—that in Christ's total offering of Himself God's salvific will has come to full expression and irrevocably so.[116] "To Jesus' life and death can be ascribed a causality of a quasi-sacramental type for us insofar as they are the cause of God's salvific will which makes it irreversible in the call for man's free decision."[117]

What does Rahner mean by "quasi-sacramental?" It is a term that is related to "quasi-formal causality." The term "quasi-formal causality" is a concept Rahner introduced in a 1961 essay in which he tries to explain who a person is when called by God to partake in the inner life of the Blessed Trinity. It is a concept Rahner uses to explain how God divinizes us without compromising the gratuity of grace. At the back of Rahner's mind when he introduced the term was what in scholastic theology is called "sanctifying grace." Rahner thinks that the scholastic notion does not do justice to the Scriptural way of speaking of Grace as God's gift or God's self-communication, the way the Apostle Paul did so well. Rahner also equally finds the scholastic notion of "efficient cause" to be inadequate. Since these scholastic terms are inadequate, Rahner reasons, there must be another way of explaining the relationship between nature and grace without compromising human freedom, in the same way there is a way to explain God's grace without compromising the gratuity of grace. For him, quasi-formal causality explains (i) how grace is not extrinsic to nature and (ii) how the indwelling of God who is triune resides in the human soul. Thus, Rahner thinks "quasi-formal causality" adequately serves this purpose. He thinks that by introducing the term quasi-formal causality (causality of the uncreated grace) he has resolved the problem of how God communicates God's self to human creatures without compromising both God's own transcendence and human freedom. The quasi-formal causality is "formal" (and different from the efficient causality of creation) because it is God's second act (different from God's first act—creation). The reason why Rahner adds the prefix "quasi"

---

115. McDermott, "Christologies of Karl Rahner," 112.
116. McDermott, "Christologies of Karl Rahner," 112.
117. McDermott, "Christologies of Karl Rahner," 112.

to it is to distinguish it from the formal causality (i.e., beatific vision that the blessed and the saints enjoy at the end of time) of the scholastics. Thus, on the basis of this argument, Rahner makes the following determinations:

- only the *Logos*-Jesus, the Second Person of the Blessed Trinity, can become incarnate (the Father and the Spirit cannot become incarnate).
- the supernatural self-communication of God should be understood as a kind of quasi-formal causality that God exercised on God's creature.
- The *Logos* is quasi-formally related to the Second Person of the Blessed Trinity.
- Contrary to what the scholastics taught, the self-communication of God, which we receive as creatures, does not happen as a result of efficient causality, but because of the quasi-formal causality.[118]

Thus, Rahner further adds, "Moreover, we must also reflect later upon the fact that the 'absolute savior,' as understood in this way in his quasi-sacramental reality as sign, actually has by this very fact the soteriological efficacy which church doctrine asserts of the destiny of Jesus, presupposing that this redemption is not understood in a mythological way as causing some change of mind on God's part."[119]

Christology and Trinity

In the next chapter, we will flesh out the triadic structure of reality in the phenomenological categories of the American pragmatist and philosopher, C. S. Peirce (1839–1914). The chapter will examine how Peircean scholars, like Andrew Robinson, have appropriated Peirce's metaphysical categories and derive from them "vestiges of the Trinity in creation." This, as we will see, stands in sharp contrast to Rahner who sees the "vestige" of the Trinity only in the Incarnation. For Rahner, the Incarnation is the real symbol of Jesus's human nature through which He expresses Himself as He really is. Jesus's whole life is revelatory of the Second Person of the Blessed Trinity.[120] Rahner thinks that without the Son's Incarnation we cannot have even the remotest abstract idea of God's proximity and absolute self-communication.[121]

Rahner criticizes Neo-Scholastic Christology for incoherence on this matter; an incoherence he thinks is even more evident in the Neo-Scholastic treatment of the Trinity. He thinks Neo-Scholasticism has done

---

118. See Rahner, "Some Implications of the Scholastic Concept of Uncreated Grace."
119. Rahner, *Foundations of Christian Faith*, 211.
120. McDermott, "Christologies of Karl Rahner," 105.
121. McDermott, "Christologies of Karl Rahner," 105.

a disservice to Christian theology by sharply separating Christology and Trinity. In his work, *The Trinity*, Rahner criticizes Neo-Scholastic theology for disconnecting the doctrine of the Trinity from soteriology and human experience. The universe, for Rahner, is a result of the exchange of love between the divine persons. Here Rahner's view is supported by the English theoretical physicist, John Polkinghorne (1930–), who also thinks that the universe is "deeply relational in its character and unified in its structure, because it is the creation of the one true God, Father, Son, and Holy Spirit."[122]

Neo-Scholasticism, which Rahner criticizes for incoherent treatment of the Trinity, begins its treatment of God under two heading: *De Deo Uno* (On the One God) and *De Deo Trino* (On the Triune God). This separation, according to Rahner, is what has led to the misconception that the Trinity is a mystery, which cannot be explained. This misconception, according to Rahner, makes the doctrine of the Trinity seem purely speculative and not essential to the Christian faith. Most importantly, it disconnects the Trinity from Christian life and spirituality.[123] The scholastic, Thomas Aquinas (*Summa Theologiae* III, q. 23. A. 2), had argued that any of the divine Persons could have become man, if God had willed it. Rahner disagrees with this assertion, arguing instead that God did not become incarnate, it was only the Second divine person who became incarnate. For Rahner, Jesus Christ is not God in general but the incarnate word.[124] Here Rahner is following Scotus and the ancient Logos theology. According to this view, the incarnation is not dependent on sin, which needed atonement, but was always intended by God from the beginning.[125] Rahner, following this view, argues that the incarnation is the "total actualization of human reality."[126] In other words, Rahner sees the incarnation as essential to God's unique plan of divinization of the world. He writes, "Where grace as the supernatural participation of man in God's inner life through God's true self-communication to men is supposed to be, there must also be the incarnation."[127] He will use his theology of the Incarnation to reconnect the doctrine of the Trinity with the doctrine of grace and salvation.

The scholastics also distinguished between the economic Trinity (God's activity and presence in salvation history) and immanent Trinity (the inner divine essence that is hidden from us). Rahner again disagrees with

---

122. Polkinghorne, *Trinity and an Entangled World*, 12.
123. See Rahner, *Trinity* (1999), x.
124. Rahner, *Trinity* (1999), xii.
125. McDermott, "Christologies of Karl Rahner," 106.
126. Rahner, "On the Theology of the Incarnation," 110.
127. As quoted by McDermott, "Christologies of Karl Rahner," 106.

the scholastic distinction, suggesting rather emphatically that the immanent Trinity is the economic Trinity and the economic Trinity is the immanent Trinity.[128] This affirmation is known as Rahner's rule or *Grundaxiom*. Rahner's rule or axiom stems from Rahner's theology of grace—that God is always communicating God's-self to creature, and God cannot but communicate God's-self. God, therefore, communicates God's-self as Father, Son, and Holy Spirit. "The economic Trinity manifests the personal self-communication of God under the conditions of time and history, hence in the missions of Christ and the Spirit."[129] Thus, Rahner's axiom that the economic Trinity is the immanent Trinity and vice versa means that "there is only one Trinitarian self-communication, which has both eternal and temporal aspects."[130] One of the imports of Rahner's *grundaxiom* is that the unity in the Godhead also implies that there is relationality within the Godhead and God's relations with the physical universe. Polkinghorne, whose view comes close to Rahner's on this matter, will argue that it is this "relationality" in the Godhead that provides an opening for dialogue between quantum physics and Trinitarian theology.[131]

Rahner's Theology of Symbols

Rahner was one of the early contemporary theologians who showed interest in the theology of symbols, although he uses the concept "symbol" in a variety of ways and in different contexts.[132] One of these contexts is the sacrament of the Church. He thinks the sacraments are "the highest stages in the word of grace in the Church in its character as exhibitive and as event."[133] Rahner's more elaborate and sustained discussion of the theology of symbols is in his essay on "theological ontology of the symbol."[134] The basic principle he enunciates in this ontology is that all beings, God included, "are by their nature symbolic, because they necessarily 'express' themselves in order to attain their own nature."[135] Relating *Realsymbol* (which he will later identify as

---

128. Rahner, *Trinity* (1999), 22.
129. Rahner, *Trinity*, xiv.
130. Rahner, *Trinity*, xiv.
131. See the collection of essays in Polkinghorne, *Trinity and an Entangled World*. See also Simmons, *Entangled Trinity*.
132. Buckley, "On Being a Symbol," 457.
133. Rahner, "What is a Sacrament?" 144.
134. See Rahner, "Theology of the Symbol," 221–52.
135. Rahner, "Theology of the Symbol," in *Theological Investigations*, 4:224.

Christ) to the sacraments, Rahner argues that symbol is the means through which transcendent reality realizes itself or attains its own nature.[136]

Although Rahner uses the concept "symbol" in a variety of ways and in different contexts, one can still discern a consistent trend in his discourse on symbols. In his early writings, the notion of symbol plays a much broader role in Rahner's system. In his later writings, the context of his use of symbols is largely "to explicate what is involved when devotional discourse says that the heart of Jesus is a symbol of his love."[137] In contributing to the contemporary discussion on Jesus's Sacred Heart, Rahner argues to the effect that the Sacred Heart is a concrete symbol of a metaphysical ground.[138] Peter Fritz has helpfully summarized Rahner's metaphysics of symbol into six propositions:

> The first two propositions are meta-propositions about (1) being's necessary self-expressiveness and (2) symbolic being as realization in another. They speak to reality as a whole. The third and fourth propositions are transitional. They concern (3) theology's general need for the concept of the symbol in order (4) to make sense of God's saving action. The last two propositions are specific to the human person, namely, the symbolic relationship between body and soul (5 and 6). All six propositions center on Rahner's general definition of symbol: "the representation which allows the other to be there."[139]

We can view Rahner's interest in symbols—the relationship between language and reality- as a reflection of his awareness of the limitations of traditional ways of doing theology.[140] Dissatisfied with the rigidity and distorting effects of conventional theological discussion, Rahner sees in symbols "a more flexible matrix for ordering perceptions."[141] For Rahner, theology is incomprehensible unless it is essentially a theology of symbols.[142] "All beings are by their nature symbolic, because they necessarily 'express' themselves in order to attain their own nature."[143] Rahner sees all the events in the life of Jesus as having symbolic significance, at least in the Gospel of John. In fact, in addition to the hermeneutics of Martin Heidegger

---

136. Rahner, "Theology of the Symbol," in *Theological Investigations*, 4:224ff.
137. Buckley, "On Being a Symbol," 458.
138. Fritz, "Karl Rahner, Friedrich Schelling, and Original Plural Unity," 301.
139. Fritz, "Karl Rahner, Friedrich Schelling, and Original Plural Unity," 301.
140. Clasby, "Dancing Sophia," 51.
141. Clasby, "Dancing Sophia," 51.
142. See Rahner, "Theology of the Symbol," in *A Rahner Reader*, 120–31.
143. Rahner, "Theology of the Symbol," in *Theological Investigations*, 4:224.

(1889–1976) and Joseph Marechal (1878–1944) whom Rahner relied on for his ontology of symbols, Rahner's understanding of symbols and language also stems largely from his understanding of the Prologue of John's Gospel. "These sources support his conviction that *logos* is inadequate as a principle of form, because it is derived from a static model of existence that fails to account for being as a process."[144]

Symbols, for Rahner, are not mere signs or ordinary agreements between the signifier and the signified. Rather, symbols have a distinct reality apart from the reality they symbolize. "A genuine symbol is the 'supreme and primal representation;' it is 'the representation which allows the other "to be there."'[145] In an apt description of the relationship between the symbol and the reality symbolized, Rahner writes, "the symbol is the reality, constituted by the thing symbolized as an inner moment of itself, which reveals and proclaims the thing symbolized, and is itself full of the thing symbolized, being its concrete form of existence."[146]

In spite of the limitations of transcendental analysis, which he employs as the starting point of his theology, Rahner was moving in the right direction with respect to the ontology of symbols. Critiques are quick to point out that he didn't quite get it right. But he at least recognized that in a symbolic representation there is plurality of distinct realities, including the symbol and the symbolized.[147] Rahner, to his credit, also recognized that in spite of their multiplicity, symbolic representation still possess a unity with that which it represents.[148] Logically, it makes sense to see that Rahner extends his symbolic language to the Trinity. "Just as there is both unity and plurality in the Trinity, so our plurality also reveals a unity: 'these plural moments in the unity of a being must have an inner agreement among themselves on account of the unity of the being, even though the plurality of moments in a being must be constituted by the reciprocal diversity of these moments.'"[149] In fact, the backdrop of Rahner's discussion of symbol all along is the Trinity. The unity of God, he says, is like that of a symbol: the Father attains own nature (in the self-possession of love: the Spirit) in expressing self (in the Word).[150] The humanity of Jesus is another example

144. Clasby, "Dancing Sophia," 51–52.

145. Little, "Anthropology and Art in the Theology of Karl Rahner," 942; quoting Rahner, "Theology of the Symbol," in *Theological Investigations* 4:225.

146. Rahner, "Theology of the Symbol," 251.

147. Little, "Anthropology and Art in the Theology of Karl Rahner," 942.

148. Little, "Anthropology and Art in the Theology of Karl Rahner," 943.

149. Little, "Anthropology and Art in the Theology of Karl Rahner," 943. Quoting Rahner, "Theology of the Symbol," in *Theological Investigations* 4:227.

150. Buckley, "On Being a Symbol," 461.

of symbol. It is in fact the supreme symbol. Because of the intrinsic symbolic nature of Christ's life, the symbolic event of Christ's life are salvifically symbolic for all of humanity.[151]

CONCLUSION

We have deliberately ended our foray into Rahner's theology with his theology of symbols because it sets up the argument to be taken up in the next chapter. Rahner moving in the direction of the ontology of symbols and conceiving the humanity of Jesus as a symbol helps, at least, our semiotic analysis. In the next chapter, we will draw from the work of Andrew Robinson who used Peircean categories to go further than Rahner—that the person and the life Jesus lived in a particular social and historical context embodied the very quality of the being of God and that the Incarnation is therefore an iconic qualisign in that the life of Jesus acts as a sign of God's transforming presence.[152] On the level of symbolic representation of signs, Robinson's argument sheds light on what Rahner is trying to say with respect to the Incarnation. Jesus Christ is not just an index of the Father, just because He derives from the Father. He is an index of the Father because the Father is in Him and He is in the Father (John 14:10).[153] Ordinarily, an index may have direct connection with the object it represents without necessarily sharing in the nature of the object it signifies. But in the case of Jesus, He does not just represent the Father in some respect; rather He represents the Father in all respects. For Robinson, therefore, Jesus represents the Father iconically: "He is the image of the invisible God (Col 1:15), "the exact imprint of God's very being" (Heb 1:3)[154]

Robinson did in fact praise Rahner's ontology of symbol as "implicitly semiotic in character."[155] Robinson himself attests to the fact that both he and Rahner agree on what he (Robinson) calls horizontal dimension of Christology, i.e., "the identity of Jesus as a puzzle to be solved in the context of fixed notions of God and the world."[156] The New Testament is not concerned with the horizontal dimension of Christology and therefore does not provide information about Jesus as a puzzle to be solved, but rather presents Jesus as a new paradigm for understanding God's relationship

151. Buckley, "On Being a Symbol," 461.
152. Robinson, *God and the World of Signs*, 124.
153. Robinson, *God and the World of Signs*, 126.
154. Robinson, *God and the World of Signs*, 127.
155. Robinson, *God and the World of Signs*, 134.
156. Robinson, *God and the World of Signs*, 133.

with the world.¹⁵⁷ The crucial issue here is actually one of ontology: How did God become man? How is the created fabric of the world the dwelling place of the transcendent creator?¹⁵⁸ Robinson finds Rahner's position that humanity has a capacity to accept God and that God is always communicating God's-self very satisfying. He accepts Rahner's thesis that God does not merely communicate things about God's self to creature, but rather that God communicates God's-self. He thinks this has implications for creation—that material reality of creatures has in itself the capacity to embody the *Logos* and agrees with this anti-docetic position.¹⁵⁹

Where Robinson and Rahner disagree is on what Robinson calls vertical dimension of Christology—which involves both ontology and epistemology.¹⁶⁰ The disagreement stems from their respective approaches. Rahner speaks of the Incarnation as *Realsymbol*, while Robinson speaks of the Incarnation as the iconic *qualisign* of God's being. For Rahner, all entities are symbolic because first, they necessarily express themselves and second, by expressing themselves entities constitute themselves. Ontology of symbol, for Rahner, reflects a universal metaphysical principle that each being is primarily symbolic.¹⁶¹ Rahner's ontology of symbols also reflects the distinction he made between "real" (genuine) symbols and "representational" (arbitrary signs and codes) symbols.¹⁶² For Rahner, only a "real symbol" genuinely expresses the entity signified.¹⁶³ The *Logos* is therefore, the *realsymbol*, for Rahner. Unlike Rahner's ontology of symbols where entities "express" themselves, in Peirce's semiotics, which Robinson adopts, "although the relation between sign and object exists prior to the interpretation of the sign, it is only when the sign is interpreted as a sign of the object that the sign-relation is fully realized."¹⁶⁴ Summing up his own differences with Rahner, Robinson writes:

> Rahner assumes that taking interpretation to be an essential aspect of the sign-relation would leave symbols (signs) as merely arbitrarily, extrinsically, related to their objects. Peirce's

---

157. Robinson, *God and the World of Signs*, 133.
158. Robinson, *God and the World of Signs*, 130.
159. Robinson, *God and the World of Signs*, 134. See also Rahner, *Theological Investigations* 4:229–30.
160. Robinson, *God and the World of Signs*, 133.
161. Robinson, *God and the World of Signs*, 136.
162. Robinson, *God and the World of Signs*, 136. See also Rahner, *Theological Investigations* 4:224–25.
163. Robinson, *God and the World of Signs*, 136.
164. Robinson, *God and the World of Signs*, 137.

semiotics shows this to be an unnecessary assumption. Rahner in effect assumes that the only kind of interpreted sign is (in Peirce's terms) a symbol, whose relation to its object is given by convention. He does not allow for indexes (whose connection with their objects are direct or causal), or icons (which are connected to their objects by virtue of intrinsic resemblances).[165]

Thus, Robinson admits that the difference between his own approach and that of Rahner is that Rahner's Christology, as developed in the concept of *Realsymbol*, is Christology "from above," whereas "the semiotic model allows for much more reciprocal relation between the bottom-up and top-down approaches. This is because a Peircean semiotic metaphysics allows, in principle, for continuity between human religious understanding, everyday human knowing, and non-human sign-use."[166] Thus, Robinson concludes that in spite of Rahner's long held interest in cosmological evolution, Rahner's ontology of symbol cannot offer an evolutionary account of the origin of the capacity to know anything or fundamental reality.[167]

---

165. Robinson, *God and the World of Signs*, 137.
166. Robinson, *God and the World of Signs*, 137–38.
167. Robinson, *God and the World of Signs*, 138.

Chapter Six

The Trinity

CHRISTOLOGY MUST BEGIN WITH the person and mission of Jesus, but its basic question has to be about his unity with God.[1] Thomas Aquinas's Trinitarian treatise, which speaks to the unity of God, is humorously characterized in the formula 5–4–3–2–1–0: five characteristics or notions, four relations, three persons, two processions, one God, and zero proof. Hence, the formula 5–4–3–2–1–0. The five characteristics or notions refer to the ingenerateness of the Father (who is the origin of the Son and Spirit) plus the 4 relations. The four relations refer to the four divine relations, i.e., paternity (relation of the Father to the Son), Filiation (relation of the Son to the Father), Active Spiration (relation of the Father and Son to the Spirit), and Passive Spiration (relation of the Spirit to the Father and the Son). The three Persons refer to the three Persons in the Godhead (Father + Son + Holy Spirit). The two Processions refer to the procession of the Son from the Father and the procession of the Spirit from the Father and the Son. One God refers to the three Trinitarian Persons constituting one God. The zero proof is meant to suggest that Aquinas did not intend his treatise to be a proof of Trinitarian faith.[2] The latter point (i.e., that it was not intended by Aquinas to be a proof) made Bernard Lonergan refer sarcastically to the zero in the formula 5–4–3–2–1–0 to mean "zero comprehension." He was caricaturing clerical students who were memorizing (rather than attempting to comprehend) the essentials of the Thomistic doctrine of Trinity.[3]

---

1. Pannenberg, *Jesus—God and Man*, 36.
2. See Ormerod, *Trinity*, 18.
3. See Marmion and Van Nieuwenhove, *Introduction to the Trinity*, 16. See also

5-4-3-2-1-0
- **5 Notions**: Ingenerateness of the Father + 4 Relations
- **4 Divine Relations**: Paternity + Filiation + Active Spiration + Passive Spiration
- **3 Divine Persons**: Father + Son + Holy Spirit
- **2 Processions**: Procession of the Son from the Father + Procession of the Spirit from the Father and the Son
- **1 God**: Trinitarian God-head
- **0 Proof**: Not intended to be an intellectual proof.

This chapter builds on Karl Rahner's ontology of symbols, as well as the dialogue between Rahner and the Peircean scholar, Andrew Robinson, begun in the last chapter. We shall situate Robinson's innovative Trinitarian thought[4] within the context of Rahner's critique that inadequate theologies of incarnation and grace characterizing much of contemporary theology has separated Trinitarian theology from Christian spirituality and experience.[5] Working out of the architectonic system of the American philosopher, scientist, and semiotician, Charles S. Peirce (1839–1914), and mindful of Rahner's critique that Neo-Scholasticism has been a stumbling block in the Church's attempt to formulate a viable and intelligible doctrine of the Trinity that could be connected to Christian faith, practice, and spirituality,[6] Robinson charts a new direction—one in which Peirce's metaphysical categories can illuminate and bring clarity to disputed questions in Trinitarian theology. Before Robinson's fresh ideas, some Peircean scholars have been attempting connections between Peirce's semiotic triads and the Trinity. Peirce's own specific references to any possible links between his categories and God remain at best ambiguous.[7] The consensus remains, however, that while Peirce may have been "reluctant to identify God with any of his categories"[8] and that while he also may never have systematically developed possible links between his categories and the Trinity, his scanty remarks

---

Dadosky, "God's Eternal Yes," 398 (see n7).

4. See Robinson, *God and the World of Signs*.

5. See Rahner, *Trinity* (1999). See also Rahner, "Remarks on the Dogmatic Treatise 'De Trinitate,'" 77–102.

6. Rahner, *Trinity* (1999), ix.

7. Robinson, *God and the World of Signs*, 109. Both Robert Corrington and Donald Gelpi think that Peirce thought his triadic semiotics had Trinitarian implications, even if Peirce never fully explored it. See Corrington, *Introduction to C. S. Peirce*, 4; Gelpi, *Gracing of Human Experience*, 183. For other views on the subject see Raposa, *Peirce's Philosophy of Religion*.

8. Robinson, *God and the World of Signs*, 110.

regarding parallels between his semiotics and the Christian doctrine of the Trinity lend itself to the kind of conclusion Robinson suggests.

In juxtaposing Robinson's ideas with Rahner's, we probe whether the application of a semiotic model to the Trinity enhances our understanding of the economy of salvation or whether this is just another "abstruse kind of metaphysical speculation" of the relations within the immanent Trinity.[9] The overall context remains Rahner's critique of the psychological analogy of the Trinity as found in his small but highly influential writing, *The Trinity*—a tiny volume "that spells out a theological agenda for liberating Trinitarian theology from its Neo-Scholastic bondage and renewing interest in the Trinity."[10] Neo-Scholasticism, in spite of its richness, can be rigid and unimaginative. It at times oversimplifies the troves of treasures and diversity to be found in the medieval Church.[11] In addition, Neo-Scholasticism has the tendency to be unhistorical and out of touch with modern culture. Critics point out how it is not in tune with the findings of modern science. There are also some who find it to be "overly focused on lifeless concepts as opposed to experience." For these reasons, they find it to be "ill-equipped to deal with the modern turn to the subject."[12] In the previous chapter, we pointed out that the traditional Christian doctrine of the Trinity, following the Chalcedonian definition, was constructed using the resources of the metaphysical frameworks of the philosophical system of the time. We then posed the question: "What happens to Christology when the metaphysical superstructure on which much of its logical consistency was based has been consigned to the philosophical dustbin?"[13] This was not a question Scholasticism was ready to answer. Scholasticism was not concerned with how to incorporate new frameworks, even in the face of shifting metaphysical presuppositions of modern culture. We are, therefore, faced with the reality that we need to leave Scholasticism behind and confront head on how to articulate the traditional Christian doctrine anew using resources of contemporary ontology of meaning.

Contemporary skepticism about the place of metaphysics in rational thought leaves one with one of two possible options: reconfigure traditional Trinitarian thought without any reference to metaphysical assumptions or frameworks,[14] or reinvent metaphysics to cohere with contemporary ways

---

9. Robinson, *God and the World of Signs*, 113.
10. Ormerod, "Two Points or Four?" 663.
11. Rahner, *Trinity* (1999), vii.
12. Rahner, *Trinity* (1999), vii-viii.
13. See Robinson, *God and the World of Signs*, 133–34.
14. Robinson, *God and the World of Signs*, 133–34.

of understanding and ontology of meaning. Rahner has blamed Neo-Scholasticism for producing a "unitarian" theology and non-Trinitarian theology of grace. As one trained in scholastic theology himself, Rahner was one of the early twentieth century theologians to re-configure the traditional Trinitarian thought with a nuanced view of the metaphysical assumptions of Neo-Scholasticism. Beginning with a different approach drawn from his preferred idiom of divine self-communication and the two processions of the Son and the Spirit,[15] Rahner developed the thesis (known as the Trinitarian axiom or Rahner's rule) that the immanent Trinity is the economic Trinity and the economic Trinity is the immanent Trinity.[16] In other words, for Rahner, God's own inner unity (three Persons) is not any different from what is manifested in salvation history. Rahner's rule was accepted as paradigmatic by many theologians and it went unchallenged for a long time.[17] To underscore how influential Rahner's rule is to contemporary Trinitarian theology, some theologians have gone as far as characterizing the differences among major Trinitarian theologians strictly along the lines of how they interpret and implement Rahner's rule in their theology.[18]

Robinson is one of the few exceptions. He adopts a different approach, following Peirce's re-invention of metaphysics as a form of inquiry. Metaphysics fell out of favor in the nineteenth century largely because the a priori assumptions on which it was based were assumed by modern scholars to hinder inquiry. Some critics also thought it was based on authoritarianism that made every area of inquiry subservient to an "overarching metaphysical structure."[19] It was to Peirce's credit that he began the process of re-inventing metaphysics. His dictum: "Do not block the way of inquiry," admonishes against apriorism and authoritarianism in the task of inquiry.[20] The structure of knowledge, in Peirce's non-foundationalist epistemological framework, is always hypothetical and provisional at every level of inquiry, including the level of metaphysics.[21]

Unlike Rahner whose own theology of the Trinity is virtually a synthesis of early Greek Patristic and Augustinian-Thomistic teachings on the subject, albeit "advanced beyond the categories of Neo-Scholasticism and

---

15. See Ormerod, "Two Points or Four?" 662.

16. Rahner, *Trinity* (1999), 22.

17. One of the few critiques to the Rahner rule can be found in the book by Fowler, *Karl Rahner's Trinitarian Axiom*.

18. See Lincicum, "Economy and Immanence," 111 and Braaten, "Triune God," 415–27.

19. Robinson, *God and the World of Signs*, 279.

20. Robinson, *God and the World of Signs*, 279.

21. Robinson, *God and the World of Signs*, 279–80.

informed by the distinctively modern concerns of history, personhood, subjectivity, and relationality,"[22] Robinson's Trinitarian theology is informed by parallels he draws from Peirce's metaphysical categories of Firstness, Secondness, and Thirdness, which he relates to the theological understandings of the Father, Son, and the Holy Spirit.[23] These parallels inform Robinson's argument that some of the perennial theological problems associated with the way we approach Trinitarian Persons and Intra-Trinitarian relations can be constructively approached by an appeal to a semiotic model of the trinity. This chapter will show how the ideas derived from Peirce, which Robinson appropriates for speaking of the Trinitarian relations (immanent and economic Trinity), are both similar and different from Rahner's. The suggestion here is that their similarity is mainly in terms of how they both attempted to overcome the problem posed by the traditional psychological analogy. Like Rahner who was mindful of the dangers of subordinationism, Robinson was motivated by the need to seek ground for the unity of the triune God. He thought by correlating the Peircean phenomenological categories to the Trinitarian Persons, one would easily eliminate subordinationism. In the Peircean semiotic model that Robinson adopts, it is logically and phenomenologically impossible to isolate the reality of any one of the categories from the co-reality of the other two.[24] Thus, Robinson adopts Peircean language and uses it to re-word the Nicene-Constantinople Creed, not only to make it metaphysically coherent, but also to bring it in consonance with Christian Scriptures and Tradition. Robinson's distinctive contribution lies in the way he uses his re-wording of the Creed to reconcile the East-West divide on the *filioque* problem. In the end this much becomes clear: if Rahner's rule has "driven contemporary Trinitarian theology into the cul-de-sac of demanding that salvation history function as the role, silent witness to the Triune God,"[25] Robinson's semiotic model uniquely offers both an application and a challenge to Rahner's rule, notwithstanding that Robinson did not intend his semiotic model to be a challenge to Rahner's axiom.

22. Rahner, *Trinity* (1999), viii.
23. See Robinson, *God and the World of Signs*, particularly ch. 2.
24. Robinson, *God and the World of Signs*, 103.
25. See Sanders's review of Dennis J. Fowler's *Trinitarian Rule*, 370–72.

INTRA-TRINITARIAN RELATIONS AND THE PROBLEM OF THE PSYCHOLOGICAL ANALOGY

The second half of the twentieth century witnessed explosion in Trinitarian theology— what has been termed a Trinitarian renaissance.[26] The revival has largely been credited to the work of two theologians: Karl Barth (1886–1968) who put the doctrine of the Trinity at the center of his *Die christlichen Dogmatik im Entwurf* and Karl Rahner's *grundaxiom*—that the economic Trinity is the Immanent Trinity and vice versa.[27] The Trinitarian revival of both Barth and Rahner is implicitly a critique of the natural theology typical of Western theism that sees God as a super-being, utterly different from the world, and self-sufficient, immutable and independent of the world.[28] In moving away from this tendency, both Barth and Rahner show a tendency towards a historicization or dynamicization of the God-head, i.e., one in which God's being is in becoming.[29]

The old Western Christian conception of the Trinity from which Rahner departs conceives of the Trinitarian Persons solely in terms of their functions: the Father is associated with creation, the Son with Justification, and the Spirit with sanctification. In the Trinitarian theology deriving from the Cappadocian Fathers, and after them St. Augustine, the distinction between the Trinitarian Persons are constituted by their relations, a form of mutual indwelling of the Trinitarian Persons to one another that the Cappadocian termed *perichoresis*. In spite of the efforts of the Cappadocian Fathers to make the Trinity more comprehensible, the functionalization of the Persons of the Trinity do not make the Trinity as comprehensible as it should be.[30] Perhaps this is why the recent surge of interest and creativity in Trinitarian theology has been simultaneously accompanied by a rejection of the psychological analogy of the classical Latin West.[31]

Although there are variations of the psychological analogy developed by Augustine, one common characteristic among them is the use of human intellect and will as a way of explicating the mystery of the Trinity and the processions in the Godhead.[32] Although we are gradually witnessing a shift from the psychological analogy to one that emphasizes personal, relational,

---

26. See Schwobel, "Renaissance of Trinitarian Theology," 1–30. See also O'Collins, "Holy Trinity," 1–25.

27. See Barth, *Die Chrisliche Dogmatik im Entwurf.*

28. Wisse, *Trinitarian Theology Beyond Participation*, 5.

29. Wisse, *Trinitarian Theology Beyond Participation*, 4.

30. Wisse, *Trinitarian Theology Beyond Participation*, 5.

31. Hunt, "Psychological Analogy and Paschal Mystery in Trinitarian Theology," 198.

32. Hunt, "Psychological Analogy and Paschal Mystery in Trinitarian Theology," 198.

and social aspects of being, the notions of processions, mission, relations, and person that form the bulwark of the classical Latin doctrine has hardly ever been jettisoned; they are at times reframed in non-classical categories.[33]

In the prima pars of the *Summa Theologiae* where he presents a systematic treatise of the Trinity, Aquinas begins with a treatise of the one God (QQ.2–26) and followed it up later with a treatise on the Triune God (QQ.27–43).[34] One of the criticisms against Aquinas's Trinitarian theology is that his presentation of the Trinity appears to be nothing more than a rational demonstration of the divine Persons.[35] "Philosophical concerns rather than the revelation of God in Christ are assumed to be the basis for the discussion of this doctrine since all divine works *ad extra* are common to the three Persons and accordingly give us no information about the Person's proper identities."[36] Among these critics was Rahner who thinks the Thomistic Trinitarian theology, together with Augustine's *De Trinitate*, are symptomatic of the problem of the Latin Trinitarian tradition that "begins with the one God, the one divine essence as a whole, and only afterwards does it see God as three in persons."[37] Rahner, like other critics, thinks the Augustinian-Thomistic tradition separate the immanent life of God from the rest of the Christian faith, thereby rendering it irrelevant to the Christian faith and life.[38] They contend that Aquinas specifically "derives the divine Persons from the essence by means of psychological speculations" and that by "introducing the processions of divine Persons as acts of knowledge and love, Thomas appears to have pursued the same troublesome path paved by Anselm."[39] Anselm was invariably caught in this dilemma of multiplying divine Persons through psychological analogies in his *Monologion* (particularly chapters 61–63),[40] where such attempts at

---

33. Hunt, "Psychological Analogy and Paschal Mystery in Trinitarian Theology," 198, see n2. The Swiss, Hans Urs von Balthasar, is a good example of one who rejected the classical psychological analogy and re-thought the processions, not in classical categories, but in terms of what, for Balthasar, was revealed in the paschal mystery—self-emptying, self-sacrificing and dynamic nature of God's love. In other words, where classical analogy sought to explicate God in terms of absolute being, *Actus Purus*, Balthasar thought, not in terms of *Ipsum Esse Subsistence* but *Ipsum Amare Subsistence*. For more on Balthasar's critique of Augustinian-Thomistic psychological analogy, see Buckley, "Balthasar's Use of the Theology of Aquinas," 517–45.

34. See Aquinas, *Summa Theologica*.
35. Smith, *Thomas Aquinas' Trinitarian Theology*, 1.
36. Smith, *Thomas Aquinas' Trinitarian Theology*, 1.
37. Smith, *Thomas Aquinas' Trinitarian Theology*, 1; quoting Rahner, *Trinity*, 19.
38. Smith, *Thomas Aquinas' Trinitarian Theology*, 1.
39. Smith, *Thomas Aquinas' Trinitarian Theology*, 2.
40. See Anselm of Canterbury, *Complete Philosophical and Theological Treatises*.

multiplication "invariably leads to a multitude of processions, since each (resulting) Person will have his own knowledge and love."[41]

In fairness to Aquinas, there is no doubt that he vigorously advanced Christian Trinitarian theology "by reorganizing and clarifying certain key issues that had been poorly addressed by his predecessors."[42] But it is beyond the scope of this paper to attempt to determine the accuracy of the criticisms against his psychological analogy of the Trinity. That endeavor has been undertaken by Timothy L Smith whose refutation of criticisms against Aquinas would be too lengthy to discuss here.[43] What is relevant here is that Rahner has produced, in *The Trinity*, "the most original contemporary contribution to the theology of the Trinity"[44] that castigates mainstream Catholic theology for its dual ways of thinking about God. The essence of his argument is that the separation of Christian life and spirituality from the doctrine of the Trinity was a habit inherited from scholastic theology, particularly Thomas Aquinas. For Rahner, the habit of thinking about God under two headings, *De Deo Uno* (On the One God) and *De Deo Trino* (On the Triune God), which we have pointed out is a characteristic feature of Aquinas's theology, has not been helpful because it encourages a way of thinking about the Trinity as an addendum.

To be clear, it is not as if Rahner does not see the need to treat both topics. What he objects to, rather, is their separation, which he thinks has fueled the neglect of the latter, i.e., "On the Triune God." His reasoning is that in this disjunction, by the time we begin with a treatment of the first, i.e., On the One God, and walk our way up to the second, On the Triune God, it seems "as if everything which matters for us in God has already been treated in the treatise On the One God."[45] Shedding light on this important point, LaCugna writes that in Rahner's view, "Thomas Aquinas' approach, as taken over by Neo-Scholasticism, hardened the legitimate distinction between the treatises into two separate tracts, thereby making it possible for Christian theology to treat, first, God's unity, the divine essence, divine attributes, and divine names, and only secondarily consider matters distinctive to the divine persons (processions, relations, persons, *propria*, missions)."[46]

---

41. Smith, *Thomas Aquinas' Trinitarian Theology*, 2.

42. Smith, *Thomas Aquinas' Trinitarian Theology*, 10.

43. For a detailed refutation, see Smith, *Thomas Aquinas' Trinitarian Theology*, particularly ch. 5.

44. Congar, *I Believe in the Holy Spirit*, 11.

45. Rahner, *Trinity* (1999), 17.

46. Rahner, *Trinity* (1999), ix.

The Neo-Scholastic arrangement, in Rahner's view, creates "a false disjunction between faith and reason" in such a way that makes the tract on the Trinity seem as if it is not very essential to Christian faith.[47] For this reason, Rahner expresses the concern that "despite their orthodox confession of the Trinity, Christians are, in their practical life, almost mere 'monotheists.'"[48] Again Rahner thinks that the Augustinian tradition of thinking of God in terms of categories borrowed from Platonic philosophy, i.e., intellect-will-memory (psychological analogy) is certainly to blame for this disjunction of the "One God" and the "Triune God."[49] Needless to say that *The Trinity* is part of Rahner's wider "theological agenda for liberating Trinitarian theology from its Neo-Scholastic bondage."[50]

To achieve the goal of his Trinitarian theology, which is to restore to prominence a stress on the Trinity in the doctrinal and practical life of the Christian,[51] Rahner distances himself from the two ways to thinking of the Trinity, stemming again from scholastic distinction between economic Trinity (Trinitarian Persons as they are known to us when God reveals God's-self in the history of salvation) and immanent Trinity (Trinitarian Persons as they eternally are in themselves).[52] While not doubting the reasoning behind the psychological analogy, Rahner doubts its appropriateness, listing the following as a reason to jettison it: (1) The analogy uses a circular reasoning.[53] (2) The psychological analogy "isolates the doctrine of the Trinity from other major theological themes."[54] (3) The analogy "postulates from the doctrine of the Trinity a model of human knowledge and love, which either remains questionable, or about which it is not clear that is be more than a model of human knowledge precisely as finite."[55] (4) The analogy "neglects the experience of the Trinity in the economy of salvation in favor of a seemingly almost Gnostic speculation about what goes on the inner life of God."[56] (5) In relation to the Incarnation, the analogy makes

47. Rahner, *Trinity* (1999), ix.

48. Rahner, *Trinity* (1999), 10.

49. See Ables, "Decline and Fall of the West?," 164; referencing Rahner, "Some Implications of the Scholastic Concept of Uncreated Grace," 319–46; Rahner, "Remarks on the Dogmatic Treatise 'De Trinitate,'" 77–102 ; and Rahner, *Trinity* (1999).

50. Ormerod, "Two Points or Four," 663.

51. Lincicum, "Economy and Immanence," 112.

52. Ables, "Decline and Fall of the West?" 164.

53. Lincicum, "Economy and Immanence," 112.

54. Ormerod, "Two Points or Four?" 663.

55. Ormerod, "Two Points or Four?" 663; quoting Rahner, *Trinity* (1999), 117–18.

56. Lincicum, "Economy and Immanence," quoting Rahner, *Foundations of Christian Faith*, 135.

it possible for only "one'" of the Trinitarian Persons to take flesh "without attending to the specificity of the Word becoming flesh."[57]

Rahner thus fortifies his own alternative approach, laying bare an argument he calls *Grundaxiom*: that "The 'economic' Trinity is the 'immanent' Trinity and the 'immanent' Trinity is the 'economic' Trinity."[58] Rahner's essential argument (in the so-called Rahner's rule) in seeking a unity or relationship between the scholastic treatises on the One God and on the Triune God is that God did not just become incarnate, only the Second divine person became incarnate. As Catherine LaCugna writes in her introduction to *The Trinity*, "Rahner is critical of all those, including Thomas Aquinas (cf. *Summa Theologiae* III, q. 23, a. 2), who took the position that *any* divine person could have become incarnate."[59] Rahner reasons that if this were true then the incarnation does not tell us much about the intra-Trinitarian relations. In other words, if it was true that any of the divine persons could have become man, if God freely so decided, "then the incarnation of the Son would tell us nothing about the unique identity of the Son in his mission of Incarnation."[60]

Yves Congar has suggested three reasons why Rahner's *Grundaxiom* must be taken seriously. First, the Trinity is a mystery of salvation that was revealed to us. "Our recognition of this fact enables us to establish a relationship and even a unity between the treatises which to a great extent lacked this. This implies, however, that the Trinity in itself is also the Trinity of the economy."[61] Second, if there is a fundamental affirmation Rahner's *Grundaxiom* at least makes, it is regarding the incarnation—that "there is at least one 'sending,' one presence in the world, one reality in the economy of salvation which is not merely appropriated to a certain divine person, but is proper to him."[62] Third, the history of salvation is not just the history of God's revelation of God's-self, it is also a history of God's communication of God's-self and God's-self is the content of that self-communication. "The economic Trinity (the revealed and communicated Trinity) and the immanent Trinity are identical because God's communication of himself to men in the Son and the Spirit would not be a self-communication of God if what God is for us in the Son and the Spirit was not peculiar to God in himself."[63]

---

57. Ormerod, "Two Points or Four?" 663.
58. Rahner, *Trinity* (1999), 22.
59. Rahner, *Trinity* (1999), xii.
60. Rahner, *Trinity* (1999), xii.
61. Congar, *I Believe in the Holy Spirit*, 11.
62. Congar, *I Believe in the Holy Spirit*, 12.
63. Congar, *I Believe in the Holy Spirit*, 12.

Despite its wide acceptance, Rahner's axiom has not gone unchallenged and has even come under severe criticism, particularly from those theologians who think his position lends itself to modalism.[64] There is also the criticism that Rahner fails to adequately distinguish between the person and the nature of the Word, which makes his theology of Incarnation, according to those critics, to oscillate between Monophysitism and Nestorian alternatives.[65] Other critics wonder, if any of the divine Persons, for example, the Father, cannot become incarnate, whether that does not mean imperfection? Rahner had dismissed any suggestion of imperfection as "pure nonsense."

> He who denies that the Father or the Spirit too might have become man deny them a "perfection" only if it had first been established that such a possibility is a real possibility, hence a "perfection" for the Father or for the Spirit. But precisely this is not sure. Thus it is, for instance, a perfection for the Son as Son to descend from the Father. But it would be pure nonsense to conclude thence that the Father as such should also possess this perfection.[66]

Rahner is firm that the Father, by definition, is the Unoriginate, the one who in principle is "'invisible,' who reveals himself and appears precisely by sending his Word into the world. The Word is, by definition, immanent in the divinity and active in the world, and as such the Father's revelation."[67] Rahner's position has so many implications, which Robert Shillaker has summarized as follows:

> 1) It implies that there is nothing unique about the immanent Son-Father relationship that made the historical event of the incarnation of the Son, in particular appropriate. 2) What we can know of the Trinity we are told, by implication, not shown. So the immanent Trinity can be derived only from direct statements, and not from economic actions. 3) The terms "Father" and "Son," e.g., are not related to the economic action. This appears to make them a useless analogy: in what way is the Second Person the "Son," if he could equally have sent the Father to become an

---

64. See Moltmann, *Trinity and the Kingdom of God*, 144–48; Congar, *I Believe in the Holy Spirit*; Kasper, *God of Jesus Christ*; Dallvalle, "Revisiting Rahner," 213–27.

65. Ormerod, "Wrestling with Rahner on the Trinity," 213–27.

66. Rahner, *Trinity* (1999), 29; see n25.

67. Rahner, *Trinity* (1999), 29.

incarnate baby? If the term "Son" merely means that he became incarnate, then it is a truism about the economic action.[68]

What Rahner was after "is a way of eliminating any arbitrary relation between the divine nature and the Trinitarian processions, so that God's self-communication in history really corresponds to God's eternal being."[69]

Very much in the mold of Rahner who shows how a doctrine of grace must be consistent with a theology of God's-self-revelation in Christ, Robinson attempts to help Christian theology move away from a narrow understanding of the doctrine of the Trinity. A narrow view understands the doctrine primarily in terms of the intra-Trinitarian relations of the Father, Son, and Holy Spirit. Robinson wants something akin to Rahner's *Grundaxiom*. More importantly, Robinson's approach "draws on and develops the idea that it may be possible to find 'vestiges of the Trinity' in the created order."[70] By "vestige," Robinson does not mean "trace," since that implies a "weak or tenuous connection between the thing in question and its origin."[71] But by "vestige," he means "mark" or "imprint," in so far as it implies that there is a likeness between the created reality and God and also "that the likeness occurs by virtue of the manner in which that thing has been created."[72] Robinson's view here runs counter to that of Augustine who thought of "vestige" in terms of "trace" and who did not attempt to connect his idea of vestiges "with his reflections on the Trinitarian mediation of creation."[73] Robinson's idea also contrasts with Aquinas who also held that though the image of God is to be found in the faculties of knowing and willing possessed by rational creatures, "in other creatures there are lesser resemblances, mere vestiges of the creator."[74] Thus, Robinson's essential argument is that the Augustinian-Thomistic psychological analogy has led Christian theology to a "weaker" understanding of vestiges of the Trinity in creation.[75] He therefore suggests a stronger alternative using Peircean categories. I must admit that the structure of Robinson's argument is complex, but easy to understand once one gets over the first strand of the argument that is unpacked. I will attempt a synthesis of Peircean categories before presenting Robinson's alternative semiotic model of the Trinity.

68. Shillaker, "Rahner's Axiom," 35.
69. Ables, "Decline and Fall of the West?" 164.
70. Robinson, *God and the World of Signs*, 221.
71. Robinson, *God and the World of Signs*, 260.
72. Robinson, *God and the World of Signs*, 260.
73. Robinson, *God and the World of Signs*, 260.
74. Robinson, *God and the World of Signs*, 260.
75. Robinson, *God and the World of Signs*, 260.

Revisiting the Peircean Categories

In the next section we will exposit Robinson's use of Peirce's philosophy to show coherence with Christian teaching on the Trinity, intra-Trinitarian relations to be precise, with a view to showing how the semiotic model, as interpreted by Robinson, clarifies some age-long difficulties in Christian understanding of the Trinitarian persons and relations. Such an enterprise, in fairness, should be preceded by an annotation of Peirce's semiotics, the philosophy in which Peirce's metaphysical categories are embedded. But because a detailed discussion of Peirce's semiotics will be too far-fetched here, We shall offer only a skeletal outline—one that is germane to the semiotic model of Robinson— before delving into the Peircean metaphysical categories of Firstness, Secondness, and Thirdness. It is on these categories that Robinson hinges his bet on resonances of the categories with the Trinitarian Persons. Robinson is convinced that Peirce himself alluded to parallels between his triadic logic (including semiotics) and the Christian doctrine of the Trinity, as far back as the 1860s when "his categories were not yet fully worked out and his semiotics was at a very early stage of development."[76] Peirce was understood to have remarked in 1866 that "in many respects this trinity," i.e., his triadic logic and still to be worked out categories "agrees with the Christian trinity; indeed I am not aware that there any points of disagreement."[77]

While Robinson is correct about Peirce's remark about resonances of the Trinity in his triadic logic, what Robinson does not do sufficiently enough is offer a critique of Peirce's own thoughts. Peirce at times makes confusing and even contradictory statements that make it difficult to situate his thoughts, particularly since his thoughts were always evolving. While it is beyond the scope of this paper to offer a lengthy critique of Peirce's thoughts, a modicum of critique is however necessary to fully understand the extent to which his theory of signs can be appropriated in our understanding of the Trinity. There is no doubt that Peirce was an original and independent investigator who dealt with many complex and difficult subjects ranging from mathematics to logic, physics, astronomy, psychology, ethics, philosophy and science. He wrote for "a motley of variety of readers, ranging from scientific specialists and technical philosophers to the lay audience of his public lectures."[78] The complex nature of his thoughts and variety of audience for whom he wrote make him very difficult to read and less easy to understand. He also often invented his own technical terms (tychism,

---

76. Robinson, *God and the World of Signs*, 61.

77. Robinson, *God and the World of Signs*, 61. See also Peirce, *Charles S. Peirce Papers*.

78. Peirce, *Selected Writings*, ix.

agapism, and synechism, for example), often employing a vocabulary "remote from both ordinary and scientific discourse."[79] All these make him difficult to understand. It is no wonder, to quote the editor of his *Selected Writings*, tragically enough, he became "a solitary thinker exploring ideas beyond the range of most of his contemporaries."[80] These notwithstanding, a systematic organization of Peirce's thought, particularly his philosophic ideas, can play a leading role in clarifying some contentious philosophical and theological issues of our time. His analysis of signs in everyday and scientific usage, particularly his penetrating discussions of the triads of icons, index, and symbols, creatively addresses perennial problems of theory of knowledge and meaning.[81]

A) Peirce's Semiotics

Peirce devoted many years to the logical theory of signs and evolution of human thought throughout history. He, in fact, identified the historical evolution of thought with signs.[82] He thought of the universe generally as "perfused with signs."[83] Sign, for him, is "anything which determines something else (its interpretant) to refer to an object to which it itself refers (its object) in the same way, the interpretant becoming in turn a sign."[84] This means, for Peirce, that a sign consists, not of dyadic relation of the sign to its object, but of triadic elements: *representamen* (i.e., the sign-vehicle itself), the *object* (what is signified or referred to by the sign), and *interpretant* (that which is determined by the sign). In this triadic relation, the sign-vehicle in and of itself does not signify anything, "but is able to signify something (an object) to the extent that its relation to the object is such that an interpreting entity or agent may make a purposeful response to the sign."[85] The sign exists, irrespective of whether the interpreter is conscious of it, which means the interpretive response may be a response that is made consciously or unconsciously.[86] The relationship between the sign-vehicle-object-interpretant, the interpretant in turn yields another triad: an icon (a sign in which the

---

79. Peirce, *Selected Writings*, ix.
80. Peirce, *Selected Writings*, ix.
81. Peirce, *Selected Writings*, xii.
82. Peirce, *Selected Writings*, 380.
83. Robinson, *God and the World of Signs*, 15. See also Peirce, *Essential Peirce*, 2:394.
84. Peirce, *Collected Papers of Charles Sanders Peirce* (Citations refer to volume number and paragraph).
85. Robinson, *God and the World of Signs*, 18.
86. Robinson, *God and the World of Signs*, 18.

sign-vehicle has some qualitative resemblance to the object),[87] an index ("a sign in which the sign-vehicle stands for the object by virtue of a direct connection of a sort that manifests the brute actuality of Secondness"),[88] and a symbol (a sign "whose sign-vehicle stands for the object by virtue neither of resemblance or causation").[89]

A sign, in the Peircean sense, is not a special kind of thing, but anything which functions in a certain special way such that it can relate to a third thing. "Not only can anything function as a sign, but the very same sign vehicle can signify differently in different contexts."[90] The semiotic triads, for Peirce, are not static structures, but "moments in the dynamic flux of *semiosis*, a continuous process of semiotic growth."[91] A sign is so called only by virtue of the functional role it plays in the continuous process where signs interpret other signs endlessly.[92] Logically, then, there is no first or last sign, since we are involved in endless process of semiosis where one thing interprets the other. Peirce conceived the sign process as "a process without logical end and without logical beginning. Inasmuch as every sign, to be a sign, must potentially give rise to an interpretant which is itself a sign, obviously there can be no such thing as a last sign"[93] This is important for the argument that Robinson will develop regarding the immanent Trinity—that the order of the Trinitarian relations is a logical order, not an ontological order. We have already pointed out that the Trinitarian renaissance effected by both Barth and Rahner was motivated by the desire to move away from the traditional Western conception (substance-ontological thinking) in which God is self-sufficient unto God's-self and independent of the world to a relational ontology in which something is determined by its relations to another.[94] This relational ontology, in my view, are fleshed out in the semiotic triads that are underpinned by the three metaphysical categories of Firstness, Secondness, and Thirdness.[95] For Robinson cleverly uses this Peircean taxonomy of signs, particularly the way they are shaped by the scheme of categories to argue "that this dynamic interpenetration of the categories

---

87. Robinson, *God and the World of Signs*, 38.
88. Robinson, *God and the World of Signs*, 39.
89. Robinson, *God and the World of Signs*, 39.
90. Delaney, *Science, Knowledge, and Mind*, 135.
91. Robinson, *God and the World of Signs*, 20.
92. Delaney, *Science, Knowledge, and Mind*, 135.
93. Delaney, *Science, Knowledge, and Mind*, 139.
94. Wisse, *Trinitarian Theology beyond Participation*, 5.
95. Robinson, *God and the World of Signs*, 20.

in the world of signs offers an analogy for the perichoretic indwelling of the Trinitarian persons in the being of God."[96]

Peirce Taxonomy of Signs

Sign-Vehicle or *Representamen*	Object	Interpretant
Icon	Index	Symbol

B) The Categories

Peirce was motivated by a concern to develop a list of categories as a backbone or ground for his logic. Working out of the philosophical strictures of Immanuel Kant (1724–1804), Peirce was convinced "that philosophy needed a new set of categories if it was going to comprehend reality as revealed by science."[97] In 1867 when he was elected to the American Academy of Arts and Sciences Peirce presented three papers on logic. "These papers were the culmination of a very intense philosophical project that grew out of his reflections on Kant. They involved a fundamental critique of Cartesianism in all its guises, a critique informed by his developing views on the logic of science."[98] The third of the three papers titled "On a New List of Categories" Peirce proclaimed his "one contribution to philosophy."[99] It was also this paper that Peirce dubbed his gift to the world.[100] Peirce's aim in presenting the list of categories Firstness, Secondness, and Thirdness "was to identify a new set of universal a priori concepts intended to supersede those of Kant."[101] Elsewhere he calls these categories "cenopythagorean categories" because they are his own attempt to characterize what Hegel sought to characterize as his three stages of thought.[102] "They also correspond to the three categories of each of the four triads of Kant's table."[103] In his famous "Letters to Lady Welby," Peirce defined Firstness, Secondness, and Thirdness thus: "Firstness is the mode of being of that which is such as it is, positively and without reference to anything else. Secondness is the mode of being of that which is such as it is, with respect to a second but regardless of any third.

---

96. Robinson, *God and the World of Signs*, 43.
97. Delaney, *Science, Knowledge, and Mind*, 8.
98. Delaney, *Science, Knowledge, and Mind*, 8.
99. Robinson, *God and the World of Signs*, 21.
100. Robinson, *God and the World of Signs*, 21.
101. Robinson, *God and the World of Signs*, 21.
102. Peirce, *Selected Writings*, 384.
103. Peirce, *Selected Writings*, 384.

Thirdness is the mode of being of that which is such as it is, in bringing a second and third into relation to each other."[104]

Firstness can never be fully grasped. The nature of Firstness is that of being abstractable from relation or reference to anything else.[105] Secondness occurs when we encounter a phenomenon that involves otherness or difference.[106] As Peirce described it, "the Second is precisely that which cannot be the first. It meets us in such facts as Another, Relation, Compulsion, Effect, Dependence, Independence, Negation, Occurrence, Reality, Result. A thing cannot be other, negative, or independent, without a first to or of which it shall be other, negative, or independent."[107] Thirdness is a category that introduces the possibility of mediation, which cannot arise from Firstness or Secondness.[108] Since a "Third is something which brings a First into relation to a Second,"[109] the category of Thirdness, for Peirce, "bridges over the chasm between absolute first and last, and brings them into relationship."[110]

In sum, Firstness is characterized by "airy-nothingness," Secondness is characterized by the "Brute Actuality of things and facts," and Thirdness being the source of meaning and intelligibility in the universe establishes "connections between different objects."[111] The categories, as Peirce intended them, are comprehensive in the sense that they are sufficient in themselves and can encompass all possible phenomena without further expansion.[112] Like Peirce's triadic signs, the categories are also irreducible.[113] These characteristics of self-sufficiency and irreducible distinctiveness of the categories are important for Robinson's claim of strong similarities to the Christian doctrine of the Trinity.

---

104. Peirce, *Selected Writings*, 383.
105. Robinson, *God and the World of Signs*, 22.
106. Robinson, *God and the World of Signs*, 22.
107. Robinson, *God and the World of Signs*, 22. Quoting Peirce, *Essential Peirce*, 1:248–49.
108. Robinson, *God and the World of Signs*, 22.
109. Peirce, *Selected Writings*, 389.
110. Peirce, *Essential Peirce*, 1:249.
111. Robinson, *God and the World of Signs*, 23.
112. Robinson, *God and the World of Signs*, 23.
113. Robinson, *God and the World of Signs*, 23.

Peirce's Metaphysical Categories

Firstness	Ingenerate	Abstractable
Secondness	Otherness or difference	relation, negation
Thirdness	Mediation	bridges chasm between entities

Robinson does a fine job of showing that though the categories are derived metaphysically, Peirce also approached them in phenomenological terms. "The a priori and phenomenological derivations of the categories both give rise to the conclusion that the presence of one of the categories always carries with it the latent involvement of the others."[114] In other words, our encounter with Firstness necessarily gives rise to Secondness and Thirdness. In Peirce's own words, "Not only does Thirdness suppose and involve the ideas of Secondness and Firstness, but never will it be possible to find any Secondness or Firstness in the phenomenon that is not accompanied by Thirdness."[115] Firstness may be phenomenologically and logically prior to Secondness and Thirdness, but the logical priority does not necessarily equate to causal priority. In other words, "the logical priority of Firstness should not be understood to mean that all phenomena originate causally from Firstness."[116]

Relation of Sign-Vehicle to the Categories

Firstness	Sign-Vehicle or *Representamen*
Secondness	Sign-Object relation
Thirdness	Sign relation to Interpretant

Towards an Alternative Semiotic Model

Catherine LaCugna reminds the reader in her introduction to Rahner's *Trinity* of how the Neo-Scholastic dogmatic structure made Trinitarian theology merely speculative in the way it presented a Trinitarian theology that was disconnected from the revelation and experience of Father, Son, and Spirit in salvation history.[117] LaCugna sees Rahner's project in

---

114. Robinson, *God and the World of Signs*, 28.
115. Robinson, *God and the World of Signs*, 28. Quoting Peirce, *Essential Peirce*, 2:177.
116. Robinson, *God and the World of Signs*, 30.
117. Rahner, *Trinity* (1999), x.

the *Trinity* as part of a larger effort to make the doctrine intelligible (as opposed to shrouded in unexplainable mystery) and part of the effort to recover the biblical, creedal, liturgical and Greek emphasis on the diversity of the divine persons in salvation by an appeal to how the doctrine of the Trinity and the doctrine of salvation are one.[118] We see the same dual motives in the Peirce-derived semiotic model, which according to Robinson, yields a Trinitarian account of relations, as opposed to a relational account of the Trinity. "The three *hypostases* are distinct, and the possibility of this distinctiveness is derived from the distinction (Secondness) of the Son from the Father. The Father is not the Son, and the Son is not the Spirit, and the Spirit is not the Father, and all of these negations depend on the otherness that is grounded in the source of otherness, the Son."[119] For Robinson, all three Trinitarian persons are in communion with one another and these relations of communion are mediated by the Spirit, who is the source of all mediation.[120] There are then three kinds of relations, Firstness, Secondness, and Thirdness, which according to Robinson, can be understood analogously as *perichoresis* (the being-in-one-another or "permeation without confusion"). The Peircean system of categories or semiosis, in other words, models for Robinson a *perichoresis*.[121]

Relation of the Categories to the Trinitarian Persons

Firstness	abstractable, ingenerateness	Father is ingenerate
Secondness	otherness, difference	Son is other than the Father, uncreated
Thirdness	mediation, unifier	Spirit mediates between Father and Son and source of unity

As I have already hinted earlier, Christian discussions about the intra-Trinitarian relations often oscillate around two dangers: subordinationism (privileging the Father over and against the Son) and Tri-theism (three substances). Robinson thinks his semiotic model overcomes these dangers.

a) Overcoming Subordinationism

Robinson addresses the intra-Trinitarian relations by noting that God's revelation of Father, Son, and Holy Spirit must be understood as a genuine revelation of God's-self and that God's Threeness must also be understood

---

118. Rahner, *Trinity*, x.
119. Robinson, *God and the World of Signs*, 106.
120. Robinson, *God and the World of Signs*, 106–7.
121. Robinson, *God and the World of Signs*, 107.

as eternally real, not merely an appearance.[122] Once this is understood, the eternal Threeness, he insists, "must be spoken of in such a way as to avoid any implication that this is a contingent, rather than essential, feature of God."[123] In my view, it is in this respect that the semiotic model that Robinson employs becomes particularly helpful because of the distinct and enduring reality that each of the three of Peirce's categories possess. In Peirce's semiotics, Firstness, Secondness, and Thirdness are enduringly real in the world analogous to the way the Father, Son, and Spirit are eternally distinct in the being of God. Robinson's particular emphasis is that here "the ultimate ground of being is neither a neo-Platonic oneness (Firstness) or a Hegelian absolute intelligibility (Thirdness),"[124] but their enduring reality. This is why, for Robinson, the semiotic model "complies with the further desideratum of being consistent with the necessary (as opposed to contingent) Threeness of God because Peirce's categories are found to be phenomenologically comprehensive."[125] There is the further point that in Peirce's explication of the categories, no further categories are required beyond those of Firstness, Secondness and Thirdness in order to encompass all the observed characters of experience. It is for these reasons that Robinson thinks the semiotic model is "arguably superior" to the traditional psychological analogy and the contemporary alternatives to the psychological analogy, the social analogy of the Trinity,[126] to which I shall return later.

b) Overcoming Tri-theism

In keeping with his argument that the Threeness of God must be understood to be an essential, not an accidental attribute, Robinson appeals to and builds on the argument that the Cappadocian Fathers employed in defending themselves against suspicions of tri-theist tendencies in their way of speaking of three *hypostases*. These Fathers, particularly Basil, pointed out that there is a sense in which the category of numbers is inapplicable to the Godhead and that even if one were to apply numbers to God then one must do it "reverently."[127] Basil also pointed out "that although each of the persons is spoken of as 'one,' this does not imply that they can be taken as numerically equivalent in the sense that they may simply be added together."[128]

122. Robinson, *God and the World of Signs*, 103.
123. Robinson, *God and the World of Signs*, 104.
124. Robinson, *God and the World of Signs*, 104.
125. Robinson, *God and the World of Signs*, 104.
126. Robinson, *God and the World of Signs*, 104.
127. Robinson, *God and the World of Signs*, 104.
128. Robinson, *God and the World of Signs*, 104.

Robinson uses the semiotic model to add nuance to this argument by Basil. Robinson deduces that though we may speak of three categories, "the very notion of a three-fold distinction of categories draws on the category of Secondness, without which the difference (otherness) of the categories would not be recognized. Without Secondness counting to three (or to any other number) would not be possible: counting depends on distinguishing one thing from another, this number from the next."[129] Numbers must partake in the category of Thirdness to have any generality. In other words, the distinctive feature of the number three is that it is the number that allows other numbers to function.[130] Applied to the Trinity, this means that "the category of numbers arises from within the relations between the Trinitarian persons, not from outside them."[131]

c) Overcomes the Difficulties of the Psychological and Social Analogies

Augustine is credited with developing the now famous psychological analogy of the Trinity that originally stemmed from Gregory of Nyssa. Augustine used the triadic faculties of the human psyche: mind-knowledge-love, memory-understanding-will, and remembering-knowing-loving.[132] In Augustine, as Robinson understands his analogy, "the triad of mind-knowledge-love expresses the way in which the unified functioning of the psyche is constituted by an irreducibly threefold relation between elements that differ from one another and yet have no existence independent of the whole."[133] One of the merits of the psychological analogy is that it offers a way of thinking about the Three Persons of the Trinity without undermining their unity—a humanly constructed way of speaking of plurality in unity in the Godhead.[134] But from the evidence provided thus far, it is clear that the psychological analogy is not flawless, even by Augustine's standard. "Augustine himself acknowledged that his psychological analogies were imperfect because, although the various triads are found within the human being, they are not together sufficient to constitute the human psyche, whereas the Trinity is God, not something in God."[135] Critics have pointed out that the psychological analogy runs the risk of conceiving God

---

129. Robinson, *God and the World of Signs*, 105.
130. Robinson, *God and the World of Signs*, 105.
131. Robinson, *God and the World of Signs*, 105.
132. Robinson, *God and the World of Signs*, 315.
133. Robinson, *God and the World of Signs*, 315.
134. Robinson, *God and the World of Signs*, 315.
135. Robinson, *God and the World of Signs*, 320.

as an "isolated autonomous individual."¹³⁶ The latter criticism stems from the idea that as persons human beings are always in relation to other persons, which the psychological analogy does not address.¹³⁷ The same criticism is equally applicable to the Thomistic psychological analogy. It is fair to say that it is the recognition of the pitfalls of the Augustinian-Thomistic psychological analogy that made Robert Doran and Neil Ormerod to draw from Bernard Lonergan's work to start moving in a direction Doran calls a unified field structure.¹³⁸ Central to the structure, as Ormerod describes it "is a four-point hypothesis found in a recently published English translation of Lonergan's writings, which relates the supernatural realities of beatific vision, grace, and incarnation to the four inner Trinitarian relations as four created participations of the divine nature."¹³⁹

Whether or not the hypothesis is, as Ormerod has argued, "a radical advance on previous theological approaches that have sought a similar unification,"¹⁴⁰ there are critics who are bent on alternative model entirely—a social model that focuses on the Trinity as a community of persons and its implications for the human social community. Although there are hints of the social analogy of the Trinity in the writings of the Cappadocian Fathers, depending on how one reads them, the social model of the Trinity derives more specifically from the medieval works of Richard of St. Victor (1110–1173) who suggested that in order to be free from selfishness perfect love must involve three persons. More recently the social analogy has been developed more fully in the work of the German reformed theologian, Jürgen Moltmann (1926 –), who advanced the social analogy as an alternative to the psychological analogy of the Trinity. Like Rahner, Moltmann was deeply aware of the tension between monotheism and Trinitarianism in Christian theological thought. Again like Rahner, Moltmann deplores the classic approach to the doctrine of God that begins with a discussion of the One God before proceeding to a discussion of the Triune God.¹⁴¹ The problem, as another thinker in the mold of Moltmann has carefully illustrated it, is simply this:

> If the most important and foundational claims about the Living God can be made before the actual divine Persons are even

---

136. Robinson, *God and the World of Signs*, 316.

137. Robinson, *God and the World of Signs*, 316.

138. See Doran, "Starting Point of Systematic Theology," 750–76 and Ormerod, "Two Points or Four?" 661.

139. Ormerod, "Two Points or Four?" 661.

140. Ormerod, "Two Points or Four?" 662.

141. See Moltmann, *Trinity and the Kingdom of God*, 16–17.

mentioned, to what extent can such a doctrine of God claim to be genuinely Trinitarian? If the so-called essence of God is defined a priori, in advance of a careful investigation of the Three Persons who actually are the Living God, then we must expect that our thinking about God will tend to default to a kind of monotheism.[142]

Moltmann's social doctrine of the Trinity is intended to ameliorate this concern, which we have repeatedly pointed out is prevalent in the psychological analogy. The social doctrine of the Trinity will also avoid, for Moltmann, the danger of conceiving God as an "absolute subject."[143] Thus, Robinson is on the mark in assessing that social Trinitarians "hold that the relational basis of human personhood is a 'likeness' of the being of God. In other words, God has intentionally created human social relations in such a way as to resemble something about God's own being. Social Trinitarians, of course, then take the further step of suggesting that this likeness consists in a likeness of the relations between human persons to the relations between the Father, Son and Spirit."[144]

There is no doubt that there are varieties of the social model of the Trinity; each with its own particular emphasis. But as a unit what the social model seeks to refute is the suggestion that each of the three Persons of the Trinity does not possess its own distinct "center of consciousness."[145] Stanley Grenz has suggested that in so far as the social model of the Trinity "speaks of God as subsisting in three subjective centers of action, it has met not only remarkable applause but also rigorous critique."[146] In Balthasar we see an instance of the applause and critique Grenz is referring to. Balthasar, as already pointed out, rejects the psychological analogy as the primary analogy of the Trinitarian Persons. Yet Balthasar was equally critical of the social model deriving from Richard of St. Victor whom he thinks fails to "take into account the crude anthropomorphism involved in a plurality of beings."[147] In Balthasar's formulation of the model, for example, it is doxology, not praxis that is important. This is because Balthasar considers faith to be primarily an aesthetic act—seeing and beholding the glory of God

---

142. See Blackham, "Trinity in the Hebrew Scriptures," 36; referencing Watson, *Body of Divinity*.

143. Moltmann, *Trinity and the Kingdom of God*, 157.

144. Robinson, *God and the World of Signs*, 316–17.

145. Robinson, *God and the World of Signs*, 317; quoting Moltmann, *Trinity and the Kingdom of God*, 146.

146. Grenz, *Social God and the Relational Self*, 4.

147. Hunt, "Psychological Analogy and Paschal Mystery," 200; quoting Balthasar, *Dramatis personae*, 527.

precedes both belief in it and its expression in praxis.[148] Balthasar conceives the Trinitarian relations in terms of a kenotic community based on mutual self-giving and self-emptying of the Trinitarian Persons, as evidenced in the death of Christ on the Cross.[149] But Robinson contends that it is in this insistence that each of the Trinitarian Persons possesses a distinct center of consciousness that the flaw in the social model becomes more apparent—that the social analogy implies a tri-theism because it does not adequately account for the unity of God and, most importantly, "the desideratum of giving an account of the distinctiveness of the persons and their limitation to three in number is much more difficult for social models than it is for psychological analogies."[150]

Although he does not fully favor the psychological analogy, left with two alternatives, i.e., the psychological analogy and the social analogy, Robinson sees more resonances of his semiotic model in the psychological analogy than in the social analogy. First, in the semiotic model, as in Augustine's psychological analogy, "the three *hypostases* are understood as corresponding to what may be regarded as aspects of the internal structure of thought. . . According to Augustine, perception involves three elements: (1) the external objects; (ii) the mind's interpretation of the object; and (iii) 'the intention or act of focusing the mind.' These three elements arguably have some similarities with the Peircean triad of object, sign-vehicle (in this case mental sign), and interpretant (a mental 'act') respectively."[151] Second, the Thomistic variation of the psychological analogy also has, according to Robinson, Peircean resonances. While the parallels between Aquinas's *verbum mentis* (word in the mind) may not be exact with Peircean terms, "the semiotic model and Aquinas' concept of the *verbum mentis* have in common the possibility of giving an account why the second person of the Trinity is called the Word and why the origin ("procession") of the Spirit is different from the generation (begetting) of the Son."[152] For Robinson, in other words, the Peircean triads of Firstness-Secondness-Thirdness and object-sign-interpretant are functionally equivalent to Augustine's psychological analogy, and like the psychological analogy, the semiotic model seeks to offer a way of understanding how the Trinitarian Persons "are irreducibly distinct from one another, and why they are limited to three (not four, five, or more.)"[153]

148. Hunt, "Psychological Analogy and Paschal Mystery," 188–89.
149. See Balthasar, *Mysterium Paschale*.
150. Robinson, *God and the World of Signs*, 317.
151. Robinson, *God and the World of Signs*, 318.
152. Robinson, *God and the World of Signs*, 319.
153. Robinson, *God and the World of Signs*, 320.

While there are resonances between the semiotic model and the psychological analogies, the semiotic model, for Robinson, is also an improvement on the psychological analogies because "it is based on an account of mental processes that claims to be an intrinsically (rather than arbitrarily) triadic in structure."[154] Also Peirce semiotics not only holds the possibility of demonstrating consonance with contemporary approaches to psychology and neurobiology, but can also contribute to current investigations in cognitive science and philosophy of mind, things that the psychological analogies cannot do.[155]

Ramifications for *Filioque* Controversy

Robinson is convinced that the semiotic model can contribute to an understanding of the troublesome concept of "procession" of the Spirit that is at the heart of the problem between the East-West divide and by so doing make a useful contribution to the *filioque* debate. His argument here begins with a historical analysis, which correctly traces the origin of the *filioque* controversy to the Trinitarian orthodoxy that took shape in the second half of the fourth century, led largely by the Cappadocian Fathers, a group that played an important role in advancing Christian thinking about the Spirit. Even before the Cappadocian Fathers, Athanasius had led the way by developing a pneumatological reflection geared towards countering the position of the Tropici or Pnuematochians (a name that literally means "Spirit-fighters"), as they are sometimes called—a group that affirmed the divinity of the Son, but denied divinity of the Spirit.[156] The Pneumatochians, in Robinson's apt summary of their position, held "that no other form of relationship could be conceived of within the Godhead other than that of the Father-Son: therefore, the Spirit must either be another unoriginated principle alongside the Father or a generated brother of the Son."[157] Athanasius rejected the view that the Spirit was a creature. Following on his theology of the Word that was accepted at Nicea (325 CE), Athanasius developed the argument "that, if our salvation depends on a relationship with God that is grounded in the work of the Spirit, then the Spirit must, like the Son, be of one substance (*homoousios*) with the Father." This view became the orthodox position of the Council of Alexandria (362 CE).[158] While Athanasius's view became a

---

154. Robinson, *God and the World of Signs*, 320.
155. Robinson, *God and the World of Signs*, 320.
156. Robinson, *God and the World of Signs*, 90.
157. Robinson, *God and the World of Signs*, 91.
158. Robinson, *God and the World of Signs*, 90–91.

reference point for Catholic orthodoxy thereafter, the matter of the Spirit's divinity was far from settled.

The Cappadocian Fathers took upon themselves the task of responding to the objection of the Pneumatochians and advancing the full divinity of the Spirit. First, they rejected the view that the *homoousion* of the Spirit implied that the Father had two Sons.[159] Basil of Caesarea led the way by distinguishing between "the generation of the Son and the breathing of the Spirit (cf. John 20:22)."[160] Following Basil, Gregory of Nazianzus used the vague term "procession" to speak of the origin of the Spirit.[161] But as Robinson points out, Gregory can no more explain what "procession" means any more than his adversaries can explain what "the Father's *agennesia* or the Son's generation" means.[162] Gregory of Nyssa's own contribution was to provide a definitive statement: "that the Father is the *cause* of the Son and Spirit, who are themselves both *caused*; and that the Son and Spirit are further distinguished by the Son being produced from the Father *directly*, whilst the Spirit *proceeds* from the Father *through* the Son."[163] Although the Council of Constantinople adopted Gregory of Nazianzus's position that the Spirit "proceeds" from the Father, the standard teaching of the Eastern Church, that the Spirit proceeds out of the Father through the Son, according to Robinson, follows from this definitive statement of Gregory of Nyssa's.[164]

What would later be known as the *filioque* controversy stems from different understandings of the East and West on the Nicene-Constantinople creedal statement that the Spirit "proceeds" from the Father. In the West this was understood to mean the Spirit "proceeds" from the Father and the Son, as in the examples of Tertullian and Hillary of Poitiers who taught that the Spirit originated from the Father through the Son.[165] The East, according to Robinson, had no difficulty in accepting the formulations of Tertullian and Hilary. But the seed of the problem was sown when Augustine taught that the Spirit proceeds from the Father "and from the Son (*filioque*)."[166] It would seem that Augustine, without intending it, had sown the seed of a bitter divide between the Eastern and Western churches. As Robinson remarked:

---

159. Robinson, *God and the World of Signs*, 91.
160. Robinson, *God and the World of Signs*, 91.
161. Robinson, *God and the World of Signs*, 91.
162. Robinson, *God and the World of Signs*, 91.
163. Robinson, *God and the World of Signs*, 91.
164. Robinson, *God and the World of Signs*, 91.
165. Robinson, *God and the World of Signs*, 92.
166. Robinson, *God and the World of Signs*, 92.

Augustine's position on the procession of the Spirit was, in fact, quite nuanced. He developed the idea that the Son's agency was necessary for the production of the Spirit but emphasized that this was only "through the gift of the Father," thus retaining the principle that the Father is the ultimate origin of the Trinitarian persons. It was not until the sixth or seventh centuries that Spanish theologians began to add the *filioque* to the Creed, possibly with the original intention of opposing modalist heresies by emphasizing the distinctiveness of the Father and the Son, or of refuting Arian tendencies by affirming their equality. From the ninth century the phrase was commonly used in Western liturgy and it was formally added to the Creed in the West in the eleventh century. Unfortunately, the nuances of Augustine's position had now been lost and the *filioque* had become one (though not the only) cause of the schism between East and West.[167]

Why does the *filioque* clause matter? The East objected to the clause on two grounds: "that it undermines the unity of God by replacing the single unoriginated source of divinity (the Father) with two equal sources (Father and Son)"[168] and that the clause "is an illegitimate unilateral addition to the Creed agreed at the ecumenical Council of Constantinople."[169] The West, on the other hand, favors the clause on the grounds "that it is not intended as a denial of the monarchy of the Father, but as an acknowledgment of the equality and inter-relatedness of all three Trinitarian persons."[170]

There are accordingly three possible ways of resolving the *filioque* controversy, in principle at least, in Robinson's view. The first approach would be to decide unequivocally in favor of one side (East or West) or the other based on the merit of theological arguments alone.[171] The second approach would be "to favor one or the other version of the creed in liturgical use, but to argue that it may in fact be interpreted in such a way as to address the concerns of adherents to the alternative version."[172] The third approach would be for both sides "to agree to a mutually acceptable re-wording of the Creed."[173] Assuming it is feasible to adopt anyone of these approaches, it is still doubtful if any of the approaches can resolve the ecclesiological impasse that led to the separation of the East and West. Moreover, "while any of

---

167. Robinson, *God and the World of Signs*, 92.
168. Robinson, *God and the World of Signs*, 92.
169. Robinson, *God and the World of Signs*, 92.
170. Robinson, *God and the World of Signs*, 92–93.
171. Robinson, *God and the World of Signs*, 93.
172. Robinson, *God and the World of Signs*, 93.
173. Robinson, *God and the World of Signs*, 93.

these three possible approaches might be capable of patching up some of the theological difficulties posed by the *filioque* it seems that any of them would face considerable barriers to full acceptance by both sides of the dispute, at least as long as they are based on the affirmation that the origin of the Spirit is by 'procession.'"[174] The main obstacle, for Robinson, therefore, remains what is meant by the word "proceed," a word that even the Patristic writers that first employed it were not clear about its meaning.

Robinson suggests that a first step towards resolving the controversy is to drop the "mysterious term 'procession'"[175] and replace it with "a positive account of the nature of the Spirit as the source of mediation and interpretation."[176] In Robinson's semiotic model, "the Spirit is acknowledged to be logically dependent on the Father and the Son (in that order) in the same way that Thirdness is logically dependent on Secondness, and Secondness on Firstness."[177] In this way of conceiving it, the Spirit may then be understood as arising from the Father (Firstness) and the Son (Secondness), "but not in a way that undermines the unique unoriginateness of the Father."[178] Robinson insists that this way of conceiving "procession" avoids any danger of subordinationism because the logical order of Father, Son, and Spirit, like the logical order of Firstness, Secondness, and Thirdness, is to be understood as mere "logical taxis, not an ontological hierarchy."[179] The logical taxis also puts to rest the claim of the Pneumatochians (that the Father had two Sons) "because the Spirit is understood to have an entirely distinctive mode of origination from, and relation to, the Father (and the Son)."[180] The Son is the ground of otherness and related to the Father by being different. The Spirit is the ground of mediation by related to the Father and Son by mediating between them.[181]

Robinson's next step, related to the first, is to offer a clarification, philosophically, on what is meant by the word "procession." This entails re-interpreting the word "proceed" to mean that the Spirit is related to the Father and the Son analogously to the way Thirdness is related to Firstness and Secondness in Peircean metaphysics.[182] The Holy Spirit would be understood here as

174. Robinson, *God and the World of Signs*, 93.
175. Robinson, *God and the World of Signs*, 94.
176. Robinson, *God and the World of Signs*, 94.
177. Robinson, *God and the World of Signs*, 94.
178. Robinson, *God and the World of Signs*, 94.
179. Robinson, *God and the World of Signs*, 94.
180. Robinson, *God and the World of Signs*, 94.
181. Robinson, *God and the World of Signs*, 94.
182. Robinson, *God and the World of Signs*, 94.

the "gift of the Father" (John 14:26; 15:26). This is in line with Peirce's account of the irreducibility of Thirdness.[183] As the "gift" of the Father, the Spirit is the ground of all mediation given by the Father to the Son.[184] For Robinson, "there is no fundamental ontological reason to suppose any of giver, receiver or gift to be necessarily inferior to any of the others (though in creaturely giving the value of a gift may, of course, be less than that of either)."[185] The Spirit is the gift of the Father to the Son, but the Spirit is also the ground of its own giving, analogously to the way there can be no mediation without Thirdness and similar to the way there can be no otherness without Secondness (Son).[186] "Thus the Father is the source of the Spirit as *gift* to the Son, but is only able to be the source of the gift by virtue of the reality of *otherness* (grounded in the Son) and *mediation* (grounded in the Spirit)."[187] This changes the pneumatological clause of the creed to read as follows:

Nicene-Constantinople Pneumatological Clause

> We believe in the Holy Spirit,
> the Lord, the giver of life,
> who proceeds from the Father and the Son...

Semiotic Pneumatological Clause

> We believe in the Holy Spirit,
> the Lord, the giver of life,
> who is the gift of the Father through the Son...[188]

What Robinson accomplishes by the statement the Spirit is the "gift" of the Father is identify the Spirit's distinct mode of origination, i.e., that the Spirit is "given" by, not "begotten" by. "The reworded clause thus refers to the immanent Trinitarian relations as well as their outworking in the economy of salvation."[189]

---

183. Robinson, *God and the World of Signs*, 95.
184. Robinson, *God and the World of Signs*, 96.
185. Robinson, *God and the World of Signs*, 96.
186. Robinson, *God and the World of Signs*, 96.
187. Robinson, *God and the World of Signs*, 96.
188. Robinson, *God and the World of Signs*, 95.
189. Robinson, *God and the World of Signs*, 96.

CONCLUSION

The renaissance in Trinitarian theology effected by Barth and Rahner involves reflections on the revelation of the triune God who is "for us fully revealed and fully concealed in His self-disclosure."[190] From this Trinitarian renaissance we learn, not only that the doctrine of the Trinity is central to a theologian's overarching task, but also that the doctrine of the Trinity "must have an explanatory and regulatory use in the whole of theology."[191] This brings us to the matter of adequacy of the various analogies for understanding the Trinity. The adequacy or appropriateness of an analogy lies in the kind of theology it produces.[192] Rahner and Moltmann both reject the psychological analogy because it makes Christians seem, to use Rahner's word, "Unitarians." As others have pointed out, "the primary problem is that the analogy's inward direction affirms the tendency to look for the essence or ontological foundation within or behind the three persons."[193] Although Rahner has squarely put the blame for the abstract speculation about the being of God on the door steps of Augustine and Aquinas, Rahner himself has been plagued by the limitations of the same psychological analogy he relied on to advance a discussion of what it means to speak of what God is in God's self and what God is for us.[194]

Not to take anything away from Rahner who, to his credit, developed his *Grundaxiom* as a way of refuting the idea of maintaining an ontological difference between economic and immanent Trinity. For Rahner, God truly is as God reveals God's-self to be and God's-self is truly as God has revealed God's-self to be.[195] Thus, the *Grundaxiom* throws light on our understanding of the Trinitarian relations and processions. According to LaCugna, the axiom stems not from a priori principles, but from salvation history. In other words, the axiom is more properly "a methodological rather than ontological insight: the order of theological knowledge must adhere to the historical form of God's self-communication in Christ and the Spirit."[196] However, the axiom does not address the important matter of "how to maintain the freedom of God's Trinitarian self-communication," since "divine freedom was

---

190. Metzger, "Introduction," 5; quoting Barth, *Church Dogmatics*, 341.
191. Metzger, "Introduction," 5.
192. Robinson, "Trinity," 57.
193. Robinson, "Trinity," 57.
194. Robinson, "Trinity," 57; referencing LaCugna, *God For Us*, 222.
195. Rahner, *Trinity* (1999), xiv.
196. Rahner, *Trinity* (1999), xv.

not the issue around which he formulated the axiom."[197] More importantly, to quote LaCugna, Rahner's rule "fails to shed light on an adequate way to maintain both the ontological difference between God and creation, and the ontological relatedness of God to creation."[198]

The social model of the Trinity has not been iron-clad either. One major difficulty with the social model is that it tends to view the human community as a mirror of the divine community. "While we may speak of the persons of the Trinity in communion with one another, or perichoretically united to one another, such unification cannot be equated with human concepts of unity because we know that God is one in a way that humans cannot be."[199] Apart from missing the intrinsic difference between the human community and the divine community, the social analogy's quest to seek community or communion that can be applied equally to both God and humanity "results in the same problems that are seen with the psychological analogy, where the emphasis is on a shared ontological basis found in both divine and human being."[200]

The alternative to the psychological analogy or the social model of the Trinity may not necessarily be the semiotic model. But the Peirce-derived semiotic model, which Robinson applies to Christian anthropology and Christology answers some key questions Rahner's axiom leaves unanswered. Most importantly, the semiotic model sheds light on the matter of divine freedom in creation and, if further explored, can lead to the idea that it is possible to find "vestiges of the Trinity in the created order."[201] In the final analysis, the doctrine of the Trinity is in constant need of fresh insights in order to make the doctrine intelligible and applicable to Christian practice and life. This is precisely what Robinson has done creatively well, appropriating the semiotic model, and using it to depict means by which the triune God may become accessible to rational thought.

197. Rahner, *Trinity* (1999), xv.
198. Rahner, *Trinity* (1999), xv.
199. Robinson, "Trinity," 57.
200. Robinson, "Trinity," 57.
201. Robinson, *God and the World of Signs*, 221.

Chapter Seven

Soteriology

WE HAVE OFFERED REASONS why the starting point of Christology should not be an abstract metaphysical speculation of who Jesus is or was. We have argued rather that the starting point of Christology should be an experiential metaphysics that can grasp the highest grades of reality. This is not only because of the openness to verification of such a metaphysics of presence, but also because it is in tune with the scientific temper of our age. We located this experiential metaphysics in the works of the philosopher-semiotician C.S Peirce and found its cognate in the work of the philosopher-theologian Bernard Lonergan. In some ways, this idea also resonates in the works of some contemporary theologians, like Wolfhart Pannenberg (1928–2014), Gerhard Ebeling (1912–2001), Jürgen Moltmann (1926–), Karl Rahner (1904–1984), Hans Kung (1928–), Walter Kasper (1933–), Edward Schillebeeckx (1914–2009), Jon Sobrino (1927–), and Gerald O'Collins (1932–). In spite of their methodological differences, these theologians all share the idea that the point of departure of Christology should not be abstract metaphysical speculation of divine Sonship of Jesus, but the life, death, and resurrection of Jesus as found in the New Testament writings.[1] Karl-Josef Kuschel has spoken of this as an ecumenical consensus.[2]

This concluding chapter is about soteriology. Almost all Christological conceptions throughout history have had soteriological motifs.[3] Soteriol-

---

1. Byrne, "Christ's Pre-existence in Pauline Soteriology," 308.

2. Byrne, "Christ's Pre-existence in Pauline Soteriology," 308. See also Kuschel, *Born before All Time?*, 424–28.

3. Pannenberg, *Jesus—God and Man*, 39.

ogy pertains to how various realities are ordered to follow each other: why salvation follows on Jesus's suffering, why punishment follows sin, and how the Cross of Christ helps our present trials and tribulations.[4] If ever there was an ecumenical consensus on the starting point of Christology, the consensus has not yet been extended to soteriology. The lack of ecumenical consensus regarding the starting point of soteriology has led one writer to suggest that what we have in soteriology today is a "confusion of tongues." In other words, the way theologians understand the saving work of Christ is more dependent on their methodological standpoints and basic assumptions than on anything else.[5] While there is no attempt here to dismiss completely this position, this chapter sees more evidence to the contrary—that it is in the arena of Soteriology that ecumenical consensus is even clearer. One reason why the latent ecumenical consensus in soteriology has not been as apparent as it should is due to the neglect of semiotics. The chapter intends to show that both the Scriptures and the writings of the Fathers on soteriology anticipate a semiotic understanding and that the traditional exposition of Christian view of atonement will benefit from a revision that reflects this semiotic understanding, if the ecumenical consensus we seek on the matter is to be made clearer.

New Testament scholars no longer explore metaphors exclusively with respect to the parables of Jesus; they now connect the language of soteriology with metaphors.[6] Jesus's whole life included numerous signs of different kinds: his words (symbols), parables (icons), death on the Cross (indexical of his obedience to the Father).[7] It is precisely because they understand the symbolism of Christ's life and death that the New Testament writers employ the language that was accessible to ordinary people, using images and metaphors to convey their message. In the sections that follow, we will trace the soteriological understandings of the Scriptures and the Church Fathers, as well as the soteriological understandings of Protestantism, and even of some contemporary critics of medieval soteriology. We will highlight their implicit semiotic motif. Using these as a heuristic or antecedent probability (to borrow Newman's phrase), the chapter will show why the language of these texts should be read symbolically. The very fact that their imageries are multivalent offers a clue. It is by doing so that the ecumenical consensus in soteriology can be made clearer and starker. There is a long-standing tradition in the German-speaking world that goes back to Georg F. Hegel

---

4. Mooney, "Lonergan's Soteriology," 24.
5. Bloesch, "Soteriology in Contemporary Christian Thought," 132–44.
6. Cimala, "Paul's Metaphorical Soteriology," 354–55.
7. Robinson, *God and the World of Sign*, 125.

(1770–1831) and Friedrich W. Schelling (1775–1854) and through them to David Strauss (1808–1874), Ludwig Feuerbach (1804–1872), Arthur Schopenhauer (1788–1860), and Friedrich Nietzsche (1844–1900)—that mythology and symbol are the keys to religion. Building on the efforts of these predecessors, Sigmund Freud (1856–1939) suggested somewhat correctly that religion was a metaphor, notwithstanding that he meant it as an attack on religion.[8] Our use of symbols and metaphors with regard to soteriology have positive resonances and is in no way intended in the Freudian sense. One of the benefits of semiotics is that it moves soteriology away from what has long been known to be the "original sin of religion"—literalism.[9]

SOTERIOLOGY OF THE SCRIPTURES

In keeping with our diachronic and synchronic approach, we begin our examination of soteriology by investigating how the early Christian writers thought and spoke of salvation. It is hard to dispute Gustaf Aulen's assertion that the early Church did not have a well-developed doctrine of atonement.[10] But that is not to say that theology of atonement was not part of the New Testament Christology. The patristic writers, whose reflections on the significance of Christ's redemptive work became classic, relied heavily on the New Testament. Earlier in chapter three, we saw how the early disciples of Jesus employed symbolic narratives to describe their understanding of the man they called Christ. Drawing from the symbols and imageries of their Jewish and Hellenistic backgrounds, they became convinced that Jesus is Lord, the Son of Man, the pre-existent *Logos*, the Wisdom of God, the Suffering Servant, and the Messiah. Based on their understandings of who Jesus is in himself and for them, they developed a symbolism that thought of themselves as the New Israel. Within these narratives, which they found congenial both for themselves and their conception of Jesus, "soteriology found expression at the level of image and metaphor."[11]

a) Soteriology of the Gospels

The first four Gospels and Acts use a cluster of metaphors, like "save," "liberation," "healing," "restitution," and "reconciliation," to speak of the physical and spiritual restoration the Christ-event brings. These first five

---

8. Tacey, *Religion as Metaphor*, 15.
9. Tacey, *Religion as Metaphor*, xi.
10. Aulen, *Christus Victor*, 1.
11. Loewe, "Jesus the Savior."

books of the New Testament use the metaphor of "expiation of sin" and the "cultic sacrifice" of Jesus the eternal High Priest to speak of the redemption brought about by Jesus's act of sacrifice. Foundational to each of these texts is the event of the death of Jesus.[12] At the heart of the Johannine soteriology is the key text of John 3:16 (a close conceptual parallel of 1 John 4:9): "For God so loved the world that he gave His only begotten Son that whosoever believes in him shall not perish but have eternal life."[13]

b) Soteriology of the Pauline and Petrine Epistles

New Testament scholars are now beginning to identify thematic correspondence between the Gospels, Mark especially, and Paul in the area of soteriology. They point to their shared emphases on the event of the Cross—that the death of Jesus is the supreme eschatological event for humanity.[14] Mark also has a thematic correspondence with Peter in their shared emphases on Christ's compassion, His transcendent presence, and His personal commitment towards the faithful. They both depict the risen Jesus, not only as eternally committed to the faithful, but also as "presently available to them in a deeply solicitous and beneficent fashion."[15] New Testament scholars have also identified the presence of "compassionate soteriology"[16] in Mark and I Peter (as well as the letter to the Hebrews). The presence of "compassionate soteriology" can equally be extended to the Pauline letters.

New Testament scholars have a long history of interest in the nature of Jesus's death and its articulation in Paul's theology as penal substitution.[17] The connection between soteriology and symbolic language here cannot be denied. In Paul where the traditional concepts of salvation are largely derived, the movement from non-salvation to salvation, which Christ effected, is depicted in symbolic imagery drawn from everyday life.[18] Paul uses imageries like "justification," "reconciliation," "redemption," "forgiveness," and "adoption." In Pauline letters where salvation is multidimensional, soteriology focuses on the relation between Christ's death on the Cross, his resurrection, and human salvation.[19] Paul treats

---

12. McCruden, "Compassionate Soteriology," 41.
13. Frick, "Johannine Soteriology and Aristotelian Philosophy," 415–21.
14. McCruden, "Compassionate Soteriology," 42. See also Marcus, "Mark—Interpreter of Paul," 479.
15. McCruden, "Compassionate Soteriology," 55.
16. McCruden, "Compassionate Soteriology," 51.
17. Williams, "Violent Atonement in Romans," 579.
18. See Theissen, "Soteriologische Symbolik," 282–304.
19. Cimala, "Paul's Metaphorical Soteriology," 352.

soteriology as essentially Trinitarian because it includes what the Father has done through Christ to deliver humanity from sin and death, by participation in the spirit.[20] Although salvation has already taken place in Christ, it also has an eschatological dimension. It is a promise already accomplished and yet still anticipated (Rom 8:19–25)—a promise with "an already not yet" character."[21] The eschatological or apocalyptic character of Paul's soteriology, i.e., the tension between the already and the yet to be, is not in Paul's thought a dialectic, but a consequence of us finding ourselves in an unfinished plot line.[22] It is not a dialectic, but a semiosis—it is already here, but still unfinished. Paul hinges his soteriological narrative on the death and resurrection of Jesus. He sees Jesus's death as both an expression of God's love and Jesus's own act of fidelity.[23] Thus, in Paul, salvation can be couched in both positive and negative terms—as a transfer from an old evil state to a new good state; from slavery, under sin and death, to freedom, adopted children of God with inheritance rights.[24] In this the subjective and objective character of salvation is made manifest. Salvation is a divine redemptive action: "In Christ God was reconciling the world to Himself (2 Cor 5:19). The divine response also demands human response: "We entreat you on behalf of Christ, be reconciled to God" (2 Cor 5:20).[25] Thus, Paul's soteriological narrative is participatory—salvation is guaranteed in so far as we respond to God's offer of love.[26] "A participatory soteriology ensures that salvation always has an Ecclesial character: we are not saved as solitary individuals, but we become incorporate in Christ, so that our fate is bound together not only with him but also with our brothers and sisters in him. Second, participation in Christ entails conformity to the pattern of self-sacrificial love that he embodied and enacted on our behalf (as Gal 2:19b–20 elegantly suggests)."[27]

Thus, the images used by Paul to speak of the transition from one sinful state of bondage to the devil to a grace-filled freedom in Christ Jesus are very symbolic. Paul uses ordinary imagery to bring out profound significance. This profound significance of Paul's imagery is sometimes called

20. Cimala, "Paul's Metaphorical Soteriology," 352.
21. Cimala, "Paul's Metaphorical Soteriology," 353.
22. Hays, "Christ Died for the Ungodly," 48–68, 61.
23. Hays, "Christ Died for the Ungodly," 62.
24. Cimala, "Paul's Metaphorical Soteriology," 353.
25. Cimala, "Paul's Metaphorical Soteriology," 353.
26. Hays, "Christ Died for the Ungodly," 62.
27. Hays, "Christ Died for the Ungodly," 62.

"metaphorical soteriology."[28] In general, what we see in Paul is a plurality of imageries and metaphors for speaking about soteriology. Paul's theological language of soteriology is grounded in a story—a first order kerygmatic narrative about Jesus.[29]

The epistles of Peter, like the Pauline ones, speak of salvation as a realized and a future event, with emphasis, however on the future event. In the realized dimension of salvation, Peter uses metaphors to speak of the ways individuals are incorporated into God's kingdom.[30] It makes use of descriptors like, "born again" (1 Pet 1:3; 23), "redeemed by the blood of Jesus" (1 Pet 1:18–19), "chose" (1 Pet 1:1; 2:9); and "called" (1 Pet 1:15; 2:9). Those captured by these descriptors essentially have a new birth, which makes them "a chosen race, a royal priesthood, a holy nation, a people for whom God has reserved his possession" (1 Pet 2:9).[31] Peter also invokes subsidiary images, like sheep returning to the shepherd (1 Pet 2:25; 5:2) and the mortally wounded being healed (1 Pet 2:24).[32] The metaphor of "born again" is used to indicate the change of status by which people outside of God's kingdom become a part of God's people (1 Pet 2:10) and the language of transformation is used to indicate the change in identity that causes people to be incorporated into Christ (1 Pet 3:16).[33] "The transformation is caused by God's initiative and is possible because of the death of Christ on the Cross for sins (1 Pet 1:19; 2:24)."[34] However, Salvation in I Peter is primarily a future event to be revealed at the "end" of time, which is drawing near (1 Pet 4:7). It will be realized when Christ returns to the earth to bring salvation one last time (1 Pet 1:5:7).[35] The descriptors "end," "final judgment," "Christ's revelation," "grace," "blessing," "glory," and "joy" used in 1 Peter capture the "yet to be" pole of soteriology.[36]

In sum, in 1 Peter, soteriology includes "both a future consummation linked to Christ's eschatological return and a present inauguration described as a new birth because in Christ the salvation temporarily reserved for the

---

28. Cimala, "Paul's Metaphorical Soteriology," 355; see also Theissen, "Soteriologische Symbolik," 282.

29. Hays, "Christ Died for the Ungodly," 64.

30. Stewart, "When are Christians Saved and Why Does it Matter? 223.

31. Stewart, "When are Christians Saved and Why Does it Matter? 223.

32. Stewart, "When are Christians Saved and Why Does it Matter? 223. See also Rensburg, "Metaphors in the Soteriology in I Peter," 418–33.

33. Stewart, "When are Christians Saved and Why Does it Matter?" 223.

34. Stewart, "When are Christians Saved and Why Does it Matter?" 223.

35. Stewart, "When are Christians Saved and Why Does it Matter?" 225.

36. Stewart, "When are Christians Saved and Why Does it Matter?" 230.

new age has decisively broken into the present."[37] The two poles (future/present or realized/not yet) are connected by the initiative of the Triune God and human response to this initiative. God gives new birth, redeems, calls, and chooses and humans respond in faith and obedience.[38] "Christians must persevere through all of the sufferings of this present time and must pursue holiness, putting away sin in all of its forms while embracing love and humility in interpersonal relationships in order to survive the eschatological judgment and inherit salvation."[39] The relationship already initiated by the Triune God is what enables Christians to persevere to the end.

2 Peter calls Jesus "master" and speaks of Him as one who has purchased us as slaves. The author, however, does not say anything about how Jesus made this purchase and from whom He made the purchase. We are left to imply that we were slaves of corruption and defilements of this world (2 Pet 2:19–20) and that the purchase Christ made was through His blood.[40] To be a slave of corruption is to be self-destruct.[41] "Corruption" here is used to mean physical corruption—defilements of this world, living in error, and being prone to licentiousness. "Corruption" here is also used in a metaphorical or symbolic sense—that metaphorical or symbolic corruption is what leads to physical corruption.[42] Followers of Jesus appropriate the salvation won by Jesus, according to 2 Peter, by answering Jesus's call (i.e., faith) and recognizing Him as one called them by His own glory and excellence (2 Pet 1:3).[43] "The author presupposes that Jesus' death has transferred human beings from enslavement to corruption to his own service. However, this transfer does not take effect until it is known to have occurred."[44] The salvation procured by Jesus is a present reality. There is also a future final reality that will take place at the end of the world. Since the world has yet to come to a final end, it is possible to lose the present salvation by returning to sin. Jesus, however, will return at the end of the world and deliver a final eschatological judgment. This event will happen unexpectedly (2 Pet 3:10).[45]

The tendency in Church history, sad as it is, has been to favor one metaphor over the other, even though no one metaphor fully conveys

---

37. Stewart, "When are Christians Saved and Why Does it Matter?" 231.
38. Stewart, "When are Christians Saved and Why Does it Matter?" 231.
39. Stewart, "When are Christians Saved and Why Does it Matter?" 234.
40. Callan, "Soteriology of 2 Peter," 550.
41. Callan, "Soteriology of 2 Peter," 551.
42. Callan, "Soteriology of 2 Peter," 552.
43. Callan, "Soteriology of 2 Peter," 553.
44. Callan, "Soteriology of 2 Peter," 553.
45. Callan, "Soteriology of 2 Peter," 558.

what Paul or authors of the epistles of Peter are trying convey regarding the salvation brought about by Christ. Protestant tradition finds Paul's use of "justification" more attractive, the same way most of Western culture find the language of "freedom" and liberation" in Paul's soteriology more attractive.[46] No one single theological paradigm of metaphor or symbolism is sufficient for understanding the Christ-event in Pauline letters. How else might we interpret this text and the whole of Pauline's soteriology in ways consistent with what Paul wants to say about the saving event of Christ without invoking a violent model? The semiotic model, which enjoins us to see images or signs as open-ended, can challenge in a constructive way both the paradigms and metaphors of traditional soteriology. The language of soteriology is a language of metaphors. Most of these metaphors are often not clearly defined. All together, the New Testament uses a myriad of imageries to speak of salvation: salvation is the ushering in of God's kingdom (Matt 4:17), the entrance into the joy of the Lord (Matt 25:21–23), rebirth as children of God (John 1:12), justification and rescue from God's wrath (Rom 5:9; 3:23–25), the vision of God (1 Cor 13:12), union with Christ (Gal 3:27), filial adoption (Rom 8:15), reconciliation to God (2 Cor 5:18–21), a new creation (2 Cor 5:17), and sanctification in Christ (1 Cor 1:2, 31).[47] Far from being literal, these are symbolic terms in need of further refinements and understandings.

SOTERIOLOGY OF THE FATHERS

It is not the epistles of Peter, but Paul's epistles that the patristic writers relied on for their soteriology. In their exegesis and preaching, the Fathers expounded and shed light on Paul's soteriology, which they found helpful. But the extent to which they illuminated Paul's soteriology remains very much a matter of debate.[48] We must acknowledge that what the soteriology of the patristic era largely expanded on was the New Testament imagery that they sometimes literalized and adapted to their audience "for whom hearing sermons was, among other things, a pastime."[49] One imagery they employed frequently was the theme of the wiles of the devil, who is considered an enemy. In combating the devil, "Christ's humanity becomes the

---

46. Cimala, "Paul's Metaphorical Soteriology," 373.
47. Duffy, "Southern Baptist and Roman Catholic Soteriologies," 436. See also Duffy, *Graced Horizon*.
48. See Blackwell, *Christosis*.
49. Loewe, "Jesus the Savior."

worm on the book of His divinity or the bait in a mousetrap."[50] Patristic theology generally thought of the divinity of Jesus as having a direct saving significance. Irenaeus of Lyons (AD 130–202), for example, developed the idea that the Son of God became what we are so that we might receive a share in his perfection.

Irenaeus the theologian may not have had the brilliant style of Tertullian or the philosophical erudition of Clement or Origen or even the religious depth of Augustine, yet the choice of him as the starting point among the Fathers is justifiable on many grounds.[51] He was, at least, astute in developing the basic tenets of the Christian faith. He was also the first patristic writer to develop a clear and comprehensive doctrine of atonement and redemption.[52] Irenaeus's theology was developed in the context of his writings against Gnosticism. In the patristic era, especially at the time of Irenaeus, Christianity was confronted with the gnostic problem. Gnostic writers developed numerous myths to account for human origin and destiny. Using Christianity as a guise, the Gnostics drew images and symbolisms from the Old Testament to explain what they thought was the true meaning of the teachings of Jesus.[53] They conceptualized them along their own elitist and dualistic conceptions of reality: saved vs reprobate; soul vs body; and spirit vs. matter. In his fight against gnostic dualism, as detailed in *Adversus haereses* (written ca. AD 180) and his later work *Demonstratio praedicationis apostolicae* (written ca. 190), Irenaeus emphasized that salvation is not meant only for the soul, but for the body as well.[54] Using the language of "corruption" to capture humanity's sinful condition, Irenaeus speaks of salvation as freedom from sinful condition to a life of immortality.[55] He describes salvation in three ways: that salvation is the conquering of humanity's foe; it is our becoming sharers in incorruptibility; and our becoming sharers in adoption as sons.[56] It was on the basis of how he unmasked Gnosticism and exposed it as pseudo-Christian that Irenaeus has been acknowledged by many to be the founder of Christian theology and the first to express in dogmatic terms the essentials of the Christian doctrine.[57] His view of atonement is constitutive of the classical idea of atonement: (i) that

50. Loewe, "Jesus the Savior."
51. Aulen, *Christus Victor*, 16–17.
52. Aulen, *Christus Victor*, 17.
53. See Loewe, "Jesus the Savior."
54. Fairbairn, "Patristic Soteriology," 294.
55. Fairbairn, "Patristic Soteriology," 294.
56. Fairbairn, "Patristic Soteriology," 296.
57. See Loewe, "Jesus the Savior."

work of atonement is carried out by God who is the effective agent from the beginning to end (ii) that God, in Jesus, enters into the world of sin and death to reconcile the world to Himself (iii) that incarnation and atonement are not antithesis, but belong inseparably together and (iv) that the work of atonement is depicted in dramatic terms, i.e., conflict with the powers of evil, which God overcomes and conquers by reconciling the world to Himself.[58]

Like Irenaeus, Origen of Alexandria (AD 184–253) also wrote to refute Gnosticism. However, the target of his defense of human freedom in *De Principiis* was not gnostic dualism, but gnostic fatalism—its insistence that the newly born are born into a particular class, which renders human action virtually meaningless.[59] Origen postulates the pre-existence of the soul, arguing that all but the soul of Jesus sinned in their preexistent state. The souls cast down in the physical universe long for reunion with God from whom they originated originally.[60] Origen then goes on to describe salvation in personal terms—as a communion with God through adoption by which God shares with the human person incorruptibility.[61] He uses the language of participation to describe this share of life of incorruptibility. In *De Principiis*, Origen also expounds on his eschatological doctrine of *apokatastasis*—the doctrine of the universal salvation of all people, which he dubiously arrived at on the basis of Acts 3:21. Many of the arguments for this doctrine of *apokatastasis* are grounded in Scripture, particularly the Pauline text that "God will be all in all" (1 Cor 15:21–28), which Origen read allegorically, as well as philosophical argument deriving from Platonism.[62] The Pauline text was important for Origen (and Gregory of Nyssa after him) "because it is connected with the final elimination of evil, an assumption that turns out to be completely consistent with his metaphysical doctrine of the non-substantiality of evil from the ontological point of view."[63] Thus, on the basis of his Neo-Platonic assumption, Origen posits the idea that evil is nothingness, and that since "human freedom is never definitive, hell is medicinal and temporary."[64] When Origen's opponents accused him of teaching unorthodox doctrine that the devil will be saved Origen denied it,

---

58. Aulen, *Christus Victor*, 34–35.
59. Fairbairn, "Patristic Soteriology," 297.
60. Fairbairn, "Patristic Soteriology," 298.
61. Fairbairn, "Patristic Soteriology," 298.
62. Ramelli, "Christian Soteriology and Christian Platonism," 314.
63. Ramelli, "Christian Soteriology and Christian Platonism," 315.
64. Egan, "Hell," 60.

countering that "not even a madman would accuse me of this."[65] Despite the denial, Origen's later writings leave open this question.[66]

Later Church Fathers, like John Chrysostom and Augustine, refuted Origen's doctrine of *apocatastasis*. The doctrine was also condemned at a local council of Constantinople (AD 563).[67] The Christian Church would also refute Origen's view that souls preexisted in time and affirm that all creatures were created in time. The Fourth century bishop and Cappadocian Father who shares some methodological and philosophical presuppositions with Origen, Gregory of Nyssa (AD 335–394), was one of the first to reject the view that souls were preexistent and declared that all souls are created in time. He, however, seemed to have continued Origen's doctrine of *apokatastasis* in his works, *De Anima et Resurrectione* and *In Illud: Tunc et ipse Filius*, written several years after *De Anima*, using allegorical interpretation of some key Pauline texts to support his position, like Origen did before him. Interpreting the Philippian text of all knees in heaven and on earth bending to acclaim Jesus as God (Phil 2:9–10), "Gregory sees there an allusion to the ultimate salvation of all rational creatures, angels, humans, and—as already Origen maintained—even demons, who, 'after long cycles of ages, when evil will have vanished and there will remain nothing else than the Good,' will return to God and submit to Christ."[68] The submission to God by all rational creatures will eventually coincide with their salvation, at least so Gregory taught.[69] Following Origen, Gregory held that sin and death will be completely annihilated and the kingdom of Satan will be destroyed.[70]

There is also Athanasius's (fourth century) writings on the incarnation of the Logos—that humanity was originally created to participate in the divine Logos and that this destiny was fulfilled in Jesus.[71] For Athanasius, human sinfulness can be removed only through penance, which makes the incarnation of God necessary. There are several other examples, such as the formula that derives from Origen, which Gregory of Nazianzus (fourth century) used in his Christological dispute: What has not been assumed has also not been saved. In other words, the whole of humanity would not have been saved, had the divine Logos not become man.[72]

---

65. Egan, "Hell," 61.
66. Egan, "Hell," 61.
67. Egan, "Hell," 61.
68. Ramelli, "Christian Soteriology and Christian Platonism," 324.
69. Ramelli, "Christian Soteriology and Christian Platonism," 325.
70. Ramelli, "Christian Soteriology and Christian Platonism," 338.
71. Pannenberg, *Jesus—God and Man*, 40.
72. Pannenberg, *Jesus—God and Man*, 40.

The high point of patristic thinking on salvation as participation was reached with Cyril of Alexandria (AD 378–444) whose main emphasis was on salvation as participation. "Like virtually all Church Fathers, Cyril does see salvation as a participation in God's qualities: he emphasizes that God grants us to share in his own incorruption and holiness."[73] Cyril's soteriological ideas were foisted in the context of his dispute with Nestorius in the aftermath of Theotokos outbreak of AD 328.[74] Cyril was clear in his defense against Nestorius that in Christ the human and divine natures are inextricably bound in one person or hypostasis. The divine and human nature exist side by side, forming the composite personality of Christ.[75] In Cyril's doctrine of hypostatic union are two soteriological arguments that are intrinsically related. First, if the Word is to free us from death, then he must be divine. Second, in order to conquer death for our sake, the Word must genuinely experience suffering and death.[76] "Cyril understands Christ's conquest of death through the divinization of human nature as the result of the *communication idiomatum*. The incarnation of the Word frees humanity from death by communicating the incorruptibility of the divine nature to the corruptible and passible human flesh."[77] The consequences of the hypostatic union are on both the divine and human axes. The primary effect being that the Word experiences the weakness of human nature by emptying Himself (Philippians 2).[78] On the flip side, by Christ's kenosis our humanity partakes both in the life-giving and sanctifying power that is proper to divinity.[79] Thus, by his kenosis and condescension Christ exalts human nature, effecting thereby a "great exchange" between God and humanity.[80] "Cyril's Christology forces him to acknowledge that in the fully integrative unity of the divine and human in Christ, the divine Word genuinely experiences the limitations of our humanity, including suffering, and at the same time preserves the perfection of his divine nature, including its impassibility, in order to heal fallen human nature."[81]

What do we learn from patristic thinking on soteriology? There is a long held view that there are two basic thought patterns in patristic view of

73. Fairbairn, "Patristic Soteriology," 304.
74. See McGuckin, *Cyril of Alexandria*.
75. Smith, "Christ's Passion in Cyril of Alexandria's Soteriology," 467.
76. Smith, "Christ's Passion in Cyril of Alexandria's Soteriology," 466.
77. Smith, "Christ's Passion in Cyril of Alexandria's Soteriology," 466.
78. Smith, "Christ's Passion in Cyril of Alexandria's Soteriology," 467.
79. Smith, "Christ's Passion in Cyril of Alexandria's Soteriology," 468.
80. Smith, "Christ's Passion in Cyril of Alexandria's Soteriology," 468.
81. Smith, "Christ's Passion in Cyril of Alexandria's Soteriology," 469.

soteriology: juridical and deification. This assumption has now been called into question. The mistaken notion was influenced by Adolf van Harnack's monumental *History of Dogma* (published 1885–1889), which detailed twentieth century interpretation of patristic theology.[82] According to Donald Fairbairn who has aptly refuted this claim, "Harnack approaches his subject with a passionate and barely-controlled hatred for the Eastern Church, coupled with an almost reverential attachment to two Western Fathers, Tertullian and Augustine."[83] Following Harnack's facile characterization of East and West,[84] those who hold on to the idea of two patterns of salvation in patristic thought speak of the juridical or legal as focused on forgiveness of sins and that this is represented by the Western Church. A more Eastern pattern was thought to see salvation as participation in God or deification. Fairbairn rubbishes such a notion, suggesting instead that there were at least two distinct ways of understanding deification or participation in the patristic period.[85] One understanding focused primarily, though not exclusively, on participation (deification) by which one shares in God's qualities and incorruptibility. Eastern theology would later conceive this in terms of "energies," something that corresponds somewhat to what Western theology would refer to as the "attributes" of God.[86] This focus on sharing in God's qualities makes soteriological pattern seem impersonal.[87] The other understanding of salvations also employs the same terms of "participation" and "deification" but understands them primarily in personalist terms. "Church fathers who hold to this view still speak of salvation as sharing in God's incorruption, but their dominant emphasis falls on our sharing in the personal communion between the persons of the Trinity."[88] Deification, according to this understanding, does not mean being absorbed into God, but being adopted as children of God. Thus, Fairbairn surmises that later Eastern and Western soteriological developments would follow each of these trajectories without making anyone exclusively Eastern or Western. A semiotic understanding can help overcome the bifurcation of juridical (forgiveness of sins) v deification (participation) with respect to the soteriology of the Fathers. A semiotic understanding does not think in

82. Fairbairn, "Patristic Soteriology," 290.

83. Fairbairn, "Patristic Soteriology," 290. On Harnack's fascination with Augustine, see Harnack, *History of Dogma*, 5 and 14–15.

84. See Campenhausen, *Fathers of the Greek Church*, 176 and Burns, "Economy of Salvation," 599–600.

85. Fairbairn, "Patristic Soteriology," 289.

86. Fairbairn, "Patristic Soteriology," 293.

87. Fairbairn, "Patristic Soteriology," 293.

88. Fairbairn, "Patristic Soteriology," 293.

terms of either-or but in terms of both-and. The both-and approach was already implicit in the thought of the Fathers.

ANSELM'S *CUR DEUS HOMO?*

There is still an unresolved question of whether Anselm of Canterbury (1033–1109) should be considered a patristic writer. In any event, Anselm acts like a bridge between the patristic and medieval theologians in all matters theological. Gustaf Aulen thinks Anselm marks the real beginnings of a well thought out doctrine of the atonement.[89] Although we do not consider him a patristic writer as some do, if for the sake of argument he is viewed as a patristic, Anselm's satisfaction theory in *Cur Deus Homo* becomes the only exception to the patristic idea that the divinity of Jesus has direct saving significance. This significant difference alone is enough to make us see that Anselm ushers in a new era in Christian soteriology quite different from the Fathers. The idea behind Anselm's satisfaction theory is simple in some sense— that anyone who has unjustly defrauded another must make recompense in proportion to the wrong done and as well as in proportion to the pain inflicted. By freely yielding to the devil, humans have violated the honor due God and must either undergo punishment involuntarily or make voluntary satisfaction.[90] Coming from a feudal society, Anselm adopts the master-slave and lord-servant imagery to depict human responsibility for the Fall. He illustrates it in *Cur Deus Homo* with this hypothetical situation:

> Suppose one should assign his slave a certain piece of work, and should command him not to throw himself into a ditch, which he points out to him and from which he could not extricate himself; and suppose that the slave, despising his master's command and warning, throws himself into the ditch before pointed out, so as to be utterly unable to accomplish the work assigned; think you that his inability will at all excuse him for not doing his appointed work?[91]

Anselm argues that because of our sinfulness we are obligated to offer God satisfaction for our sins. There have been different renditions of Anselm's satisfaction theory over the years. One of the most plausible is Wolfhart Pannenberg's rendition of what Anselm is trying to say:

---

89. Aulen, *Christus Victor*, 1.
90. Kereszty, *Jesus Christ*, 217.
91. As cited in Nuth, "Two Medieval Soteriologies," 611.

The sinner is held fast in the condition of sin by the duty to bring satisfaction. It is not enough for man to stop sinning, but over and beyond this he must offer satisfaction to God for the sin he has already committed. Such satisfaction can consist only of something that man does not already owe God. It can consist only in a work that goes beyond his obligation, that is, in a merit. The ordinary man cannot, however, accomplish such a thing, because he already owes His creator everything he has. Only the man Jesus, born without sin, can offer God a work of superogation, the gift of his life.[92]

Anselm's satisfaction theory has come under severe attack by scholars who see it as a time-conditioned theory reflective of the feudal society of the time in which Anselm lived.[93] Anselm, in truth, employed the feudal images of "honor" and "debt" to explain how human sinfulness (disobedience) disrupted the harmony of God's order. This disobedience, according to Anselm, cannot go unpunished. To restore the honor due God, human beings must either be punished or make recompense. In truth, the Anselmian theory lends itself to criticism, and justifiably so. But before examining some of the criticisms, it is pertinent to present a context for understanding Anselm so we do not distort his position, as some critics have done. There is a suggestion, traceable to none other than Karl Rahner, that we "consult the writings of mystics and saints as authentic sources of doctrinal theology in order to repair the rift that exists between 'lived piety and abstract theology.'"[94] The rift Rahner had in mind was the rift between medieval scholastics and mystics who wrote in an atmosphere of piety.[95] Although scholastic theology, like monastic theology, began with the practice of *lectio divina*, it moved away in due time from the context of Scripture and prayer. The result of this move was an abstract theology that concerned itself mainly with arid quiddities. But monastic theology, on its part, continued to nurture spiritual development and contemplative experience.[96] Anselm belongs to both camps, i.e., scholastic theology and monastic theology. "The juxtaposition of thought and feeling in Anselm can be seen in the Proslogion, where Anselm's prayerful outpourings of emotion are interspersed with the construction of the highly abstract ontological

92. Pannenberg, *Jesus—God and Man*, 42.
93. Kereszty, *Jesus Christ*, 219.
94. Nuth, "Two Medieval Soteriologies," 612–13; referencing Rahner, *Theological Investigations* 16:72, see n12.
95. Nuth, "Two Medieval Soteriologies," 613.
96. Nuth, "Two Medieval Soteriologies," 613.

argument."[97] Thus, to understand Anselm's theory of atonement, it is helpful to read *Cur Deus Homo*, together with his other works, in the context of his monastic devotion.[98] "While the Cur Deus Homo has been studied extensively, receiving eminence as a precursor of scholasticism, Anselm's prayers have been ignored. As a result, the Cur Deus Homo has been subject to misinterpretation and distortion."[99] With the growing interest in the passion of Christ that reemerged in the twelfth century, Anselm helped to shape this development in two ways: through his prayers, which detailed the suffering of Christ with "poignancy and passionate intensity" and through his theological treatise, *Cur Deus Homo*, "which grounded such devotion in a reasoned explanation of the necessity of the Incarnation."[100] What Anselm tried to do in *Cur Deus Homo*, therefore, was "simply to provide a satisfactory answer to the question why God became human to save us."[101] It was never his intention to give "human reason an absolute, demonstrative power over the truths of faith."[102] Taking faith as a starting point, he emphasized the power of natural reason to offer coherent rational argument for the truths of faith—something that will later develop into what would be known as Scholasticism.[103]

With this context in mind, we now turn to some criticisms of Anselm's argument in order to determine the extent to which the criticisms can be considered fair. The Orthodox Archbishop, Lazar Puhalo, has been credited with offering a scathing castigation of the concept of Jesus's atoning sacrifice: "A god who demands the child-sacrifice of his own son to satiate his own wrath? That is not Jehovah. That is Molech."[104] Other critics have joined this chorus, castigating the Anselmian model of atonement for perpetuating violence—"that schemes which include Christ's sacrifice as satisfaction for sin put violence in the heart of God."[105]

One of the criticisms of this traditional view of atonement, i.e., salvation consists of "payment" or satisfaction made to God, has centered on the fact that it portrays God as an angry God in need of appeasement. However, this theory of satisfaction needs to be nuanced. Since Anselm, there has

---

97. Nuth, "Two Medieval Soteriologies," 614.
98. Nuth, "Two Medieval Soteriologies," 614.
99. Nuth, "Two Medieval Soteriologies," 615.
100. Nuth, "Two Medieval Soteriologies," 617.
101. Nuth, "Two Medieval Soteriologies," 619.
102. Nuth, "Two Medieval Soteriologies," 620.
103. Nuth, "Two Medieval Soteriologies," 620.
104. As quoted in Erdman, "Sacrifice as Satisfaction, Not Substitution," 461.
105. As quoted in Erdman, "Sacrifice as Satisfaction, Not Substitution," 461.

been a tendency to identify satisfaction with redemption, something that Bernard Lonergan recognized as problematic and aimed to correct by distinguishing satisfaction from redemption.[106] For Lonergan, the essence of redemption is not in satisfaction, but in the transformation of the world. Although satisfaction is important in the redemptive process, it belongs mainly within consciousness or subjectivity because satisfaction belongs to the redemptive process where people are involved consciously in responding to God's gift in Christ.[107] Thus, satisfaction belongs to the realm of interpersonal relations, notwithstanding that it happens under grace.[108] As something that happens in the realm of interpersonal relations, Lonergan sees satisfaction in the relationships between Christ and the Father, between Christ and the sinner, and between Christ and the justified.[109]

Satisfaction can be vicarious when it is done for others in detestation of sin and grief over it.[110] Vicarious satisfaction "applies both to our Lord satisfying for our sins and to that aspect of the sufferings of this world by which Christians can offer satisfaction not only for their own sins but for those of other people."[111] Lonergan's notion of vicarious satisfaction derives from a principle in Aristotle in which Aristotle (*Ethics* 13.3, 122b) stated that love makes two people one in affectivity such that what we do through our friends is thought to be done by us.[112] "This union in affectivity throws some light on how Christ's sufferings count as our sufferings, and our sufferings count as the sufferings of those for whom we pray. When Lonergan invokes this principle, he speaks mainly of Christ's satisfying for others. He does not say much about Christians offering satisfaction for others, but he does refer to it in passing."[113] Thomas Aquinas, like many other scholastics, incorporated Anselm's theory of satisfaction and atonement as found in *Cur Deus Homo?* But moving beyond Anselm, Aquinas developed the idea of *Christus Victor*—Christ triumphant over the devil and all evil powers. This theme of Christ's victory over the devil, although ancient, would play a major role in Thomas's soteriological work.[114]

---

106. Mooney, "Lonergan's Soteriology," 26.
107. Mooney, "Lonergan's Soteriology," 26.
108. Mooney, "Lonergan's Soteriology," 26.
109. Mooney, "Lonergan's Soteriology," 27.
110. Mooney, "Lonergan's Soteriology," 31.
111. Mooney, "Lonergan's Soteriology," 31.
112. Mooney, "Lonergan's Soteriology," 31.
113. Mooney, "Lonergan's Soteriology," 31.
114. See Morgan, "Christus Victor Motifs," 409–21.

SOTERIOLOGY OF PROTESTANTISM

Edward Oakes has made the bold claim that there would be no Protestant Reformation without "the Christology of Martin Luther in its specific and unique contours."[115] Oakes bases his claim largely on the argument that Christology was a key element that gave expression to Luther's Reformation ideas. In the light of this claim, it will be helpful to examine some of Luther's Reformation ideas, such has his theology of grace, his doctrine of justification, what he thought about the sacraments of the Church, and his doctrine of sanctification. These reformation ideas of Luther were in fact condemned by the Council of Trent. They were considered incompatible with the Catholic doctrine.

(a) Doctrine of Grace

Like Paul and Augustine, two great teachers from whom he developed his doctrine of grace, what would become Luther's theology of grace grew out of a traumatic experience that haunted him throughout his life, i.e., his depraved condition. He felt helplessly depraved in the face of an angry God. He became an Augustinian monk out of fear of the wrath of God. He thought becoming a monk was a meritorious work that would earn him a divine approval and forgiveness only to discover later that it was not possible to secure peace of mind by such a method. He later came to discover "that the only road to peace lay in repudiating all righteousness of his own, and depending wholly upon the free grace of God in Christ."[116] The Catholic idea, which Luther rejected, thought of grace as a divine substance bestowed on a person by God. In the scholastic theology, which Luther was trained in, grace was conceived as a *habitus* or *qualitas*. It was thought to have been received *gratia infusa* (by a gradual process of infusion). But for Luther, grace is not infused. Rather, grace is to be understood only in the biblical terms of divine favor. For Luther, what grace does is restore to the sinner the favor of God. Where scholastic thought placed emphasis on salvation as something that depended on human merit (albeit assisted by grace), Luther insisted that salvation is totally dependent on *sola gratia*, *sola fidei*, for grace is the forgiveness of sin *per Christum* and *propter Christum* (not out of one's merit).

(b) Justification and Sanctification

Luther relies almost exclusively on Paul for his theology of justification. One who is forgiven *propter Christum* is justified by grace and faith. This

---

115. Oakes, *Infinity Dwindled to Infancy*, 223.
116. McGiffert, *Protestant Thought before Kant*, 21.

means that Justification cannot be by works, but only by the word of God. In the word of God is God's promise of grace and faith. Luther stresses that justification comes from faith in Christ Jesus and that *sola gratia* is intrinsically related to *sola fide* because of the God who unleashes divine favor on the sinner as an act of assistance. The depraved is justified only when one accepts this favor in faith. Faith, for this reason, is *fides justificans* (a certain and sure trust and assent to Christ). Faith does not remain indifferent. Rather, it perpetually vivifies and justifies the depraved.[117] Faith leads to predestination. The grace that comes from Christ is the foundation of all grace. The forgiveness that comes from the grace of Christ comes by hearing the Word of God. Hence, *sola Scriptura* is as important as *sola fide*.

(c) The Sacraments of the Church

For Luther, the sacraments are a means of grace only when they proclaim the Word of God. A sacrament without the Word is nothing. The depraved can be saved without the sacrament, but not without the word. The sacraments are only effective when the words they proclaim are believed. The Christian is *simul Justus et peccator*. Luther insists that there are strictly speaking only two sacraments: baptism (which is freely bestowed by grace and in the case of the infant by infused faith) and the Lord's Supper (which when rightly administered and received in faith makes the depraved holy by the forgiveness of sins that comes from the presence of Christ under the appearance of bread and wine).[118]

Viewed in the context of abuses in ecclesial life to which Luther and the reformers took exception, it is easy to mistake the catalogue of ecclesial abuses and critique of ecclesial life they presented as leading to a radically different teaching on atonement. Granted that Luther and reformers presented a radically reformed theology of the church and of salvation that we may say places ecclesiology and soteriology in dynamic tension,[119] their teaching on atonement was not commonly assumed to be one of the controversial issues of the Reformation. In particular, Luther's teaching on atonement had not been as polemical as his doctrine of Justification.[120] The man who worked the closest with Luther in the Reformation movement, Philip Melanchthon (1497–1560) stated in his *Loci Praecipus Theologici*

117. See Luther, *Werke*.

118. See Greaves, "Luther's Doctrine of Grace," 385–95; Kerr, *Compend of Luther's Theology*; Dillenberger, *Martin Luther*; Niesel, *Reformed Symbolics*; Plass, *What Luther Says*.

119. Bender, "Martin Luther and the Birth of Protestant Ecclesial Vision," 268

120. Aulen, *Chrisus Victor*, 125.

(1541) that their doctrine of Atonement was fundamentally in accord with the scholastic scheme.[121]

It is widely held in some Protestant circles today that at the time of the Protestant Reformation Justification by faith was considered the *articulus stantis et cadentis ecclesiae* (the article by which the church stands or falls).[122] Luther's famous song, "Ein fest Burg ist unser Gott" [A Mighty Fortress is our God] (1928), which most Lutheran congregations sing at the anniversary of the Reformation, captures his view of the world as a battlefield, which Jesus must conquer and take from the devil, in order to save true believers.[123] Christ's final victory over sin, death, hell, and the devil, although has taken place on the Cross, will be consummated on the last day when Christ returns to claim victory over the devil. Even where doubt persists whether the doctrine of Justification is an *articulus stantis*, there is no doubting that classical Lutheran theology considers it a "regulative idea" or criterion for true theology.[124] There are five central emphases in Luther's theology of the Cross. The emphasis on: (i) the majesty of God as revealed through creation (ii) the hiddenness of God—that God hides in certain places (iii) the fact that it is through suffering and the cross of Christ that the believer recognizes God (iv) the fact that God has hidden God's-self in the suffering of Christ and therefore can be seen only with the eyes of faith and (v) the fact that God particularly makes God's-self known through suffering, most notably through Christ's passion.[125] Thus, Luther's theology of the Cross then becomes the basis of his understanding of Justification by faith alone.[126]

Luther's theology of Justification by faith is dependent on a particular Christology—Patristic Christology.[127] What Luther meant by faith is in itself Christological. For him, "the very concept of 'saving faith' and the doctrine about Christ are logically tied to one another, mutually implicated and mutually interpreting, but in such a way that the Christology is primary and

---

121. Aulen, *Chrisus Victor*, 124.

122. Matson, "Divine Forgiveness in Paul?" 59. There is a dispute whether the doctrine of justification by faith was the *articulus stantis et cadentis ecclesiae* because there is no convincing proof that it derives from Luther himself. Some think it probably dates back to the Reformation anniversary in 1617 "where it gained entry into Lutheran confessional writings reproducing more or less accurately a statement of Luther's from memory"; see Matthias, "'Lutheran' Christology in Barth's Doctrine of Justification," 15.

123. Phillips, "Bearing the Shame of the Cross," 21.

124. Matthias, "'Lutheran' Christology in Barth's Doctrine of Justification," 15.

125. Phillips, "Bearing the Shame of the Cross," 22.

126. Phillips, "Bearing the Shame of the Cross," 21.

127. See Yeago, "Bread of Life," 257–59.

determinative."[128] Faith is adherence to Jesus as the exclusive giver of life. The force of this faith lies in its confession.[129] The soteriological implication of this, for Luther, is this: one is justified only by faith in what Jesus has done for humanity. For Luther, the logic of faith is simply this—that one clings to the concrete divine man Jesus from whom assurance of forgiveness follows.[130] This is why Luther insists that the soteriological concepts cannot be divorced from the person of Christ, as affirmed by the Councils and taught by the Fathers.[131] If there was a common ground between the soteriology of the Fathers and that of the reformers, it is in the fact that the soteriological expressions "righteousness," "justification," "redemption," and "propitiation" take center stage in the writings of the Fathers and the Protestant reformers.[132]

Earlier we sketched the theory of atonement of the Fathers, which was interpreted for a long time along juridical lines. We made clear that while Anselm may have served as a bridge between the Fathers and medieval scholasticism, the theory of atonement of *Cur Deus Homo* solidified a juridical reading of atonement of the Fathers, if one wanted to follow that line of interpretation and consider him a patristic. But Anselm was not really a patristic. He was a scholastic in the strict sense of the term. The doctrine of atonement of the reformers (Protestant orthodoxy, if you like) was by no means identical with that of Anselm or medieval scholasticism, though they do not significantly differ either. In characterizing what the similarity between Protestant orthodoxy and medieval scholasticism on the subject was, Aulen writes: "The strange thing is that the medieval doctrine of the Atonement remained, in a slightly modified form, while the penitential system and the idea of penance, on which it had originally been built, had completely disappeared."[133] Like Anselm, Protestant orthodoxy's view on the subject was dominated by the idea of satisfaction. Like Anselm, Protestant orthodoxy "states the problem in the same way, it repeats the contention that the payment of the satisfaction is the only alternative to a condonation of laxity."[134]

In the final analysis, Luther and the reformers did very little to reverse the juridical trajectory of the Western Church, at least with respect to

128. Yeago, "Bread of Life," 261–62.
129. Yeago, "Bread of Life," 263.
130. Yeago, "Bread of Life," 271.
131. Yeago, "Bread of Life," 272.
132. Longenecker, "Metaphor of Adoption in Paul's Letters," 76.
133. Aulen, *Christus Victor*, 128.
134. Aulen, *Christus Victor*, 129.

Atonement. The Reformers may have given a radically different answer to the question of how one attains a right standing before God, in the end, they did not fundamentally alter the prevailing notion that salvation is primarily juridical in character.[135] However, modern Protestant understanding of Atonement, from the time of Friedrich Schleiermacher (1768–1834), has been moving in the opposite direction. The trend seems to be towards reversing the medieval Protestant understanding of soteriology. Gradually the language of justification has been yielding to the language of forgiveness.[136] Whereas in earlier understanding, stemming from the Fathers, atonement was understood as prior to salvation, Schleiermacher reverses the order: that salvation (change in spiritual life) is prior to atonement (reconciliation or forgiveness); it is the latter that completes the former. In Schleiermacher's anthropocentric interpretation of the world, "Man comes to understand that all things are dependent on God, and therefore, that which seems to disturb the harmony of things does so only in appearance. It might be said that 'atonement' in this sense means that man is reconciled with his situation and his environment."[137] The same idea is found in Albrecht Ritschl (1822–89) and in the writings of other nineteenth century Protestant thinkers who all mount an assault on the juridical understanding of Atonement and replace it with the language of forgiveness. They all use "forgiveness" to denote the sum total and effect of the deeds of Jesus, in spite of the fact that forgiveness language is virtually absent in Paul.[138] It is beyond the scope of this work to probe why Paul was reticent in using the language of forgiveness and or whether forgiveness is the same thing as justification, at least in Paul. The point here is rather that modern Protestantism now assume "that the real object of faith is the fact of our being forgiven and accepted, rather than Jesus Christ himself, apprehended as true God and true human being."[139]

In general, what we see in Protestantism, beginning with Luther to Schleiermacher and down to Ritschl, is a tension between the language of justification and forgiveness and a struggle to unite two poles that have been made to seem like polar opposites. This brings us back to our earlier point—that these metaphors are not to be conceived as dialectical, but as semiotic. A semiotic understanding lends itself to both-and approach of soteriology as meaning forgiveness and justification, something that Protestant orthodoxy now accepts.

135. Fairbairn, "Patristic Soteriology," 307.
136. Matson, "Divine Forgiveness in Paul?" 59.
137. Aulen, *Christus Victor*, 137.
138. Matson, "Divine Forgiveness in Paul?" 59.
139. Yeago, "Bread of Life," 270.

OBJECTIONS TO THE ANSELMIAN THEORY

Allan Mann has suggested correctly that the vocabulary of soteriology should be redefined for a post-Christian and post-industrialized culture because non-Western cultures do not think in the old categories of the penal substitution used to describe the saving work of Christ.[140] As we saw with respect to Anselm's theory, the language of penal substitution has been deemed by some New Testament scholars to be violent—that it is a sharp contrast to a benevolent and loving God of the New Testament.[141] Admittedly, there are variations of the theory of penal substitution. Its rigorous version, however, states that Christ took the place of all sinners as object of God's anger who then inflicted on him the punishment of sinners.[142] Critics of the theory understandably object to it on the ground that the Cross is not God's violent solution to sin, but God's non-violent love response to the violence of Jesus's accusers.[143] The understanding here is that Jesus's death should rather be interpreted in the light of Israel's salvation history (redemption).[144] Evidence for this can be found even in Pauline soteriology where the author(s) of these letters make clear how God's saving act is not like a bolt from the blue with no relation to the story of Israel, but rather that God's act in Christ happened *kata tas graphas*; its intelligibility depending squarely on its relation to Israel's Scripture.[145]

The difficulty with penal substitution is the reason for the misgivings scholars have against Anselmian theory of atonement in *Cur Deus Homo*. The African American liberation theologian, James Cone (1938–2018), for example, rejects the theory of penal substitution in part because he considers it to be a part of abstract European doctrine that has been used to justify the oppression of African-Americans.[146] His womanist theologian counterpart, Delores William (1937–), has also suggested "that a penal substitutionary understanding of Jesus's death embraces the exploitation of black women as forced surrogates in both white and black contexts because penal substitution presents a Jesus who acts as a surrogate for those whom he died."[147] Similar protest has been on going among African Pentecostal

---

140. See ch. 3 of Manns, *Atonement for a Sinless Society*.
141. See Gorman, *Inhabiting the Cruciform God*.
142. Mooney, "Lonergan's Soteriology," 22.
143. Williams, "Violent Atonement in Romans," 581; referencing Jersak, "Nonviolent Identification and the Victory of Christ," 33.
144. Williams, "Violent Atonement in Romans," 581.
145. Hays, "Christ Died for the Ungodly," 60.
146. See Cone, *God of the Oppressed*, 42–52.
147. Williams, "Violent Atonement in Romans," 582; see also Weaver, *Nonviolent*

Churches who denounce an ecclesiology that puts suffering at the heart and center of soteriology.[148]

Charles Heffling, working out of the work of Bernard Lonergan, has described *Cur Deus Homo* as "a magnificent failure" because Anselm attempted to do something that cannot be done without adopting an intellectual perspective he knew he was not in a position to adopt.[149] Anselm, in Heffling's view, needed a theorem of the supernatural, which had not yet been discovered at the time.[150] That is not to say Anselm's aim was not noble. His aim was to understand what the Christian tradition means when it says the Incarnate Word has done *propter nos homines et popter nostrum salute* [for us men and for our salvation].[151] Heffling argues that Anselm's lack of coherent theorem of the supernatural order led him to two basic problems—one general and the other specific. "The general problem is well known: Anselm thought (or somehow said) that control of meaning was a matter of discovering necessary reasons. The second problem, which appears specifically in *Cur Deus Homo*, is that Anselm tried to conceive what was supernatural about Christ's saving work in terms of supererogation."[152] Anselm thought that in trying to uphold justice, Christ exceeded what he was obliged to do "and by so doing earned a reward that was transferred, at his own request, from himself to his human 'kindred.' The gift he gave by 'giving his life' was not so much the payment of a debt as it was an overpayment, a supplement to the honor that is justly due to God."[153] The difficulty with Anselm's argument of supererogation, for Heffling, is that "excess implies that what exceeds and what is exceeded share a common measure."[154] There is also the related incoherent view of merit in Anselm's argument—that by earning God's reward is to imply in this case that merit before God does not depend on grace.[155]

In spite of the difficulties scholars have with the idea of penal substitution, most agree that penal substitution of Rom 3:24–26 is foundational to Paul's soteriology.[156] Lonergan helpfully brings clarity to the theory

---

Atonement, 99–178. See also Williams, *Sisters in the Wilderness*.

148. See Ngong, "Protesting the Cross," 5–19.
149. Heffling, "Lonergan's *Cur Deus Homo*," 147.
150. Heffling, "Lonergan's *Cur Deus Homo*," 147.
151. Heffling, "Lonergan's *Cur Deus Homo*," 147.
152. Heffling, "Lonergan's *Cur Deus Homo*," 147–48.
153. Heffling, "Lonergan's *Cur Deus Homo*," 148.
154. Heffling, "Lonergan's *Cur Deus Homo*," 148.
155. Heffling, "Lonergan's *Cur Deus Homo*," 148.
156. Williams, "Violent Atonement in Romans," 584.

of penal substitution, a clarity that adequately addresses the concerns of Cone, Delores William, and other critics of the Anselmian theory. Lonergan points out that though materially the deprivations and sufferings, which Christ endured here on earth are the same as those humans experience on earth as punishment for their sins, they cannot be for Christ formal punishment, since he did not contract them as a result of sin.[157] Lonergan is here employing Aquinas's (ST III 14.3) distinction between deprivations as sinfully contracted and deprivations as voluntarily assumed. Punishment, according to this distinction, is not inflicted justly unless on account of one's own sin.[158] "As a result in no formal sense is Jesus punished for our sins, and in no formal sense may the theory of penal substitution be applied to the Cross."[159] Christ takes up his sufferings voluntarily in solidarity with sinners. "In this way the sufferings of Christ are transformed from being instances of God's punitive justice to being manifestations of that redemptive justice by which God is said to be just and justifying (Rom 3:26)."[160]

Anselm asked, *Cur Deus Homo*? Lonergan frames an answer to this question by appealing to the order of the universe designed by God who is ontologically prior to creation. Lonergan conceives the end of creation "in terms of mutual benevolent love, that is, in terms of friendship, with the common good to which all the friends are committed being the goodness of God. This friendship is appropriately, but not necessarily, mediated by an intermediate friend, and what is required of this intermediate friend is that he or she can mediate divine friendship and that he or she ought to enjoy it the first place."[161] One who mediates divine friendship has what Miroslav Wolf has called "a Catholic personality, a personality enriched by otherness."[162] It was Lonergan's appropriation of the theorem of the supernatural that made it possible for him to neatly sketch an intelligible account of Christ's person and work in ways that sublate the account given by Anselm.[163]

---

157. Mooney, "Lonergan's Soteriology," 22; referencing Lonergan, *De Verbo Incarnato*, 456.

158. Mooney, "Lonergan's Soteriology," 22.

159. Mooney, "Lonergan's Soteriology," 22.

160. Mooney, "Lonergan's Soteriology," 30–31.

161. Heffling, "Lonergan's *Cur Deus Homo*," 157–58.

162. Wolf, "Exclusion and Embrace," 230–48.

163. Heffling, "Lonergan's *Cur Deus Homo*," 163.

TOWARDS AND ECUMENICAL CONSENSUS

The Christian Church distinguishes Christology (the science or study of Christ) from Soteriology (the doctrine of the work of Christ). This distinction goes back to Medieval Scholasticism. It also has a basis in Scripture. During his life on earth, Jesus employed symbols and metaphors to get his message across to his audience. One of the symbols he employed often was to speak of the nearness of the Kingdom of God, urging the people to repent because the kingdom of God is near (Matt 3:3; 4:17; and Mark 1:15). He invoked this image to evoke hope and bring a final resolution to the problem of evil.[164] Contemporary discourse in soteriology can be culpably one dimensional. It sometimes reduces salvation to a single trope: liberation or substitutionary atonement.[165] But salvation cannot be a here and now event (liberation) with no reference to the eschaton or future where this liberation will be a fully realized event (atonement). Salvation is an evolutionary love that is both "already and not yet." The relationship between the already realized soteriology and the future soteriology requires a multi-dimensional approach. This multi-dimensional approach can be better grasped in semiotic terms. That is to say we must understand the metaphors or imageries used for speaking about the eschaton along the lines of icon-index-symbols that C. S. Peirce delineates.

Just as sign is related to its object, the divinity of Jesus and his redeeming significance are related in the closest way possible. Who Jesus Christ is in Himself is known virtually to us through his saving action.[166] This does not mean that the divinity of Jesus for us consists only in his saving significance. The divinity and saving significance of Jesus, though interrelated, are very distinct.[167] "The divinity of Jesus remains the presupposition for his saving significance for us and, conversely, the saving significance of his divinity is the reason why we take interest in the question of his divinity."[168] Medieval Scholastic theology was thought to have separated the divine-human person from the redemptive work of Christ until Schleiermacher reconceived it as two sides of the same reality.[169] Herein lies the consensus among the Churches today— that "in general the soteriological interest, the interest in salvation, in the *beneficia Christi*, is what causes us to ask about the figure of Jesus."[170] The

---

164. See Loewe, "Jesus the Savior."

165. See Greggs's review of "God of Salvation," 357.

166. Pannenberg, *Jesus—God and Man*, 38; quoting Philip Melanchthon's preface to the *Loci Communes* (1521).

167. Pannenberg, *Jesus—God and Man*, 38.

168. Pannenberg, *Jesus—God and Man*, 38.

169. Pannenberg, *Jesus—God and Man*, 38–39.

170. Pannenberg, *Jesus—God and Man*, 47.

Churches all want to understand what the God-man has done *propter nos homines et popter nostrum salute* [for us men and for our salvation]. Whether they use the language of "righteousness," "justification," "redemption," "propitiations" or "forgiveness," they all place meanings beyond what is apparent in these imageries. The intent is to shed light on what it means to affirm *Christus Victor*—that God in Jesus was reconciling the world to God.

The high point of soteriology, which the Churches agree, has to be what Lonergan calls the Law of the Cross. Although "law" here does have a sense of precept, it is not to be understood in a juridical sense, but as a precept at the heart of the redemptive process.[171] In Lonergan's Law of the Cross, "the order between things is determined, not primarily by the things themselves, but by the divine creative plan in the mind and choice of God, who plans all things in his loving wisdom from an eminence strictly outside time."[172] Not only are created things caused by God who is ontologically prior, the mode of their emergence and how they are related to one another are part of the divine plan.[173]

CONCLUSION

Paul, like most of the New Testament writers, understood Christ's beneficiary death as a prolepsis of the eschatological judgment in which the old existence will be terminated, opening up the possibility of a newly created humanity in Christ.[174] This is in line with understandings in theological anthropology that on the basis of the resurrection of Christ human beings are "becoming;" that they are on the way to what they are meant to be. In other words, because of the resurrection of Christ, the future is determinative for human beings.[175] Lonergan refers to this as the transformation of the world through an evolving process he calls the Law of the Cross.[176]

The soteriological tension between the present realized eschatology and future "not yet" eschatology, i.e., "the already and not yet" indicates the dynamic movement or evolution of the cosmos. The spatial reality of the world to come and the present spatial reality have been brought together at the initiative of the Triune God who intervenes in human affairs, particularly through the Christ event. It means the connection between the present and

171. Mooney, "Lonergan's Soteriology," 32.
172. Mooney, "Lonergan's Soteriology," 24.
173. Mooney, "Lonergan's Soteriology," 24.
174. Van der Watt, *Salvation in the New Testament*, 185.
175. Henriksen, "Distinct, Unique, or Separate?" 166.
176. See Lonergan, *Supplement to "On the Incarnate Word."*

the future realization of the world can be explained in soteriological terms. Salvation is a process, an on-going event in the life of the believer and the life of the cosmos. The completed "already" dimension of salvation is due to the activity of Christ whose future return will signal the final and definitive consummation of the world process.

Bibliography

Ables, T. E. "The Decline and Fall of the West? Debates about the Trinity in Contemporary Christian Theology." *Religion Compass* 6 (2012) 163–73.

Allison, Dale. *Resurrecting Jesus: The Earliest Christian Tradition and its Interpreters.* New York: T. & T. Clark, 2005.

Alston, William P. "Being-Itself and Talk about God." *Center Journal* 3 (1984) 9–25.

Anderson, Hugh. "Christology: Unfinished Business." In *Earthing Christologies: From Jesus' Parables to Jesus the Parable,* edited by James H. Charlesworth and Walter P. Weaver, 81–97. Valley Forge, PA: Trinity, 1995.

Anselm of Canterbury. *Complete Philosophical and Theological Treatises of Anselm of Canterbury.* Translated by Jasper Hopkins and Herbert Richardson. Minneapolis: Arthur J. Banning, 2000. http://jasper-hopkins.info/monologion.pdf.

Aquinas, Thomas. *Summa Theologica.* http://dhspriory.org/thomas/summa.

Aulen, Gustaf. *Christus Victor: An Historical Study of the Three Main Types of the Idea of Atonement.* Translated by A. G. Herbert. Eugene, OR: Wipf and Stock, 2003.

Balthasar, Hans Urs von. *Dramatis personae: Persons in Christ.* Translated by Graham Harrison. San Francisco: Ignatius, 1992.

———. *Mysterium Paschale: The Mystery of Easter.* Translated by A. Nichols. San Francisco: Ignatius, 1990.

Barr, James. "The Synchronic, the Diachronic and the Historical: A Triangular Relationship?" In *Synchronic or Diachronic?: A Debate on Method in Old Testament Exegesis,* edited by Johannes C. De Moor, 1–14. New York: Brill, 1995.

Barth, Karl. *Church Dogmatics, II/I, The Doctrine of God.* Edited by G. W. Bromiley and T. F. Torrance. Edinburgh: T. & T. Clark, 1957.

———. *Die Chrisliche Dogmatik im Entwurf.* Zurich: Verlag, 1927.

Bender, K. J. "Martin Luther and the Birth of Protestant Ecclesial Vision." *Perspectives in Religious Studies* 41 (2014) 257–75.

Bergeron, Joseph. "The Resurrection of Jesus: A Clinical Review of Psychiatric Hypotheses for the Biblical Story of Easter." Faculty Publications and Presentations of Liberty University. http://digitalcommons.liberty.edu/cgi/viewcontent.cgi?article=1407&context=lts_fac_pubs.

Blackham, Paul. "The Trinity in the Hebrew Scriptures." In *Trinitarian Soundings in Systematic Theology,* edited by Paul Louis Metzger, 22–35. New York: T. & T. Clark, 2005.

Blackwell, Ben. C. *Christosis: Pauline Soteriology in Light of Deification in Irenaeus and Cyril of Alexandria.* Tübingen: Mohr-Siebeck, 2011.

Bloesch, Donald G. "Soteriology in Contemporary Christian Thought." *Interpretation* 35 (1981) 132–44.
Bonhoeffer, Dietrich. *Letters and Papers from Prison*. Edited by E. Bethge. London: SCM, 1971.
Bousset, Wilhelm. *Kyrios Christos [A History of the Belief in Christ from the Beginnings of Christianity to Irenaeus]*. Translated by John E. Steely. Nashville: Abingdon, 1970.
Bracken, Joseph, SJ. "Feeling Our Way Forward: Continuity and Discontinuity within the Cosmic Process." *Theology and Science* 8 (2010) 319–31.
Braaten, Carl E. "The Triune God: The Source and Model of Christian Unity and Mission." *Missiology* 18 (1990) 415–27.
Brent, Joseph. *Charles Sanders Peirce: A Life*. Bloomington, IN: Indiana University Press, 1993.
Bridge, Edward J. "The Metaphoric Use of Slave Terms in the Hebrew Bible." *Bulletin for Biblical Research* 23 (2013) 13–28.
Brown, Raymond Edward. *An Introduction to New Testament Christology*. New York: Paulist, 1994.
———. *Jesus God and Man: Modern Biblical Reflections*. Milwaukee: Bruce, 1967.
Buckley, James J. "Balthasar's Use of the Theology of Aquinas." *Thomist* 59 (1995) 517–45.
———. "On Being a Symbol: An Appraisal of Karl Rahner." *Theological Studies* 40 (1979) 453–73.
Burns, P. J. "The Economy of Salvation: Two Patristic Traditions." *Theological Studies* 37 (1976), 599–600.
Byrne, Brendan, SJ. "Christ's Pre-existence in Pauline Soteriology." *Theological Studies* 58 (1997) 308–30.
Cain, Betty. *Gabriel Marcel's Theory of Religious Experience*. New York: Peter Lang, 1995.
Callan, Terrance. "The Soteriology of 2 Peter." *Biblica* 82 (2001) 549–59.
Campenhausen, Hans von. *The Fathers of the Greek Church*. London: A. & C. Black, 1963.
Cantens, Bernardo. "Prolegomena to Peirce's Philosophy of Religion." http://www.unav.es/gep/SeminarioCantens.html.
Carr, Anne. "Starting with the Human." In *A Rahner Reader*, edited by Gerald A. McCool, 17–30. New York: Seabury, 1975.
Casey, Maurice. *Jesus of Nazareth: An Independent Historian's Account of his Life and Teaching*. London: T. & T. Clark, 2010.
Chadwick, Henry, trans. *Origen: Contra Celsus*. Cambridge: Cambridge University, 2003.
Cimala, Peter. "Paul's Metaphorical Soteriology: Galatians as a Test Case." *Neotestamentica* 49 (2015) 351–76.
Clasby, Nancy. "Dancing Sophia: Rahner's Theology of Symbols." *Religion and Literature* 25 (1993) 51–65.
Coelho, Ivo. "The Non-Violence of Insight." *Divyadaan* 28 (2017) 29–30.
Coffey, David. "The 'Incarnation' of the Holy Spirit in Christ." *Theological Studies* 45 (1984) 466–80.
Colapietro, Vincent. *Peirce's Approach to the Self: A Semiotic Perspective on Human Subjectivity*. Albany: State University of New York, 1989.
Cone, James. *God of the Oppressed*. Maryknoll, NY: Orbis, 1997.

Congar, Yves. *I Believe in the Holy Spirit.* Translated by David Smith. New York: Crossroad, 2003.
Corduan, Winfried. "Hegel in Rahner: A Study in Philosophical Hermeneutics." *Harvard Theological Review* 71 (1978) 285–98.
Corrington, Robert S. *An Introduction to C.S. Peirce: Philosopher, Semiotician and Ecstatic Naturalist.* Lanham, MD: Rowman and Littlefield, 1994.
Crossan, John Dominic. *Who Killed Jesus? Exposing the Roots of Anti-Semitism in the Gospel Story of the Death of Jesus.* San Francisco: HarperCollins, 1995.
Crowe, Frederick E. *Appropriating the Lonergan Idea.* Edited by Michael Vertin. Toronto: University of Toronto, 2006.
Cullmann, Oscar. *The Christology of the New Testament.* Rev. ed. Translated by Shirley C. Guthrie and Charles A. M. Hall. Philadelphia: Westminster, 1963.
Dadosky, John D. "God's Eternal Yes!: An Exposition and Development of Lonergan's Psychological Analogy of the Trinity." *Irish Theological Quarterly* 81 (2016) 397–419.
Dallvalle, N. "Revisiting Rahner: On the Theological Status of Trinitarian Theology." *Irish Theological Quarterly* 68 (2003) 213–27.
Davis, Stephen T., et al., eds. *The Resurrection: An Interdisciplinary Symposium on the Resurrection of Jesus.* Oxford: Oxford University Press, 1997.
Dawkins, Richard. *The Ancestors Tale: A Pilgrimage to the Dawn of Life.* London: Weidenfeld & Nicolson, 2004.
———. *The Blind Watchmaker: Why the Evidence of Evolution Reveals a Universe without Design.* New York: Norton, 1996.
———. *A Devil's Chaplain: Selected Essays.* London: Weidenfeld & Nicolson, 2003.
———. *The God Delusion.* Boston: Houghton Mifflin, 2006.
———. *The Greatest Show on Earth: The Evidence for Evolution.* New York: Free Press, 2009.
———. *River Out of Eden: A Darwinian View of Life.* New York: Basic, 2008.
———. *Unweaving the Rainbow.* New York: Houghton Mifflin, 1998.
Delaney, C. F. *Science, Knowledge, and Mind: A Study in the Philosophy of C.S. Peirce.* Notre Dame, IN: University of Notre Dame, 1993.
Deely, John. "The Beginning of Postmodern Times: Or Charles Sanders Peirce and the Recovery of Signum." Helsinki, 2000. http://www.commens.org/sites/default/files/news_attachments/redbook.pdf.
———. "The Impact of Semiotics on Philosophy." Helsinki, 2000. http://www.commens.org/sites/default/files/news_attachments/greenbook.pdf.
Dennett, Daniel C. *Breaking the Spell: Religion as a Natural Phenomenon.* New York: Viking, 2006.
———. *Darwin's Dangerous Idea: Evolution and the Meanings of Life.* New York: Simon and Schuster, 1995.
———. *Science and Religion: Are They Compatible?* New York: Oxford University Press, 2011.
Derrida, Jacques. *Edmund Husserl's Origin of Geometry: An Introduction.* Translated by J. P. Leavey, Jr. Lincoln, NE: University of Nebraska, 1989.
———. *Positions.* Translated by A. Bass. London: The Athlone, 1987.
Dillenberger, John, ed. *Martin Luther: Selection from his Writings.* Garden City, NY: Doubleday, 1961.

Doran, R. M. "The Starting Point of Systematic Theology." *Theological Studies* 67 (2006) 750–76.

———. "Two Ways of Being Conscious: The Notion of Psychic Conversion." *Method: Journal of Lonergan Studies* 3 (2012) 1–17.

Duffy, Stephen J. *The Graced Horizon: Nature and Grace in Modern Catholic Thought*. Collegeville, MN: Liturgical, 1992.

———. "Southern Baptist and Roman Catholic Soteriologies: A Comparative Study." *Pro Ecclesia* IX (2000) 434–59.

Dulles, Avery. *The Faith of a Theologian: Marianist Award Lecture/2004*. Dayton: The University of Dayton, 2008.

Dych, William V. "Theology in a New Key." In *A Rahner Reader*, edited by Gerald A. McCool, 1–16. New York: Seabury, 1975.

Egan, Harvey D., SJ. "Hell: The Mystery of Eternal Love and Eternal Obduracy." *Theological Studies* 75 (2014) 52–73.

Eldridge, Niles, and Stephen Jay Gould. "Punctuated Equilibria: An Alternative to Phyletic Gradualism." In *Models in Paleobiology*, edited by Thomas J. M. Schopf, 82–115. San Francisco: Freeman, Cooper, 1972.

Encyclopedia Britannica. "Logos." https://www.britannica.com/topic/logos.

Erdman, Rachel. "Sacrifice as Satisfaction, Not Substitution: Atonement in the Summa Theologiae." *Anglican Theological Review* 96 (2014) 461–80.

Evans, Craig A. "Jewish Burial Traditions and the Resurrection of Jesus." *Journal of the Study of the Historical Jesus* 3 (2005) 233–48.

Fairbairn, Donald. "Patristic Soteriology: Three Trajectories." *Journal of Evangelical Theological Society* 50 (2007) 289–310.

Fischer, Mark F. "Karl Rahner's Transcendental Christology." *Philosophy and Theology* 26 (2014). https://www.pdcnet.org/collection/authorizedshow?id=philtheol_2014_0999_9_25_18&file_type=pdf.

Fowler, D. *Karl Rahner's Trinitarian Axiom: "The Economic Trinity is the Immanent Trinity and Vice Versa."* New York: Edwin Mellen, 2006.

Frey, Jörg. "Continuity and Discontinuity between 'Jesus' and 'Christ,': The Possibilities of an Implicit Christology." *RCatT* 36 (2011) 69–98. http://www.raco.cat/index.php/RevistaTeologia/article/download/244905/334226.

Frick, Peter. "Johannine Soteriology and Aristotelian Philosophy: A Hermeneutical Suggestion on Reading John 3:16 and I John 4:9." *Biblica* 88 (2007) 415–21.

Fritz, Peter Joseph. "Karl Rahner, Friedrich Schelling, and Original Plural Unity." *Theological Studies* 75 (2014) 284–307.

Gelpi, Donald L., SJ. *Grace as Transmuted Experience and Social Process, and Other Essays in North American Theology*. Lanham, MD: University of America, 1988.

———. *The Gracing of Human Experience: Rethinking the Relationship between Nature and Grace*. Collegeville, MN: Liturgical, 2001.

———. *The Turn to Experience in Contemporary Theology*. Mahwah, NY: Paulist, 1994.

———. *Varieties of Transcendental Experience: A Study in Constructive Postmodernism*. Collegeville, MN: Liturgical, 2000.

Gorman, Michael J. *Inhabiting the Cruciform God: Kenosis, Justification, and Theosis in Paul's Narrative Soteriology*. Grand Rapids: Eerdmans, 2009.

Goulder, Michael. "The Baseless Fabric of a Vision." In *Resurrection Reconsidered*, edited by G. D'Costa, 48–61. Oxford: One World, 1996.

———. "The Explanatory Power of Conversion-Visions." In *Jesus' Resurrection: Fact or Figment?: A Debate between William Lane Craig and Gerd Ludemann*, 86–103, edited by Paul Copan and Ronald K. Tacelli. Downers Grove, IL: IVP Academic, 2000.

Graffi, Giorgio. "Again on Saussure and Dilthey [Ancora su Saussure e Dilthey]." *Lingua e Stile* 30 (1995) 151–58.

Greaves, R. L. "Luther's Doctrine of Grace." *Scottish Journal of Theology* 18 (1965) 385–95.

Gregersen, N. H. "God, Matter, and Information: Towards a Stoicizing Logos Christology." In *Information and the Nature of Reality: From Physics to Metaphysics*, edited by Niels Henrik Gregersen and Paul Davies, 405–4443. Cambridge: Cambridge University Press, 2010. curis.ku.dk/ws/files/40540940/15._gregersencpt15redmgcur.doc.

Greggs, T. Review of "God of Salvation: Soteriology in Theological Perspectives." *Modern Believing* 54 (2013) 357–59.

Grenz, Stanley J. *The Social God and the Relational Self: A Trinitarian Theology of the Imago Dei*. Louisville: Westminster John Knox, 2001.

Guinard, Patrice. "Critical Analysis of Peirce's Semiotics and an Ontological Justification of the Concept of the Impressional." http://cura.free.fr/16peiren.html.

Haight, Roger, SJ. *The Future of Christology*. New York: Continuum, 2005.

———. *Jesus, Symbol of God*. Maryknoll, NY: Orbis, 1999.

Harnack, Adolf von. *History of Dogma*. Translated from 3rd German ed. by Neil Buchanan et al. New York: Russell & Russell, 1898.

Harris, Errol E. *The Foundations of Metaphysics in Science*. New Jersey: Humanities, 1993.

———. *Positions*. Translated by A. Bass. London: The Athlone, 1987.

Hays, Richard B. "Christ Died for the Ungodly: Narrative Soteriology in Paul?" *Horizons in Biblical Theology* 26 (2004) 48–68.

Heffling, Charles C., Jr. "Lonergan's *Cur Deus Homo*: Revisiting the 'Law of the Cross.'" In *Meaning and History in Systematic Theology: Essays in Honor of Robert M. Doran, S.J.*, edited by John D. Dadosky, 144–66. Milwaukee: Marquette University Press, 2009.

Heidegger, Martin. *Kant und das Problem der Metaphysik* [Kant and the Problem of Metaphysics]. Translated by James S. Churchill. Bloomington, IN: Indiana University Press, 1962.

Hengel, Martin. *Crucifixion*. London: SCM, 1977.

Henriksen, Jan-Olav. "Distinct, Unique, or Separate? Challenges to Theological Anthropology and Soteriology in Light of Human Evolution." *Studia Theologica* 63 (2013). 166–83.

Hunt, Anne. "Psychological Analogy and Paschal Mystery in Trinitarian Theology." *Theological Studies* 59 (1988) 197–218.

Janowitz, Naomi. "Rereading Sacrifice: The Semiosis of Blood." *Signs and Society* 3 (2015) 193–208.

Jersak, Brad. "Nonviolent Identification and the Victory of Christ." In *Stricken by God? Nonviolent Identification and the Victory of Christ*, edited by Brad Jersak and Michael Hardin, 13-53. Grand Rapids: Eerdmans, 2007.

Johnson, Elizabeth. "'The Right Way to Speak about God': Pannenberg on Analogy." *Theological Studies* 43 (1982) 673–93.

Johnson, J. J. "Were the Resurrection Appearances Hallucinations? Some Psychiatric and Psychological Considerations." *Churchman* 115 (2001) 227–38.

Joyce, P. M. "Synchronic and Diachronic Perspectives in Ezekiel." In *Synchronic or Diachronic?: A Debate on Method in Old Testament Exegesis*, edited by Johannes C. De Moor, 115–28. New York: Brill, 1995.
Kahler, Martin. *The So-Called Historical Jesus and the Historic, Biblical Christ*. Translated by C.C. Braaten. Philadelphia: Fortress, 1964.
Kasper, Walter. *The God of Jesus Christ*. Translated by Matthew J. O'Connell. New York: Crossroad, 1984.
Kereszty, Roch A, O. Cist. *Jesus Christ: Fundamentals of Christology*. Edited by J. Stephen Maddux. New York: Alba, 1991.
Kerr, Hugh Thomson, ed. *A Compend of Luther's Theology*. London: Student Christian Movement, 1941.
Kim, Stephen S. "The Significance of Jesus' First Sign-Miracle in John." *Bibliotheca Sacra* 167 (2010) 201–15.
Koester, Craig R. "The Savior of the World." *Journal of Biblical Literature* 109 (1990) 665–80.
Kuhn, Thomas S. *The Structure of Scientific Revolutions*. 2nd ed. Chicago: University of Chicago, 1970.
Kuschel, Karl-Josef. *Born before All Time? The Dispute over Christ's Origin*. Translated by John Bowden. London: SCM, 1992.
LaCugna, Catherine Mowry. *God For Us: The Trinity and Christian Life*. New York: HarperCollins, 1991.
Lagopoulos, Alexandros. "A Meta-Theoretical Approach to the History and Theory of Semiotics." *Semiotica: Journal of the International Association for Semiotic Studies* 213 (2016) 1–42. https://www.degruyter.com/view/j/semi.2016.2016.issue-213/sem-2015-0100/sem-2015-0100.xml.
Lee, Dorothy A. "Signs and Works: The Miracles in the Gospels of Mark and John." *Colloquium* 47 (2015) 89–101.
Leithart, P. J. "Adam, Moses, and Jesus: A Reading of Romans 5: 12–14." *Calvin Theological Journal* 43 (2008) 257–73.
Lincicum, David. "Economy and Immanence: Karl Rahner's Doctrine of the Trinity." *European Journal of Theology* 14 (2005) 111–18.
Little, Brent. "Anthropology and Art in the Theology of Karl Rahner." *Heythrop* LII (2011) 939–51.
Locke, John. *An Essay Concerning Human Understanding*. Abridged with an introduction and notes by Pauline Phemister. New York: Oxford University Press, 2008.
Loewe, W. P. "Jesus the Savior: Soteriology and the Stages of Meaning." https://rsc.byu.edu/archived/salvation-christ-comparative-christian-views/6-jesus-savior-soteriology-and-stages-meaning.
Lonergan, Bernard. "Belief: Today's Issue." In *Collected Works of Bernard Lonergan, vol. 13, A Second Collection*, edited by Robert M. Doran and John D. Dadosky, 75–85. Toronto: University of Toronto, 2016.
———. "Christology Today: Methodological Reflections." In *A Third Collection: Papers by Bernard J.F. Lonergan, S.J.*, edited by Frederick E. Crowe SJ, 74–99. New York: Paulist, 1985.
———. *Collected Works of Bernard Lonergan, vol. 8, The Incarnate Word*. Translated by Charles C. Hefling Jr. Edited by Robert M. Doran and Jeremy D. Wilkins. Toronto: University of Toronto, 2016.

------. *Collected Works of Bernard Lonergan*, vol. 3, *Insight: A Study of Human Understanding*. Edited by Robert M. Doran and Frederick E. Crowe. Toronto: University of Toronto, 1992.

------. *Collected Works of Bernard Lonergan*, vol. 14, *Method in Theology*. Edited by Robert M. Doran and John D. Dadosky. Toronto: University of Toronto, 2017.

------. *De Verbo Incarnato*. Rome: Gregorian University, 1960.

------. *Grace and Freedom: Operative Grace in the Thought of St. Thomas Aquinas*. Edited by J.P. Burns. London: Herder & Herder, 1971.

------. "The Future of Christianity." In *Collected Works of Bernard Lonergan*, vol. 13, *A Second Collection*, edited by Robert M. Doran and John D. Dadosky, 127–39. Toronto: University of Toronto, 2016.

------. "The Natural Desire to See God." In *Collected Works of Bernard Lonergan*, vol. 4, *Collection*. Edited by Frederick E. Crowe and Robert M. Doran. Toronto: University of Toronto, 1988.

------. "Revolutions in Catholic Theology." In *A Second Collection: Papers by Bernard J. F Lonergan, S.J.* Edited by W. F. J. Ryan and B. J. Tyrell. Philadelphia: Fortress, 1974.

------. *Supplement to "On the Incarnate Word."* Translated by Michael Shields SJ. Toronto: Lonergan Research Institute, 1987.

------. *Verbum: Word and Idea in Aquinas*. Edited by David Burrell. Notre Dame, IN: University of Notre Dame, 1967.

Longenecker, Richard N. "The Metaphor of Adoption in Paul's Letters." *Covenant Quarterly* 72 (2014) 71–78.

Ludemann, Gerd. *The Resurrection of Christ: A Historical Inquiry*. New York: Prometheus, 2004.

------. *What Really Happened to Jesus*. Translated by John Bowden. London: SCM, 1995.

Luther, Martin. *Werke: Kritische Gesamtausgabe*. Weimar: H. Bohlaus Nachfolger, 1883.

Lynch, William F., SJ. *Christ and Apollo: The Dimensions of the Literary Imagination*. Wilmington, DE: ISI, 2004.

Manns, Alan. *Atonement for a Sinless Society: Engaging with an Emerging Culture*. London: Paternoster, 2005.

Marcel, Gabriel. *Being and Having*. Translated by Katharine Farrer. Westminster, UK: Dacre, 1949.

------. *The Mystery of Being*, vol. 1, *Reflection and Mystery*. Translated by G. S. Fraser. London: The Harvill, 1951.

Marcus, Joel. "Mark—Interpreter of Paul." *NTS* 46 (2000) 473–87.

Marmion, Declan, and Rik Van Nieuwenhove. *An Introduction to the Trinity*. Cambridge: Cambridge University Press, 2011.

Martens, J. W. "An Empty Tomb." *America*. March 30, 2015.

Matson, D. L. "Divine Forgiveness in Paul? Justification by Faith and the Logic of Pauline Soteriology." *Stone-Campbell Journal* 19 (2016) 59–83.

Matthias, M. A. "'Lutheran' Christology in Barth's Doctrine of Justification." *Zeitschrifft fur Dialektishce Theologiae* Supplement Series 6 (2014) 12–32.

McCarthy, Michael H. *Authenticity as Self-Transcendence: The Enduring Insights of Bernard Lonergan*. Notre Dame, IN: University of Notre Dame, 2015.

Nuth, Joan N. "Two Medieval Soteriologies: Anselm of Canterbury and Julian of Norwich." *Theological Studies* 53 (1992) 611–45.

McCool, G. A., ed. *A Rahner Reader*. New York: Seabury, 1975.
McCruden, Kevin B. "Compassionate Soteriology in Hebrews, I Peter, and the Gospel of Mark." *Biblical Research* 52 (2007) 41–56.
McDermott, J. M. "The Christologies of Karl Rahner." *Gregorianum* 67 (1986) 87–123.
McGiffert, Arthur Cushman. *Protestant Thought Before Kant*. New York: Scribner's Sons, 1942.
McGuckin, John A. *St. Cyril of Alexandria: The Christological Controversy: Its History, Theology, and Texts*. Leiden: Brill, 1995.
Metz, Johann Baptist. *Faith in History: Towards a Practical Fundamental Theology*. Translated by David Smith. New York: Seabury, 1980.
Metzger, P. L. "Introduction: What Difference Does the Trinity Make?" In *Trinitarian Soundings in Systematic Theology*, edited by Paul Louis Metzger, 5–8. New York: T. & T. Clark, 2005.
Misak, Cheryl. *The American Pragmatists*. Oxford: Oxford University Press, 2013.
———. *Cambridge Pragmatism: From Peirce and James to Ramsey and Wittgenstein*. Oxford: Oxford University Press, 2016.
Molnar, P. D. "Can We Know God Directly? Rahner's Solution from Experience." *Theological Studies* 46 (1985) 228–62.
Moltmann, Jurgen. *The Trinity and the Kingdom of God: The Doctrine of God*. Translated by Margaret Kohl. London: SCM, 1981.
Mooney, R. "Lonergan's Soteriology." *Irish Theological Quarterly* 78 (2013) 19–37.
Morelli, Mark D. *At the Threshold of the Halfway House: A Study of Bernard Lonergan's Encounter with John Alexander Stewart*. Boston: Lonergan Institute, 2007.
Morgan, Jonathan. "Christus Victor Motifs in the Soteriology of Thomas Aquinas." *Pro Ecclesia* XXI (2012) 409–21.
Muck, Otto, SJ. "The Logical Structure of Transcendental Method." *International Philosophical Quarterly* 9 (1969) 342–62.
———. *The Transcendental Method*. Translated by William D. Seidensticker. New York: Herder & Herder, 1968.
Mueller, John J. *What Are They Saying About Theological Method?* New York: Paulist, 1984.
Mühlhäusler, P. "Linguistics: Diachronic." In *The Encyclopedic Dictionary of Psychology*, edited by R. Harre and R. Lamb. Oxford: Oxford University Press, 1983.
Ngong, David T. "Protesting the Cross: African Pentecostal Soteriology and Pastoral Care." *Journal of Theology for Southern Africa* 150 (2014) 5–19.
Niesel, Wilhelm. *Reformed Symbolics: A Comparison of Catholicism, Orthodoxy and Protestantism*. Translated by David Lewis. Edinburgh: Oliver & Boyd, 1962.
Oakes, Edward T., SJ. *Infinity Dwindled to Infancy: A Catholic and Evangelical Christology*. Grand Rapids: Eerdmans, 2011.
———. *Pattern of Redemption: The Theology of Hans Urs Von Balthasar*. New York: Continuum, 2005.
O'Collins, Gerald, SJ. *Christology: A Biblical, Historical, and Systematic Study of Jesus*, 2nd ed. Oxford: Oxford University Press, 2009.
———. "The Holy Trinity: The State of the Questions." In *The Trinity: An Interdisciplinary Symposium on the Trinity*, edited by Stephen Davis et al., 1–25. Oxford: Oxford University Press, 1999.
———. "The Resurrection and Bereavement Experiences." *Irish Theological Quarterly* 76 (2011) 224–37.

———. "The Resurrection Revisited." *Gregorianum* 79 (1998) 169–72.
Ormerod, Neil. *A Trinitarian Primer*. Collegeville, MN: Liturgical, 2011.
———. *The Trinity: Retrieving the Western Tradition*. Milwaukee, WI: Marquette University Press, 2005.
———. "Two Points or Four?—Rahner and Lonergan on Trinity, Incarnation, Grace, and Beatific Vision." *Theological Studies* 68 (2007) 661–73.
———. "Wrestling with Rahner on the Trinity." *Irish Theological Quarterly* 68 (2003) 213–27.
Ortlund, D. C., and G. K. Beale. "Darkness Over the Whole Land: A Biblical Theological Reflection on Mark 15:33." *Westminster Theological Journal* 75 (2013) 221–38.
Pannenberg, Wolfhart. *Basic Questions in Theology*. Philadelphia: Fortress, 1970.
———. *Jesus—God and Man*. London: SCM, 1968.
Pape, Helmut. "Searching for Traces: How to Connect the Sciences and the Humanities by a Peircean Theory of Indexicality." *Transactions of Charles S. Peirce Society* 44 (2008) 1–25.
Parker, Kelly. "C. S. Peirce and the Philosophy of Religion." *The Southern Journal of Philosophy* 28 (1990) 193–212.
Paschal, R. Wade. "Sacramental Symbolism and the Physical Imagery in the Gospel of John." *Tyndale Bulletin* 32 (1981) 151–76.
Peirce, Charles S. *The Charles S. Peirce Papers*. Cambridge: Harvard University Press, 1966.
———. *Collected Papers of Charles Sanders Peirce*. Edited by Charles Hartshorne et al. New York: Thoemmes Continuum, 1997.
———. *The Essential Peirce: Selected Philosophical Writings (1867–1893), vol. 1*. Edited by Nathan Houser and Christian Kloesel. Bloomington, IN: Indiana University Press, 1992.
———. *The Essential Peirce: Selected Philosophical Writings (1893–1913), vol. 2*. Edited by Nathan Houser and Christian Kloesel. Bloomington, IN: Indiana University Press, 1998.
———. *The Essential Writings (Great Books in Philosophy)*. Edited by Edward C. Moore. New York: Prometheus, 1998.
———. "Questions Concerning Certain Faculties Claimed for Man." *Journal of Speculative Philosophy* 2 (1868) 103–14. http://www.peirce.org/writings/p26.html.
———. *Reasoning and the Logic of Things*. Edited by Kenneth L. Ketner. Cambridge, MA: Harvard University Press, 1992.
———. *Selected Writings: Values in a Universe of Chance*. Edited with an introduction and notes by Philip P. Wiener. New York, Dover, 1966.
———. "Two Letters to Lady Welby." In *Selected Writings: Values in a Universe of Chance*, edited with an introduction and notes by Philip P. Wiener. New York, Dover, 1966.
Peterson, Gregory R. "Whose Evolution? Which Theology?" *Zygon* 35 (2000) 221–32.
Phillips, Matthew C. "Bearing the Shame of the Cross: Luther's Theology of the Cross, the Imitation of Christ, and Martyrdom." *Logia* 24 (2015) 21–26.
Piaget, Jean. *Insights and Illusions of Philosophy*. Abingdon, UK: Routledge, 2013.
Plass, Ewald M., ed. *What Luther Says, vol. 3*. St. Louis: Concordia, 1972.
Polkinghorne, John, ed. *The Trinity and an Entangled World*. Grand Rapids: Eerdmans, 2010.

Price, Robert M., and Lowder, J. J., eds. *The Empty Tomb: Jesus Beyond the Grave*. New York: Prometheus, 2005.
Rahner, Karl. "Anonymous Christian." In *Theological Investigations* 6. Baltimore: Helicon, 1961.
―――. "Anonymous Christianity and Missionary Task of the Church." In *Theological Investigations* 12. New York: Crossroad, 1971.
―――. "Currents Problems in Christology." In *Theological Investigations* 1, 149-200. London: Darton, Longmann, and Todd, 1965.
―――. *The Foundations of Christian Faith: An Introduction to the Idea of Christianity*. New York: Crossroad, 1997.
―――. *Hearers of the Word*. New York: Herder & Herder, 1969.
―――. "Jesus Christus." In *Sacramentum Mundi*, edited by Karl Rahner et.al. Freiburg: Herder, 1968.
―――. *Karl Rahner in Dialogue: Conversations and Interviews 1965–1982*. Edited by Paul Imhof et al. New York: Crossroad, 1986.
―――. "Observations on the Doctrine of God in Catholic Dogmatics." In *Theological Investigations* 9. New York: Herder & Herder, 1972.
―――. "On the Current Relationship between Philosophy and Theology." In *Theological Investigations* 13. Translated by David Bourke. New York: Crossroad, 1983.
―――. "One Christ and the Universality of Salvation." In *Theological Investigations* 16. New York: Seabury, 1979.
―――. "On the Theology of the Incarnation." In *Theological Investigations* 4. Baltimore: Helicon, 1966.
―――. "Remarks on the Dogmatic Treatise 'De Trinitate.'" In *Theological Investigations* 4. London: Darton, Longman and Todd, 1966.
―――. "Some Implications of the Scholastic Concept of Uncreated Grace." In *Theological Investigations* 1, edited by C. Ernst. Baltimore, MD: Helicon, 1961.
―――. "Theology and Anthropology." In *Theological Investigations* 9. New York: Herder & Herder, 1972.
―――. "Theology as Engaged in an Interdisciplinary Dialogue with the Sciences." In *Theological Investigations* 13. Translated by David Bourke. New York: Crossroad, 1983.
―――. "The Theology of the Symbol." In *Theological Investigations* 4. Translated by Kevin Smyth. Baltimore: Helicon, 1966.
―――. "The Theology of the Symbol." In *A Rahner Reader*, edited by Gerald McCool. New York: Seabury, 1975.
―――. "The Two Basic Types of Christology." In *Theological Investigations* 13. Translated by David Bourke. New York: Crossroad, 1983.
―――. *The Trinity*. Introduction, Index, and Glossary by Catherine Mowry LaCugna. New York: Crossroad, 1999.
―――. *The Trinity*. Translated by J. Donceel. New York: Crossroad, 1997.
―――. "What is a Sacrament?" In *Theological Investigations* 14. Translated by David Bourke. New York: Seabury, 1976.
Raposa, M. L. "Peirce and Modern Religious Thought." *Transactions of the Charles S. Peirce Society* 27 (1991) 341–69.
―――. *Peirce's Philosophy of Religion*. Bloomington, IN: Indiana University Press, 1989.

Ramelli, Ilaria L. E. "Christian Soteriology and Christian Platonism: Origen, Gregory of Nyssa, and the Biblical and philosophical Basis of the Doctrine of Apokatastasis." *Vigiliae Christianae* 61 (2007) 313–56.

Rees, D. W. "The Hallucinations of Widowhood." *British Medical Journal* 4 (1971) 37–41.

Rensburg, F. J. J. van. "Metaphors in the Soteriology in I Peter: Identifying and Interpreting the Salvific Images." In *Salvation in the New Testament: Perspectives on Soteriology*, edited by J. G. Van der Watt, 418–33. Leiden: Brill, 2005.

Robinson, Andrew J. "Continuity, Naturalism and Contingency: A Theology of Evolution Drawing on the Semiotics of C.S. Peirce and Trinitarian Thought." *Zygon: Journal of Religion and Science* 39 (2004) 111–36.

―――. *God and the World of Signs: Trinity, Evolution, and the Metaphysical Semiotics of C.S. Peirce*. Boston: Brill, 2010.

Robinson Andrew, and Christopher Southgate. "Incarnation and Semiotics: A Theological and Anthropological Hypothesis Part 1: Incarnation and Peirce's Taxonomy of Signs." *Theology and Science* 8 (2010) 265–83. http://www.tandfonline.com/doi/pdf/10.1080/14746700.2010.492620?needAccess=true.

―――. "Interpretation and the Origin of Life." *Zygon: Journal of Religion and Science* 45 (2010) 345–60.

―――. "Semiotics as a Metaphysical Framework for Christian Theology." *Zygon: Journal of Religion and Science* 45 (2010) 689–712.

Robinson, Peter M. "The Trinity: The Significance of Appropriate Distinctions for Dynamic Relationality." In *Trinitarian Soundings in Systematic Theology*, edited by Paul Louis Metzger, 49–61. New York: T. & T. Clark, 2005.

Rogerson, J. W. "Synchrony and Diachrony in the Work of De Wette and its Importance for Today." In *Synchronic or Diachronic?: A Debate on Method in Old Testament Exegesis*, edited by Johannes C. De Moor, 145–58. New York: Brill, 1995.

Sanders, Fred. Review of "Trinitarian Rule." *International Journal of Systematic Theology* 11 (2009) 370–72.

Saussure, Ferdinand. *Course in General Linguistics*. Edited by Charles Bally and Albert Sechehaye. Translated by Wade Baskin. New York: Philosophical Library, 1959.

Schineller, J. Peter. "Discovering Jesus Christ: A History We Share." In *A Rahner Reader*, edited by Gerald A. McCool, 92–119. New York: Seabury, 1975.

Schner, G. P., SJ. "The Appeal to Experience." *Theological Studies* 53 (1992) 40–59.

Schweitzer, Albert. *The Quest of the Historical Jesus: A Critical Study of its Progress from Reimarus to Wrede*. Translated by W. Montgomery. London: A. & C. Black, 1910.

Schwobel, Christoph. "The Renaissance of Trinitarian Theology: Reasons, Problems and Tasks." In *Trinitarian Theology Today: Essays on Divine Being and Act*, edited by Christoph Schwobel, 1–30. Edinburgh: T. & T. Clark, 1995.

Sebeok, T. A. *Contributions to the Doctrine of Signs*. 2nd ed. Lanham, MD: University of America, 1991.

Shillaker, Robert. "Rahner's Axiom and the Hermeneutic Foundation of Thomas Weinandy's Reconceiving the Trinity." *European Journal of Theology* 25 (2016) 33–43.

Siebenrock, R. A. "Christology." In *The Cambridge Companion to Karl Rahner*, edited by Declan Marmion and Mary E. Hines. Cambridge: Cambridge University Press, 2005.

Simmons, E. L. *The Entangled Trinity: Quantum Physics and Theology*. Minneapolis: Fortress, 2014.

Shults, LeRon F. "Transforming Theological Symbols." *Zygon* 45 (2010) 713–32.
Skiba, Paulette. *The Transcendental Christology of Karl Rahner: A Resource for Catholic Social Teaching?* PhD diss, Marquette University, 1977.
Slater, G. Review of *God and the World of Sign: Trinity, Evolution and the Metaphysical Semiotics of C. S. Peirce*. *American Journal of Theology and Philosophy* 34 (2013) 86–89.
Smith, Daniel A. "Revisiting the Empty Tomb: The Post-Mortem Vindication of Jesus in Mark and Q." *Novum Testamentum* 45 (2003) 123–37.
Smith, Joseph H. *Arguing with Lacan*. New Haven, CT: Yale University, 1991.
Smith, Stephen H. *A Sense of Presence: The Resurrection of Jesus in Context*. Leicester, UK: Troubador, 2016.
Smith, Timothy L. *Thomas Aquinas' Trinitarian Theology; A Study in Trinitarian Method*. Washington, DC: Catholic University of America, 2003.
Smith, J. Warren. "Christ's Passion in Cyril of Alexandria's Soteriology." *Pro Ecclesia* XI (2002) 463–83.
Stewart, Alexander E. "When are Christians Saved and Why Does it Matter? An Investigation into the Rhetorical Force of First Peter's Inaugurated Soteriology." *Trinity Journal* 32 (2011) 221–35.
Strauss, David Friedrich. *A New Life of Jesus*, vol. 1. London: Green and Sons, 1879.
———. *The Life of Jesus*, vol. 3. Bristol, UK: Thoemmes, 1998.
Tacey, David. *Religion as Metaphor: Beyond Literal Belief*. New Brunswick, NJ: Transaction, 2015.
Tavard, G. H. "Papacy and Christian Symbolism." *Journal of Ecumenical Studies* 13 (1976) 345–58.
Taylor, V. *The Names of Jesus*. London: McMillan, 1953.
Tejera, Vittorino. "Has Eco Understood Peirce?" *American Journal of Semiotics* 6 (1989) 251–64.
Theissen, Gerd. "Soteriologische Symbolik in den Paulinischen Schriften: Ein Strukturalistischer Beitrang." *Kerygma und Dogma* 20 (1974) 282–304.
Tillich, Paul. *Dynamics of Faith*. New York: Harper & Row, 1957.
———. "Religious Symbol and our Knowledge of God." *The Christian Scholar* 38 (1955) 189–97.
———. "Reply to Interpretation and Criticism." In *Theology of P. Tillich*, edited by G. W. Kegley. London: Macmillan, 1952.
———. *Systematic Theology*. Chicago: Chicago University Press, 1957.
———. "Theology and Symbolism." In *Religious Symbolism*, edited by F. E. Johnson, 107–16. New York: Harper & Row, 1955.
Tripole, Martin R., SJ. "Philosophy and Theology—Are They Compatible? A Comparison of Barth, Moltmann, and Pannenberg with Rahner." *Thought* 53 (1978) 25–74.
Townshend, J. "Derrida's Deconstruction of Marxism." *Contemporary Politics* 10 (2004) 127–43.
Van der Watt, J. G. *Salvation in the New Testament: Perspectives on Soteriology*. Leiden: Brill, 2005.
VanMaaren, John. "The Adam-Christ Typology in Paul and its Development in the Early Church Fathers." *Tyndale Bulletin* 64 (2013) 275–97.

Vatican Council II. *Dei Verbum, Dogmatic Constitution on Divine Revelation.* http://www.vatican.va/archive/hist_councils/ii_vatican_council/documents/vat-ii_const_19651118_dei-verbum_en.html.

———. *Gaudium et Spes.* http://www.vatican.va/archive/hist_councils/ii_vatican_council/documents/vat-ii_const_19651207_gaudium-et-spes_en.html.

Ware, James. "Paul's Understanding of the Resurrection in 1 Corinthians 15: 36–54." *Journal of Biblical Literature* 133 (2014) 809–35.

Watson, Thomas. *A Body of Divinity.* Edinburgh: Banner of Truth Trust, 1965.

Weaver, J. Denny. *The Nonviolent Atonement.* Grand Rapids: Eerdmans, 2001.

Weber, E. T. "Proper Names and Persons: Peirce's Semiotic Consideration of Proper Names." *Transactions of the Charles S. Peirce Society* 44 (2008) 346–62.

Williams, Delores S. *Sisters in the Wilderness: The Challenge of Womanist God-Talk.* Maryknoll, NY: Orbis, 1993.

Williams, Jarvis J. "Violent Atonement in Romans: The Foundation of Paul's Soteriology." *Journal of the Evangelical Theological Society* 53 (2010) 579–99.

Wisse, Maarten. *Trinitarian Theology Beyond Participation: Augustine's De Trinitate and Contemporary Theology.* New York: T. & T. Clark, 2011.

Wittgenstein, Ludwig. *Tractatus Logico-Philosophicus.* London: Routledge and Paul Kegan, 1922.

Wolf, M. "Exclusion and Embrace: Theological Reflections in the Wake of 'Ethnic Cleansing.'" *Journal of Ecumenical Studies* 29 (1992) 230–48.

Wright, N. T. "Jesus' Resurrection and Christian Origins." *Stimulus* 16 (2008) 41–50.

Yeago, David S. "The Bread of Life: Patristic Christology and Evangelical Soteriology in Martin Luther's Sermons on John 6." *St. Valdimir's Theological Quarterly* 39 (1995) 257–59.

Index of Names

Anselm of Canterbury, St., 7, 157, 172, 210–13, 217, 219–21, 225, 231
Aquinas, Thomas, St., 26, 30, 39–40, 54, 59, 127, 175, 177, 189, 195, 213, 225–26, 228, 231–32, 235–36
   argument that any of the divine persons could become man, 159
   distinction between deprivation as sinfully contracted and deprivation as voluntarily assumed, 221
   Marechal's devotion to, 12–15
   philosophical system, xi, 6
   Trinitarian treatise, 166, 172–73
Aristotle, xii, 26, 29. 39, 57, 59
   humans have five faculties, 8
   love makes two people one in affectivity, 213
   reified essences, 14, 17
Arius, 52
Athanasius of Alexandria, St., 52, 70, 190, 207
Augustine of Hippo, St., 6, 30, 54, 115, 171, 177, 186, 189, 191–92, 195, 205, 207, 209, 214, 237
   De Trinitate, 172
   psychological analogy, 189
Aulen, Gustaf, 199, 205–6, 210, 216–18, 225

Balthasar, Hans von, 172, 188–89, 225–26, 232

Barth, Karl, 7, 171, 180, 195, 216, 225, 231, 236
Basil of Caesarea, (see also Cappadocians), 53, 185–86, 191
Bonhoeffer, Dietrich, xi, 45, 226
Bousset, Wilhelm, 89, 226
Brent, Joseph, 226
Brown, Raymond, 71, 103, 226
Brownson, Orestes Augustus, 10–11
Bultmann, Rudolph, 89
Byrne, Patrick, ix, 197

Cantens, Bernando, 44, 226
Caesar Augustus, 26
Casey, Maurice, xiv, 28, 123–26, 226
Celsus, 120, 226
Chardin, Pierre Teilhard, 48, 139
Chrysostom, John, St., 207
Clement of Alexandria, St., (see also Alexandrian school), 51, 205
Comte, Auguste, 55
Crowe, Fredrick, 9, 18, 25, 227, 230–31
Cone, James, 219, 221, 226
Congar, Yves, 173, 175–76, 227
Copernicus, Nicolaus, 4
   Copernican, 12, 141
Cullmann, Oscar, 20, 75–9, 81–5, 88–96, 98,–99–101, 103, 227
Cyril of Alexandria, St., 34, 70, 87, 208, 225, 232, 236

Darwin, Charles, 55, 135–37, 139, 227
Dawkins, Richard, xv, 48, 135, 137–38, 227

INDEX OF NAMES

Dennett, Daniel, xv, 135, 137–38, 227
Derrida, Jacques, 42–43, 227, 236
Descartes, Rene, 1–2, 16

Ebeling, Gerhard, 197
Einstein, Albert, 2, 4
Emerson, Ralph Waldo, 10
Eunomius, 53
Evans, Craig, 116–18, 228

Fairbairn, Donald, 205–6, 208–9, 218, 228
Fiske, John, 55 (see also pragmatism)
Feuerbach, Ludwig, 199
Freud, Sigmund, 199

Gelpi, Donald, 5–7, 11, 31–32, 35–36, 51, 149, 228
   began his career as a devotee of Rahner's, 149–50
   identifies counterpositions in faculty psychology and transcendental Thomism, 8–20
   Marechal's work as an apologetic work, 12, 16
   Trinitarian implications in Peirce's semiotic triads, 167n7
Gould, Stephen Jay, xv, 19, 137, 228
Goulder, Michael, xiv, 121–23, 125–26, 228
Green, Nicholas St. John, 55 (see also pragmatism)
Gregory of Nazianzus, St., 98, 191, 207
Gregory of Nyssa, St., 53, 186, 191, 206–7, 235

Haight, Roger, 67–9, 229
Harnack, Adolf von, 209, 229
Harris, Errol, 17, 43, 67, 229

Heffling, Charles, 220–21, 229
Hegel, Georg F. W., 46, 49, 139, 141–42, 155, 181, 198, 227
Heidegger, Martin, 161, 229
Heisenberg, Werner, 2, 4, 49
Hillary of Poitiers, 191
Hengel, Martin, 28, 117, 229
Herodotus, 29

Holmes, Oliver Wendell, 55 (see also pragmatism)
Hume, David, 11
Husserl, Edmund, 18, 42, 227

Ignatius of Antioch, St., 34, 70
Irenaeus of Lyons, St., 86, 115, 205–6, 225–26

James, William, 8, 55–6, 232 (see also pragmatism)
Jerome, St., 115
John XXIII, Pope, 3
Josephus, Flavius, 24, 29
Justin Martyr, St., 6

Kahler, Martin, 27, 230
Kant, Immanuel, 2, 6, 9–13, 15–16, 32, 46, 48–49, 59, 66, 141–42, 181, 214, 229, 232
Kasper, Walter, 176, 197, 230
Ketner, Kenneth, 45, 233
Kuhn, Thomas, xi, xv, 136, 230
Kung, Hans, 70, 117, 197
Kuschel, Karl-Joseph, 197, 230

Lacugna, Catherine, 173, 175, 183, 195–96, 230, 234
Laplace, Pierre-Simon, 1
Lavoisier, Antoine-Laurent, xii
Leo XIII, Pope, 12
Locke, John, 2, 11, 57, 230
Lonergan, Bernard, ix–xii, 31, 35, 73, 187, 198
   analogy, use of, 39–41
   experiential metaphysics, 35–36, 197
   satisfaction and redemption, 213, 219–21, 223, 227, 229–33
   shift from a cosmological viewpoint to anthropological viewpoint, 4
   things that properly belong to Christ, 127–29
   transforms Kant's transcendental analysis, 9–10, 16–19, 25
   An Sit and *Quid Sit* pair of questions, 26
   Trinitarian formula, 166

Lubac, Henri, 7
Ludemann, Gerd, xiv, 121–23, 126, 229, 231
Luther, Martin, xvi, 70–71, 214–18, 225, 227, 229–31, 233, 237

Macquarie, John, 40, 70
Marcel, Gabriel, 32–33, 231
Marechal, Joseph, xi, 9, 12–16, 18, 66, 141, 162
Meier, John, 28
Melanchthon, Philip, 216, 222
Metz, Johann Baptist, 149, 232
Misak, Cheryl, 48, 55–6, 232
Moltmann, Jurgen, 176, 187–88, 195, 197, 232, 236
Muck, Otto, 18, 67, 232

Nestorius, 208
Newman, John Henry, Cardinal, 198
Newton, Isaac, 1, 4, 141
Nietzsche, Friedrich, 199

Oakes, Edward, 22, 24–26, 34, 36, 38–39, 71–75, 77–83, 100–105, 214, 232
O'Collins, Gerald, 1–3, 27–33, 36–37, 69, 72, 75, 83, 94–100, 102, 114–17, 119–20, 125–27, 171, 197, 232
Origen, 6, 51–2, 120, 205–07, 226, 235

Pannenberg, Wolfhart, 20, 37, 39, 70–71, 73, 76, 86–87, 89, 90, 96, 106, 127, 130–32, 166, 197, 207, 210–11, 222, 229, 233, 236
Parker, Kelly, 44, 233
Parker, Theodore, 10–11
Peirce, Charles Sanders, ix, 233–37
    connects metaphysical categories to the divine persons, xvi
    critique of European philosophy, 30–31
    evolutionary Christology, 134, 158–59, 167, 170, 178, 196–97, 222, 226–27
    fallibilist theory, xiii–xiv, 9–11, 16–17, 19, 43–45, 51

metaphysics with the highest grade of reality, 20, 32, 46–50, 54–67
pragmatism, 55–56
resurrection can be grasped by signs, 107, 110, 114, 129, 132–33, 179–84, 190
triadic logic, 16
Peterson, Gregory, 19, 136–39, 233
Piaget, Jean, 16, 233
Planck, Max, 2, 4
Plato, 6, 14, 17, 29, 39, 94, 111
Pliny the Younger, 24, 29
Polkinghorne, John, 135, 159–60, 233

Rahner, Karl, xv–xvi, 4–5, 7–9, 12–14, 18–19, 38
    Christology
        from below v. from above, 68–70
        transcendental or evolutionary, 66–67, 135, 139, 150–65
    gnoseological concupiscence, 5
    gnoseoological pluralism, 5
    Jesuit study, background information and context of, 140–50
    Rahner's Rule or *grundaxiom*, xvi, 160, 169, 171, 175, 177, 195
    Trinitarian renaissance, 167–77, 180, 183–84, 187. 195, 197, 211, 226–28, 230, 232–36
Raposa, Michael, 44, 167, 234
Rees, Dewi W., xiv, 124–26, 235
Reichenbach, Hans, 43
Reimarus, Hernan Samuel, 27, 235
Ritschl, Albrecht, xvi, 218
Robinson, Andrew, xv–xvi, 45, 57
    following Peirce's classification of signs, 61–5, 93–4, 136, 148, 156
    God became man or horizontal dimension of Christology/Trinity, 163–65. 167–70, 177–96, 198, 235
    neglect of the metaphysics of the Holy Spirit, 54–55
    Platonic resonances in Peirce's categories, 51–3
    vestiges of Trinity in creation, 158

INDEX OF NAMES

Rorty, Richard, 56 (see also pragmatism)
Royce, Josiah, 5, 8
Russell, Bertrand, 43

Saussure, Ferdinand, 20–23, 37, 57–8, 229, 235
Santayana, George, 8
Schelling, Friedrich, 161, 199, 228
Schillebeeckx, Edward, 7, 70, 197
Schiller, Ferdinand Canning Scott, 56 (see also pragmatism)
Schleiermacher, Fredrich, xvi, 7, 218, 222
Schopenhauer, Arthur, 199
Schweitzer, Albert, 27–28, 235
Scotus, John Duns, 159
Sobrino, Jon, 197
Socrates, 29
Southgate, Christopher, 45, 51, 61–62, 64–65, 235

Spencer Herbert, 137
Stewart, Alexander, 202–3, 236
Strauss, David, 27, 120–21, 199, 236
Suetonius, 29

Tacitus, 24, 29
Teilhard de Chardin, Pierre, 48, 139
Tertullian, 115, 191, 205, 209
Tillich, Paul, 40, 44–5, 60, 64–5, 236

Valentinus, 115
Volf, Miroslav, 221, 237

Watson, Thomas, 188, 237
Whitehead, Alfred North, 8
William, Delores, 219, 221
Wittgenstein, Ludwig, 36, 56, 107, 232, 237
Wright, Chauncey, 55 (see also pragmatism)
Wright, N.T., 110–13, 129–30, 237

Index of Subjects

a posteriori, 152
a priori, 8, 10, 13, 19, 152, 154, 169, 181, 183, 188, 195
   metaphysical thinking, 32, 66–67
   structure of consciousness, 13
   truths, xiii, 5, 14, 51
abduction, 16
absolute, 1–2, 5, 33, 55, 212
   absolute first and absolute last, 47, 182
   Allah the eternal absolute, 34
   God, absolute being of, 172, 188
   God of absolute closeness, 61, 148–49
   Hegelian absolute intelligibility, 185
   idealism, 49
   Jesus as absolutely incapable of sin, 128
   Jesus as absolute savior, 152, 154, 158
   power, 88
   state of absolute nothing, 50
abstract, 13, 158
   metaphysical speculation, 149, 195, 197
   modes of thinking/ideas, 20, 36, 51, 129
   theology 211, 219
Adam, 230, 236
   Christ the (second) final Adam, 3, 75, 85–87, 96
adoption, 200, 204–6, 231
African, 152, 219, 232
agapism, 48–49, 54, 179

agency, 192
   Agennetos, 52–53
   the Father *agennesia*, 191
agnostics, 27
Alexandria, Council of, 190
Alexandrian Christology, 68, 70
Alexandrian School, 51, 69
algorithms. 138
analogy, 31, 36, 38–9, 176. 195
   psychological analogy of the Trinity, 168, 170–74, 177, 181, 185–90, 195–96, 227, 229
   social analogy of the Trinity, xvi, 185–86, 187, 189, 196
Anomoeans, 53
anthropology, ix, 6, 139
   anthropological turn, 1–2, 6–7, 36, 38
   Christian anthropology, 15, 23, 141, 145–46, 148, 152, 154, 162, 196, 223, 229–30, 234–35
   shift from a cosmological to anthropological viewpoint, 4
anthropocentric interpretation, 218
Antioch, 100
Antiochene School, 68–69
apocalypse, 81, 84
Apokatastasis, 206–7, 235
apologetic, 12, 15, 24
apologists, 6, 70
Arianism, 52–53, 192
Aristotelian, xi, 6, 8–9, 14, 30, 42, 132, 140, 200, 228
ascending [Christology], xiii, 69, 153
atheist/atheistic, xv, 137–38

INDEX OF SUBJECTS

atone/atonement, xvi, 23, 81, 84, 198–200, 205–6, 210, 212–13, 222, 225, 228, 231, 237
    Luther/Protestant teaching, 215–20
    Rahner's view, 157, 159
authentic, 21, 211
Augustinian, 6, 169, 172, 174, 177, 214

Beatific/knowledge vision, xv, 40, 158, 187, 233
Bible, 24, 40, 88, 226
Biblical, xiv, 20, 22, 29, 37–38, 76, 79, 88, 106–107, 109, 112, 114, 117, 184–85, 214, 225–26, 229–30, 232–33, 235, 237
biology, xiii, 23–24
    biological, 135, 138
    biologist, 137

Cappadocians, 53–4, 171, 185, 187, 190–91, 207
categories, xiii, xvi, 4, 6, 8, 14, 17, 19, 35–36, 42, 46–49, 51–53, 59, 64, 66, 104, 110, 132, 134–35, 143, 149, 158, 163, 167, 169–70, 172, 174, 177–78, 180–86, 219
    categorical knowledge, 154
    categorical scheme, 59
Catholic (Roman), 3–4, 6
    doctrine, 214, 221, 234, 236
    theology, xi, 140, 142–3, 173, 191, 204, 229, 231–32
Chalcedonian definition, 135–36
    as Omega point, 139
    Rahner's view, xv, 142–44, 147–48, 151–57, 159–61, 163, 172, 195
    Robinson's view, 177, 189
chance, 10, 48–49, 51, 111, 134, 233
change, 26, 137, 158, 202, 218
Chemist, xii
    chemistry, 136
Christ, Jesus, ix, xi, xiii–xiv, 3, 5–6, 17, 20, 31, 61, 198–204, 207–8, 212–26, 228–31, 233–36
    hallucination theory, 120–27
    iconic sinsign, 61, 127–30, 132
    intelligibility of, xiii-xiv, 23–28
    natures of, xv, 39, 53, 69–70, 90–101, 106–7
    paradox of 34, 40–41
    pre-existence of, 6
    in Scripture, 3
    significance of, 67, 73–75, 78, 82, 84–88, 103, 110, 114–17
Christianity, xi, xiv, 5, 19, 24, 27, 34, 78, 88, 90–91, 93, 96, 106–7, 116, 120–21, 127, 140, 205, 226, 231, 234
    Eastern, 36
    what is distinctive about, 152
Christogenesis, 48, 139
Christos, 70, 89, 130, 226
classic/classical [tradition], 32, 43, 45, 112, 187, 199
    analogy, 172
    atonement, idea of, 205
    Christology, 153, 155
    Latin, 171–72
    Lutheran theology, 216
    philosophy or metaphysics, 2, 8, 14, 150
    physics, xii, 3, 17
    prophets, 77
cognition, 11, 13, 31, 46, 48, 149
    cognitional, 7, 12
collaboration [functional] ix
    community of collaborators, 19
commitment, 52, 118, 138, 200
    committed to a cause no longer believable, 122
    commitment to challenging theology's excessive reliance on ancient metaphysics, 132
    Jesus eternally committed to the faithful, 200
    satisfaction for sins committed, 84, 211, 221
    sins committed, 84
common sense, 8
conscious being/activities, 1, 77, 107, 147, 154, 228
conscious interpreter, 58–59, 133, 179
consciousness, 1, 13, 16–17, 19–20, 31, 73, 188–89, 213
    of early Christians, xiv, 103

INDEX OF SUBJECTS   245

invariant structure of, xiii, 24
consummation, 78–79, 139, 202, m 216, 224
context, 19–20, 30, 42, 57, 68, 161, 163, 167–68, 236
    Christology in new context, 35
    of culture, xi
    Hellenistic, 88–89
    of understanding, 45, 114, 205, 208, 211–12, 215
contingent/contingency, x, 18, 45, 135, 235
continuity [principle of], 45, 47–49, 72, 134, 165, 226, 228, 235
    continuous process of semiosis, 59, 180
    continuous with dogma, 106
    continuously evolving universe, 134
    Jesus' continuous revelation of divine plan, 94
conversion, 19, 122, 125, 149, 228–29
corruption, 203, 205
corruptible, 208
cosmogenesis, 139
cosmological, 153
    argument, 59
    evolution, 165
    shift from cosmological to anthropological viewpoint, 4
cosmology, 93
cosmos, 39, 93–94, 127, 143, 223–24
councils, 37, 136, 153, 217
    Alexandria, 190
    Chalcedon, xv, 35, 39, 135–36, 155, 168
    Constantinople, 52, 191–92
        local council of, 207
    Constantinople III, 156
    Nicaea, 35, 52, 170, 194
    Trent, 214
    Vatican I, 3, 31
    Vatican II, 3, 8, 140, 237
counter position, xi, 8, 141
creation, xv, 52, 82, 137–39, 148–49, 151–54, 157, 164, 196, 204, 216, 221
    of Adam, 85–86

    relates redemption to, 93–96, 98, 108
    resurrection as act of new creation, 129
    vestiges of Trinity in, 158–59, 171, 177
crisis, xv, 3–6, 12, 136
culture, 4, 6, 22–23, 26, 58, 96, 124, 168, 204, 219, 231
    cultural, 28, 125, 133, 153
    crisis, 3–6
    matrix/context, xi, 114, 123
    meanings and values, 25
    systems, 57
    turn, 36

Darwinian/Darwinism, xv, 48, 137–38, 140–41, 227
data, xii, 33
    of Christ, 22–24, 26–31, 71, 73
deconstruction, 10, 42–43, 236
    deconstructionist project, 12, 42
deduction, 13, 16
deductivist, 75
deification, xvi, 111, 209, 225
deist, 27
deity, 53, 88
descending [Christology], xiii, 69, 153
description, xii, 81, 99, 107, 118, 162
    descriptive, xii, 21
design, 48, 104, 138–39, 227
    design argument, 139
    designed, 59, 107, 221
    designer, 138
determinism, 48–9
diachronic, xii–xiv, xvi, 20–23, 25–27, 73–74, 199, 225, 230, 232, 235
dialectic, 201
    dialectical, xvi, 67, 218
dialogue, 5, 96, 148, 160, 167, 234
docetic, 164
dogma, 35, 136, 209, 229–30
    dogmatic, 7, 19, 27, 143, 167, 174, 183, 195, 205, 225, 234, 237
dyadic relations, 57–59, 179

earth, 25, 65, 78, 83, 87, 90, 95, 97, 100, 102, 111–12, 115, 128, 131, 135, 137–38, 202, 207, 221–22, 227
  earthly
    body, 115
    Jesus, 119
    work of Jesus, xiv, 75–76, 78, 82, 85, 87, 89–90, 102–4
ecumenical, 3, 136, 153, 192, 236–37
  consensus, xvi, 197–98, 222
Epicureans, 57
eschatology/eschatological, 23, 132, 223
  event, 76, 200–203, 206
  hope, 129–30
  prophet, 77–78
  sign, 108
  work of Jesus, 84, 98, 101
eschaton, 114, 129, 222
eternal, 10, 26, 34, 39, 41, 84, 108, 148, 160, 167, 177, 185, 227–28
  generation, 52
  preexistence, 95
  priesthood, 83, 200
  of the Second Person, 22
  son, 128, 156
eternally distinct, 52–53, 174, 185
emergence, 223
empirical, 16, 31, 43, 107, 133
  empirically verifiable, 32, 37
  empiricism, 38, 43
  empiricist, 1, 37
empty 6
  tomb, 115–23, 133, 231, 234, 236
Enlightenment, 140
  critique of religion, xi, 10–12, 27
episode, 29, 106, 119–20, 126
epistemic, 4, 107
epistemology, 8, 12–13, 43, 141, 164
  epistemological hypothesis/ accounts, 15, 56, 68–69, 169
Eucharist, 62, 81, 83
evil, 84, 109, 201, 206–7, 213
  problem of, 109, 222
evolution, xv, 19, 23, 48, 153–56, 227, 229, 233, 235–36
  cosmological, 165, 223

  theory of, 135–39
  of thought, 103, 134, 179
Evolutionary, 17–18, 65, 104, 165
  biologist, 137
  Christology, 134–36, 150–51, 153, 155
  love, 222
  process, xi–xii, xv, 48–9, 138–39

faculty, 12
  faculty psychology, xi-xii, 8–9, 14–16, 18, 20, 35, 149–50
  faculties of knowing, 8, 14, 20, 31, 46, 177, 186, 233
faith, xii–xiii, 22–25, 27–28, 31, 35, 61, 67, 73, 78, 89, 91–92, 100, 105–7, 109, 119–20, 149, 152, 155, 159, 166–67, 172, 174, 188, 203, 205, 228, 231–32, 234, 236
  as an act of human personality, 44
  as an act of knowledge, 44
  distinguishes theology from other disciplines, 24
  intelligible, 151, 212
  justification by, 214–17
  language of, 60
  object of, 218
  people of no faith, 142, 150
  uncritical, 140
fallibilism, 43
  fallibilist, xiii, 44
  fallibilistic 10, 17
  fallible, 32
Fathers [Church], xvi, 6, 30, 40, 86–87, 98, 102, 120, 127–28, 198, 204–5, 207–10, 217–18, 226, 236
  (see also Cappadocians)
  God as Father, xiv, 13, 52–4, 88, 93–6, 106, 119, 128, 158–60, 162–63, 166–67, 170–71, 176–77, 183–85, 188, 190–94, 198, 201, 213
filioque, 170, 190–93
  filiation, 166–67
  filial adoption, 204
fire, xi–xii, 63, 111
first principles, 8, 75

firstness, xvi, 46–8, 51–3, 134, 170, 178, 180–85, 189, 193
forgiven, 214, 218
forgiveness, 200, 209, 214–18, 223, 231
fossils, 137
foundational, 1, 10–11, 187, 200, 220
    foundationalist, 43, 169
        foundations, 12, 16, 19, 21, 34, 97, 132, 141, 195, 215
freedom, 13, 18, 54, 68, 143, 146–48, 152, 154, 157, 195–96, 201, 204–6, 231
functional, ix, xiii, 16, 72, 180
    functionalization, 171
    functionally, 138. 189

galaxy, 144
Germany, 11
gene, 138
Generalized Empirical Method (GEM), 31
Genesis, 82, 85–87, 95, 137–38
Gnostic/Gnosticism, 115, 174, 205–6
grace, xv, 6, 8–9, 17, 23, 31, 36, 67–8, 127, 167, 169, 177, 187, 201–2, 213, 228, 231, 233–34
    Anselm's argument on, 220
    available to everyone, 144, 146–52, 157–60
    Christ's grace is different from ours, 128–29, 153, 156
    Luther's theology of, 214–15, 229
grave, 80, 111, 234
gravitational. 12
Grundaxiom, xvi, 160, 169, 171, 175, 177, 195

hallucination (hypothesis), xiv, 61, 119–27
Hegelian, 49, 185
Hellenistic, xiii, 6, 29, 74, 88, 91–92, 96, 106, 110, 199
hermeneutics, 132, 161, 227, 235
    hermeneutical, xiv, 7, 106, 110, 133, 228
Heterousians, 53, (see also Cappadocians)
heuristics, 198

High Christology, 70–72
high priest, 75, 81–85, 113, 200
Hindu, 28, 152
historical
    approach, xiv, 22, 153
    antecedents, 79
    Christianity, 27
    Christology, 153
    context, 42, 163
    criticism, 138
historicity, 25–6, 116, 139
historicization, 171
homousion, 52, 190–91
Homer, 110–11
horizon, 10, 97, 150, 228
    horizontal dimension, 163
hypostasis, 37, 52–53, 184–85, 189, 208
    hypostatic union, 127–28, 141, 151, 154–56, 208
hypothesis, xii–xiv, 14, 16, 32, 51, 134, 225
hypothetical, xii, 24, 169, 210

icon, 45, 61–63, 65–66, 103, 165, 179, 181, 198, 222
    iconic, 61–62, 65, 163–64
    iconically, 110, 133, 163
idealism, 12, 43, 49, 66
    German, xiii, 46, 49, 51, 149
immanent, 14
    God's immanence, 94
    Trinity, 135, 159–60, 168–72, 174–76, 180, 194–95, 228
immutable, 39, 171
imperfection, 176
impersonal, 32, 209
implicit (Christology), xiii, 72, 228
incarnation, xv, 23, 64–5, 71, 96, 127–28, 132, 135, 151, 153–56, 158–59, 163–64, 167, 174–76, 187, 206–8, 212, 226, 233–35
    incarnately, 26
    incarnational, 11
    O'Collins' description of, 37
    Lonergan's distinction, 39
inculturated, 16

INDEX OF SUBJECTS

index, 62–63, 65–66, 103, 133, 163, 179–81, 222, 234
    indexical, xiii–xiv, 64, 107, 114, 133, 198, 233
induction, 16
innovative, 52, 167
inquiry, 9, 43, 56, 140, 231
    metaphysics as a form of, 32, 49–50, 107, 169
intellectual concepts, 56
    intellectualism, 140
Intelligibilities, xiii, 11, 24–25, 33, 47, 54, 182, 185, 219
    intelligible, 10, 39, 116, 134, 151, 167, 184, 196, 221
intentionality analysis, 9, 18, 31
interpretant, 58–61, 63, 66, 114, 134, 179–81, 183, 189
interiority, 155
    interior, 30, 120
intuition, 5, 10–11, 30–31, 46
invention, 80, 101, 169

Jews, 92, 102, 113–14, 116, 130
    pious, 112
Jewish
    apocalypticism, 127
    burial, 116–19, 228
    Christian beliefs, 122
    concept of resurrection, 129–30, 132
    conception, xiii–xiv, 24, 28–29, 65, 70, 74, 78–79, 81–83, 90–91, 93–94, 96, 98–99, 103, 106–7, 110–14
    symbols, 199
judgment, 26, 31, 130–31, 202–3, 223
    moral, 13
justice, 69, 71, 78, 82, 130, 157, 220–21
justification, 128, 134, 171, 200, 204, 214–18, 223, 228–29, 231

Kantian, 13, 32, 46, 66
    derived philosophy, xi, 5
    logic and epistemology, 8–9, 12, 14–16
    nominalism, 31
    transcendental method, 2, 18, 142

kenosis, 208, 228
    kenotic community, 189
kerygma, 35, 106, 110, 114, 236
    kerygmatic tradition, 115, 202
kingdom(s)
    ancient, 111
    of God, 65, 78, 89, 90, 102, 132, 202, 204, 222, 232
    of Satan, 207

Latin, 6, 171–72
law, 66, 113
    of the Cross, 104, 223, 229
    law-like character of the evolutionary process, 138
    Mosaic, 89, 118
    Planck's, 2, 4
Legisign, 61–63, 66
liberation, 31, 199, 204, 222
    theologian, 219
Logos, 75, 93, 158–59, 162, 164, 199, 207, 228–29
    Christology, 68–69
    of the Johannine Gospel, 93–96
    of Middle Platonism, 6, 52, 120
love, xiii, 31, 48–49, 51, 54, 73, 92, 111, 203, 213, 219, 221–22, 228
    between the divine Persons, 128, 159, 162, 172–73
    heart of Jesus as symbol of, 161
    Jesus' death as an expression of, 201
    psychological analogy as the model of, 174, 186–87
low (Christology), xiii, 70–72

machine, 1
material, 15, 39, 58, 61, 88, 109, 115, 119, 133, 151, 153, 164
materialism, 3, 46, 93, 135
mathematical/mathematics, 1, 4, 48, 56, 132, 178
    mathematician, 1, 56–57
mechanism, 151
    mechanistic, 1, 48
mediated, 2, 11, 17, 23, 25, 30, 35, 59, 68, 84, 184, 221
mediates, 47, 52, 58, 83, 184, 221

mediating, 5, 193
mediation, 134, 177, 182–84, 193–94
    mediator, 82–84, 93, 129
metaphors, xvi, 96, 198–200, 202–4,
        218, 222, 231, 235–36
    metaphorical, 40, 202–203, 226
metaphysics, 6, 8, 66, 74, 136, 143, 150,
        161, 197, 206, 229, 235–36
    Christology from above as
        metaphysical Christology, 68,
        161, 164
    classical, xi-xiii, xv, 2, 8, 12–14, 16,
        18, 64, 132, 140–43
    demise of, 6, 168
    of experience/presence, xv–xvi,
        9–11, 17, 20, 42–43, 45–46,
        48–49, 64, 66–68, 76, 158, 165,
        167–70, 178, 180, 193, 197
    Kant's assault on, 13, 32, 48
    members of the Metaphysical Club
        (see pragmatism), 55-6
    theological neglect of metaphysics
        of the Holy Spirit, 54
    theology is a religion in search of,
        5, 149–50
miracles, 103, 110, 230
    sign miracles, xiv, 107–10
modalism, 176, 192
model, 162, 174, 212, 226
    semiotic, xii, xv–xvi, 51, 53–54,
        165, 168, 170, 177–78, 183–86,
        189–90, 193, 196, 204
    social, 187–89, 196
modernism, 11
modernists, 10–12
modernity, xi, 4–6, 132, 140
Monophysitism, 155, 176
monotheism, 34, 187–88
monotheists, 174
Monothelite, 156
moral, 4, 11, 13, 85
motion, 4
Muslim, 28, 33-4, 152
mysterious, 67, 77, 82, 102, 193
mystery, 26, 29–30, 36, 39, 85, 225,
        228–29, 231
    of the incarnate Word, 3
    openness to, 149, 153–54
    of the Trinity, 159, 171–72, 175,
        184
mystic, 7, 112, 211

natural sciences, 1, 23
natural selection, 48, 136–39
naturalistic, 120, 122
naturalists, 4, 227
Neo-Darwinism, xv, 48, 137–38, 140–41
Nestorian, 176
Nestorius, 208
new atheists (see atheist and Neo-
        Darwinism)
Newtonian, 3
Nicaea, Council of (see Councils)
nominalism, 5, 11–12, 31, 36
    British, 46
noumena, 13

object, 38–39, 88, 143–44, 146, 150,
        154, 218–19
    Peircean, 44, 50, 58–66, 114,
        133–34, 163–65, 179–81, 183,
        189, 222 (see also icon, index,
        symbol)
    possibility of knowing, 1, 12, 19,
        31–33, 43
    of theology, 20
    objective character, 3–4, 11, 13, 32–33,
        56, 59, 201
    objectively, 142, 152
    verifiable hypothesis, 134
objectivity, 1–3, 11, 33, 135
    fixation with, 2
omega point, 139
ontological, xiii, 15, 51, 53, 68, 72, 134,
        180, 193–96, 206, 211, 221,
        223, 229
    ontology, xv, 11, 136, 160, 162–65,
        167–69, 180
organisms, 137–38
oxidization, xii

paleobiology, 228
paleontologists, 137
Palestine, 25, 28, 73, 117, 119, 123
pantheistic, 93
parables, 81, 98, 198, 225

INDEX OF SUBJECTS

paradigm, xiv–xv, 107, 110, 151, 163, 204
    shift, xv, 136
paradox, 26, 34, 101
perichoresis, 171, 181, 184, 196
phenomenology, xiii, xvi, 9–10, 17, 19, 42, 47, 74, 134, 150, 170, 183, 185
phenomenon, 13, 28, 47, 52, 56, 138, 182–83, 227
Phlogiston, xii
physicist, 1–2, 136, 159
physics, xii, 1–4, 12, 17, 23, 67, 136, 160, 178, 229, 235
Planck's law, 2, 4 (see also Max Planck)
Platonic, 8–10, 15, 30, 39, 42, 51–52, 94, 96, 174, 185, 206
Platonism, 6, 30, 51–52, 93, 120, 206–7, 235
Platonist, 15, 30, 52, 120
pneumatic, 115, 194
Pneumatochians, 190–91, 193
positivism, 55
pragmatism, 232
    America's home grown philosophy, 55–56
    pragmatists, 9, 45, 49, 158
preexistence, 75, 87, 103, 206–7
priest, 78, 99, 102, 113
    Jesus as, 71, 75, 81–85, 200
    priestly office, 82–5
probability (antecedent probability), 198
    low probability of evidence, 44
problem, xi, 15, 30, 32–34, 37, 39, 64, 109, 133, 217, 220, 234–35
    gnostic, 205
    of evil, 222
    of intra-Trinitarian relations, xvi, 52, 55, 157, 170–72, 187, 190–91, 195–96
    of metaphysics, 13, 21, 42, 141–42, 179, 229
prolepsis, 223
prophet(s), 28, 54–5, 78, 81, 89, 99, 108, 112–13, 132
    Jesus as, 71, 75–79, 100
Protestant, 3, 44, 55, 120, 204, 214, 216–18, 225, 232
Protestantism, xvi, 198, 214, 218, 232
providence, ix
psychological analogy of the Trinity (see analogy)
Punctuated Equilibrium (PE), 19, 137, 228

qualisign, 61–63, 65–66, 163–64
quasi [divine], 111
    quasi-sacramental/formal causality, 157–58

rabbi, 26, 71, 75, 89
randomness, xv, 138–39
real-symbol, 158, 164
realism, 11–12, 16, 19, 30–31, 140
Reconciliation, xvi, 135, 199–200, 201, 204, 206, 218, 223
redeemer, 86
redemption, 19, 64, 83–84, 93, 158, 200, 205, 213, 217, 219, 223, 232
redemptive, 72, 92, 199, 201, 213, 221–23
Reformation, 3, 214–16
reformers, 215, 217–18
relations, 3, 17, 35–36, 55, 58–59, 133–34, 141, 143–44, 160
    indexical, 107
    Intra-Trinitarian, xvi, 166–68, 170–73, 175, 177–78, 180, 184, 186–89, 194–95, 213
religion, ix, 3–4, 19, 24, 112, 142–43, 149, 152–53, 199, 225–27, 233–36
    Christianity as a religion in search of metaphysics, 5
    Enlightenment critique of, xi, 10–11
    Kant's claim that we cannot know religious truths, 13
    multi-religious world, 153
    Peircean harmony between science and, 44–5, 50, 165
    pragmatists' view, 55–6
religious language, 36–38, 40, 60, 64, 88, 94, 110, 122, 138–39
religious understanding of the Fathers, 205

relativity (theory of), 2, 4
repetition, 155
representamen, (see also sign-vehicle), 58–9, 179, 181, 183
representation, 40–41, 87, 107, 134, 161–64
revelation(s), 94–96, 100, 119, 122, 143, 147–48, 150, 156, 176–77, 183–84, 202, 237
   history of God's, 175, 195
   philosophical concerns of God's, 172
   recipients of, 45
revolution, xii, 4, 12, 17, 19, 67, 136, 138, 142, 230–31
revolutionary, 113

Sabbath, 103
sacraments, 41, 160–61, 214–15, 234
   quasi-sacramental, 157, 233
Saussurean, xii, 21–23, 59
schema, 54, 75
schematization, xiv, 76
schemes, 59, 132, 139, 142, 180, 212, 216
scientists, 9, 43, 55, 137–38, 142, 167
Scholastic, 6, 9, 16, 18–19, 30, 142, 151, 157–60, 169, 173, 211, 213–14, 216–17, 222, 234
Scholasticism, xi, 212, 217, 222
   criticism of Neo-Scholasticism, xv, 8, 140, 158–59, 167–69, 173–75, 183
Scotist, 151
secondness, xvi, 46–49, 51–53, 134, 170, 178, 180–86, 189, 193–94
selfish, 27, 187
sin, xv, 29, 36, 61, 79–81, 84, 86–7, 92, 198, 200–201, 203, 206–7, 211–14, 216, 219, 221
   Christ has no sin, 128, 159
   literalism as original sin of religion, 199
   original, xv, 128, 139
   transformation of, 83–4, 115, 202, 209–10, 213, 215, 221
sinsign, xiv–xv, 61–63, 66, 106, 110, 127–30, 133
skeptic(s), 57, 133
skepticism, 11, 32, 121, 136, 168

Social Analogy of the Trinity (see analogy)
social doctrine, 188
social sciences, 5, 23
space, 2, 17, 108, 120, 150
species, 55, 125, 136–37
statistical laws, 2
stimulus, 123, 237
Stoics/Stoicism, 6, 57, 93–94, 96, 111, 229
subordinationism, xvi, 52, 170, 184, 193
supernatural existential, 146–49, 151–52
symbol(s), 60, 62–66, 103, 140, 158, 160–65, 180–81, 199, 226, 229, 234, 236
symbolism, 65, 198–99, 204–5, 233, 236
synchronic, xii–xiii, xvi, 20–27, 73–74, 199, 225, 230, 235
synechism, 47–9, 134, 179
Synoptics, 68, 72, 89. 95, 102, 109, 126
synthesis, 26, 140, 169, 177
systematic, xv, 32, 55, 57, 64–65, 139, 167, 179, 225, 228–29, 232, 235–36
   exegesis as systematic reflection, 21–23, 26
   theological thinking, 7
   treatise of the Trinity, 172

taxonomy of signs, 64, 135, 180–81, 235
teacher (see also rabbi), 75–76, 89, 214
teleological, 139,
teutonic, xiii, 51, 67
theological method, 19, 45, 232
thirdness, xvi, 45–48, 51, 53–54, 134, 170, 178, 180–86, 189, 193–94
Thomism/Thomistic, 6, 15, 132, 153, 166, 169, 172, 177, 187, 189
transcendental, xi–xii, 6–10, 12–16, 18–20, 35, 141, 149–50, 226
tradition, 31, 70
   Christian, 6, 40, 54, 87, 98, 115, 118, 122, 124, 131–32, 143, 151, 153, 170, 172, 174, 204, 220, 225
   western philosophical, 42–43, 52, 198, 233

252 INDEX OF SUBJECTS

transcendence, 69, 94, 141, 146–49, 151–54, 156–57, 231
transcendental method, 10, 13, 16, 18–19, 35, 66–67, 141–42, 146, 149, 232
    transcendental Christology, xv, 49, 67–68, 153–54, 228, 236
    transcendental Thomists (see Thomism)
transcendentalism, 10–12
triadic
    faculties, 186
    logic, 9, 45, 75, 178
    relations, 58, 179
    signs, 58–59, 182
    structure, 19–20, 135, 158, 167, 190
Trinity (immanent), 159–60, 168–69, 171, 174–76, 180, 194–95, 228
    economic, 135, 159–60, 169–71, 174–75, 228
    vestiges of the Trinity in creation, 158, 177, 196
tychism, 48–49, 178

Uncertainty Principle (see also Werner Heisenberg), 2, 4, 49
United States, 4, 10

universe, xi, 1, 4, 6, 11–12 17–18, 38, 47–50, 63, 128, 134–35, 139, 153, 155–56, 159–60, 179, 182, 206, 221, 227, 233

value, 1, 5, 22, 34, 45, 56, 194
variation, 11, 21, 74, 137, 171, 219
Vatican Council II, (see Councils)
verifiability, 10, 43
verifiable, 11, 32, 37, 134, 142
verification, 36, 197
violence, 42, 71, 212, 219, 226
violent
    death, 118
    model, 204
    solution, 219, 237
virgin birth, 34, 127
visions, 121–24, 229

wisdom, 36, 54, 223
    in Hebrew thought, 96–98, 113
    identification with the Son, 75, 199
wonder, 37, 61, 108, 176, 179
Word (see also Logos), xv, 3, 8, 22, 26, 38–40, 52, 54, 62–64, 69, 75, 80, 84, 88–89, 93–95, 101, 112, 127, 148, 152, 156, 159–60, 162, 170, 175–76, 189–90, 193, 195, 208, 215, 220, 231, 234

www.ingramcontent.com/pod-product-compliance
Lightning Source LLC
Chambersburg PA
CBHW050346230426
43663CB00010B/2005